VISIONARY LEADERS FOR INFORMATION

T0348589

Recent publications from CiS

Practising information literacy: Bringing theories of learning, practice and information literacy together.
Edited by Annemaree Lloyd and Sanna Talja

Organising knowledge in a global society. Revised edition
Philip Hider and Ross Harvey

Exploring methods in information literacy research
Suzanne Lipu, Kirsty Williamson and Annemaree Lloyd

Libraries in the twenty-first century: Charting new directions in information services
Stuart Ferguson

Collection management: A concise introduction. Revised edition
John Kennedy

The other 51 weeks: A marketing handbook for librarians. Revised edition
Lee Welch

Archives: Recordkeeping in society
Edited by Sue McKemmish, Michael Piggott, Barbara Reed and Frank Upward

Computers for librarians: An introduction to the electronic library. 3rd edition
Stuart Ferguson with Rodney Hebels

Australian library supervision and management. 2nd edition
Roy Sanders

Research methods for students, academics and professionals. 2nd edition.
Kirsty Williamson and others

VISIONARY LEADERS FOR INFORMATION

Arthur Winzenried
with

Derek Law
Phillip Hughes
Doug Johnson
Sue Healey
David Warner
Katie Hannan, and
Giuseppe Giovenco

Centre for Information Studies

Charles Sturt University
Wagga Wagga New South Wales

Copyright © Arthur Winzenried
This book is copyright. Apart from any fair dealing for the purposes of private study, research, criticism or review as permitted under the Copyright Act, no part may be reproduced, stored in a retrieval system, or transmitted, in any form or by any means, electronic, mechanical, photocopied, recorded or otherwise, without prior permission of the copyright owner. Enquiries should be made to the Centre for Information Studies, Charles Sturt University.

ISBN 9781876938857

National Library of Australia cataloguing-in-publication data

---

Visionary leaders for information / Arthur Winzenried [et al.] – Wagga Wagga, N.S.W. : Centre for Information Studies, 2010.

1st ed.

Includes index.

9781876938857 (pbk.)

1. Information technology--Forecasting. 2. Library science--Forecasting. 3. Libraries and society. I. Arthur Winzenried. II. Charles Sturt University. Centre for Information Studies.

021

Published in 2010

Production coordinator: Chelsea Kovacs
Copy editor: Rachel Crease
Indexer: Arthur Winzenried
Cover designer: Andrew Winzenried
Printer: On-Demand, Southbank, Vic.

Centre for Information Studies
Locked Bag 660
Wagga Wagga NSW 2678
Australia
Phone: + 61 (0)2 6933 2325
Fax: + 61 (0)2 6933 2733
Email: cis@csu.edu.au
http://www.csu.edu.au/cis

Contents

Acknowledgements

I would like first and foremost to acknowledge the debt I owe to my various contributors. Without their contributions, most willingly provided, this work would certainly be much the poorer. To Giuseppe Giovenco who, as the then Director of the Centre for Information Studies, was responsible for the conception of this work, I owe so much. His encouragement, occasional discomfiture and his general willingness to debate issues and throw out wild ideas have contributed so much to my own personal development and to the development of this book. Also among the contributors I am especially indebted to Professor Derek Law for his preparedness to meet and discuss the work in its final stages. Although our meeting was disrupted by a fire alarm in our cafe in York, and resulted in a major rewrite of significant portions of the manuscript, his assistance was invaluable.

I would also be remiss if I did not acknowledge the throng of information professionals with whom it has been my pleasure to work through the years. So many have inspired me in the way that they have continued to give of their best in the middle of cash-flow problems, political infighting and generally trying situations. The dedication and commitment of so many of them has given me huge faith in a future for the industry. In so many cases they go far beyond the required in order to meet the needs of others.

To my colleagues at Charles Sturt University, a big thank you for all of the encouragement and support that was given. To Robert Pymm and Jake Wallis, in particular, a thank you for being able to cite their discussions and have the benefit of their advice, sometimes even before it was asked for.

Finally, for the ongoing support of my family I will always be grateful, but in particular for his editorial support I need to acknowledge son Andrew, severest (and perhaps rudest) of my critics but a real inspiration.

Like arrows in the hand of a warrior, so are the children of one's youth (Psalm 128:4).

To my wife, Jillienne, I give my most heartfelt thanks as without her constant encouragement to keep on regardless of the sometimes almost overwhelming discouragements. He who finds a good wife ... (Prov. 18.22)

Introducing the author and contributors

Dr Arthur Winzenried, Charles Sturt University

Arthur Winzenried holds a Diploma of Teaching (Prim), a BA (Hon) from Melbourne University, Victoria, a PhD (Arts) in history from Monash University, Victoria and a PhD (Applied Science) in Information Systems from Charles Sturt University, NSW.

His working experience has been varied in the extreme; teaching for five years tertiary, five years primary, eighteen years secondary and a teacher librarian for fifteen years. He is currently a lecturer at Charles Sturt University and providing library consultation to several schools in Melbourne.

Moving into information management in 1991. Arthur was Head of Library at Lilydale Adventist Academy for six years before moving to Eltham College as Head of Libraries. From 2000, Arthur became Facilitator to all of ELTHAM's digital developments including their revolutionary automated home reporting and student learning managements systems developed largely to his designs. This software designed for the College features secure online access to student learning content, context and assessment for all the involved stakeholders. As a truly transparent learning transaction, the system is extremely innovative whilst being of great value in an increasingly litigatious environment.

His work in the information and knowledge management field is now world recognised. Arthur loves to travel and share his research with others. A regular speaker at national and international conferences, in recent times he has addressed meetings in London, Hong Kong, Rotterdam, Eindhoven, Perth (WA) and a range of locations within Australia. In January 2010 he is to present at the International Information in Education Conference in Berlin, Germany.

Arthur is a well-published author with more than twenty monographs to his name, together with a large number of essays, book chapters and professional papers. His most recent work, published by the Australian Council for Educational Research (ACER), is *The use of instructional technology in schools* in 2009. This work is co-authored with Mal Lee and deals with the development of educational technology together with its imperatives for teaching and learning. That book has in turn led to some significant research which Arthur is currently directing into interactive whiteboards in classrooms and their effect on teacher dynamic. Earlier research, much of it presented at international conferences, focused on future predictions as to the staffing needs and duties of information provision.

A member of the Australian Council for Educational Leaders, the Australian Library and Information Association (ALIA) and the National Trust (Aust.) Arthur loves to share with his professional colleagues as well as with the community.

He is still in love with the lady he has been married to for thirty-six years and she loves him! They have two sons. His interests include reading, industrial archaeology, playing Railway Tycoon, drinking coffee in front of the open fire and spending time with his family.

Professor Derek Law, University of Strathclyde

Derek has worked in several British universities and published and spoken at conferences extensively. Most of his work has been to do with the development of networked resources in higher education and with the creation of national information policy. This has been combined with an active professional life in organisations related to librarianship and computing. A committed internationalist he has been involved in projects and research in more than forty countries. He was awarded the Barnard prize for contributions to Medical Informatics in 1993, Fellowship of the Royal Society of Edinburgh in 1999, an honorary degree by the Sorbonne in 2000, the IFLA medal in 2003, Honorary Fellowship of CILIP in 2004 and was an OCLC Distinguished Scholar in 2006. He is currently Chair of the new JISC Services Management Company and continues to teach and write.

Doug Johnson, Director, media and technology, Mankato Public Schools

Doug Johnson has been the Director of Media and Technology for the Mankato (MN) Public Schools since 1991 and has served as an adjunct faculty member of Minnesota State University since 1990. His teaching experience has included work in grades K-12 both here and in Saudi Arabia.

He is the author of four books: *The indispensable librarian, The indispensable teacher's guide to computer skills, Teaching right from wrong in the digital age* and *Machines are the easy part; People are the hard part*. His regular columns appear in *Library Media Connection* and on the Education World website. Doug's Blue Skunk blog averages over 50,000 visits a month and his articles have appeared in more than forty books and periodicals. Doug has conducted workshops and given presentations to more than 130 organisations throughout the United States as well as in Malaysia, Kenya, Thailand, Germany, Qatar, Canada, Chile, Peru, the UAE and Australia and has held a variety of leadership positions in state and national organisations, including ISTE and AASL.

Phillip Hughes, Emeritus Professor of Education, Australian National University

Phillip Hughes is Emeritus Professor of Education and Adjunct Professor at the Australian National University. He has degrees from Tasmania, Oxford and New England. Completing a Rhodes Scholarship at Oxford, he taught in high schools, technical colleges and universities. He was founding Principal of Hobart Teachers College, then Deputy Director-General of Education in Tasmania. He was the Australian member of the South Pacific Higher Education Mission in 1965, founding the University of the South Pacific. Phillip was foundation Head of the School of

Teacher Education at Canberra CAE, and foundation Chairman of the ACT Schools Authority, supervising the establishment of Australia's first new education system since 1870. He returned to Tasmania as Dean and Professor, working to achieve the amalgamation of the university with the Tasmanian College of Advanced Education. He was foundation Chief Executive Officer of the Australian Principals Centre in Melbourne. In medical education, he supervised the curriculum review for the Medical School at the University of Tasmania from1991to1995, obtaining accreditation for the School from the Australian Medical Council and receiving an honorary Doctor of Medicine.

Phillip Hughes has worked for OECD and UNESCO in Paris, Asia and the Pacific. He has written more than thirty-nine books and 200 major papers with a continuing concern to achieve an effective education for all. Becoming an Officer in the Order of Australia in 1991, he was awarded the Gold Medal of the Australian Council for Educational Administration, the 2002 Medal of the Australian College of Educators and in 2008 in Geneva received UNESCO's Comenius Medal for lifetime services to education. His interests are in music, reading, gardening, sport and the well-being of a growing flock of grandchildren and great-grandchildren.

Katie Hannan, Charles Sturt University

 Katie is passionate about librarianship. She has six years of professional library experience following four years in the IT sector. Katie has worked with a variety of different organisations; local and state government, academic and corporate. In 2007 she was selected to participate in an AusAID-funded development program called Australian Youth Ambassadors for Development. She spent five months working at a government boarding school in Vanuatu where she established a new library and trained staff and students in its use and management. This experience gave her the opportunity to write and present a paper at the 4th ALIA New Librarians Symposium where she discussed the challenges of her project in Vanuatu. It also provided her with incentive to motivate other young librarians to take on the challenge of working on a development project. Her current research interests are sustainability, libraries, government 2.0, co-collaboration and corporate social responsibility. At the time of writing her scenario, she was working as a faculty liaison librarian at Charles Sturt University, Wagga Wagga.

Sue Healey, Tintern Schools, Melbourne

Sue Healey has been involved in the development and management of information services for more than twenty-five years. Her experience extends across the school spectrum having worked in primary, secondary and TAFE library sectors. To broaden her understanding of the digital world Sue has undertaken numerous technology qualifications during the last twelve years as a way of melding technology and information services into a single school view. As Director of Information and Technology Services at Tintern Schools, Sue manages both the IT network and four school libraries across two campuses.

Whenever possible, Sue looks for opportunities to see schools from other parts of the world as well as their library services in action. In recent years, this has taken Sue to Budapest, Penang and Shanghai . Before taking up the position at Tintern, Sue had spent time in a number of Canadian schools exploring library services and the implementation of cooperative planning as well as a short stint in London working with Year 11 and 12 students.

Sue has a wealth of experience as an educator, having taught students of all ages starting from prep all the way through to adults. She is passionate about all facets of her work whether that be her work as a teacher, library manager or information technology director. Innovation and change have been a constant hallmark of her work throughout her time working in both libraries and IT.

Taking time to continue working as a classroom teacher of IT has allowed Sue to look at the changing nature of student learning and their preferred research methods. This in turn has impacted on the style and delivery of information services which are fast becoming unrecognisable from libraries twenty years ago. Sue's view of the future is that libraries are full of inspiring possibilities. 'Libraries should aspire to grow to be the symbol of a stimulating, adaptable environment that facilitates the creative work of scholars, enables both formal and informal collaboration, and is a vibrant centre of intellectual life' (http://library.nyu.edu/about/KPLReport.pdf).

Dr David Warner ELTHAM College of Education

David Warner is Principal of ELTHAM College of
Education in Melbourne, an independent, co-
educational K-12 school that has committed to
transforming to relevant and challenging schooling
for the twenty-first century knowledge era. David
has been a Senior College, TAFE and Higher
Education Director and involved in education and
labour market policy and research.

    The Australian Council for Education Research
published his book, *Schooling for the knowledge
era*, in 2006. David Warner has been a key note
speaker at international conferences in Mexico,
New Zealand, Italy, Belgium, China, UK, USA and
the UAE and invited presenter at several national
forums. David has been appointed CEO of both ELTHAM and a new P-12 CBD
school in Melbourne, Melbourne City School, operating fifty-two weeks a year and
converging caring and schooling.

Giuseppe Giovenco, information and research consultant

Giuseppe Giovenco has some thirty years
experience in the library and information fields.
His career and experience spans from public to
private and to academic and educational areas
both in the LIS and in the teaching profession.

    Giuseppe's interests lie in the area of socio-
anthropology and philosophy of LIS. He is also
focused on the essential aspects of stakeholder
involvement and relationships in the LIS field.
He brings in a specific focus of provider/client/
stakeholder relationship as drawn from an
independent and non-organisationally bound
perspective and represents the affirmation of the need for connectedness, meaning
and validity. Having experienced both traditional and non-traditional modes of
service facilitation in LIS and educational contexts he brings in cross-
representational understanding and perspectives. Giuseppe tries to make trust,
values and authentic human care and communication as his base lines.

A note about the terminology

The word 'Library'.

Throughout this book you will find the term Library. This is used in its widest sense as meaning a facility where information is connected with users. In application this facility might be a school library, public library, archive, or the information centre for a corporation, government or business.

I have deliberately used this term as an alternative to others because to me it implies a human face to information provision. One alternate term, information agency, for example, tends to carry with it constructions of facelessness and soullessness. It can easily become almost indistinguishable from any number of 'agencies' (government ones in the larger bureaucracies, for example) that can play a large and often frustrating part in modern society.

As you will see from this book, I argue most earnestly for Library to have a future. If this is to be the case, it must have a face – a very approachable, high quality front end. For all of us, Library is a sufficiently meaningful and known term. This is not to say that the future Library (or Libraries) described in this work are necessarily going to be readily recognisable to present users. However, whether recognisable or not, it will have a face that inspires confidence, provides quality service and offers helpfulness as a primary concern.

INTRODUCTION

Where have we come from?

Although few of us were there at the time, it is most likely that from the first moment that human beings began to think, they simultaneously considered ways of managing their ideas and transmitting them to others in an orderly way. Certainly from the earliest times of written language there have been related thoughts about its management.

Stueart and Moran suggest that 'as early as 3000 BC the Sumerians kept records on clay tablets' (Stueart & Moran, in Sanders 2004, p.4). They were not alone. Pictorial symbols, carving or painting on stones or in caves, strong customs that regulate traditional storytelling; all these and their many variations were early manifestations of human attempts to organise knowledge.

Among the better known attempts at formal information management was development of the library at Alexandria (see figure 1). Similar repositories include those at Nineveh, Ugarit and Nippur. There is some evidence that at Nineveh, the library of Ashburbanpil actually included a classification system (Polastron 2007, pp.2-3). In China, libraries can be traced back to at least the Qin Dynasty (221BC-206BC) (Bodde 1986).

These early libraries or archives maintained a collection of physical records in some degree of orderliness for the use of government bureaucracies and selected scholars. With restrictions on materials, writing skills and the other factors of the times, those collections were necessarily finite and thus 'manageable'.

To a large extent, this situation remained almost unchanged for the best part of two thousand years or more. Books were frequently chained to their shelves because of their value. One writer has suggested that in the fourteenth century Geoffrey Chaucer's collection of around sixty books was 'the medieval equivalent to owning a Ferrari, except with extra points for being cultured' (Turner 2005, p.21).

Figure 1 Inside the library at Alexandria, opened around the third century BC
(reproduced under creative commons licence)

Even despite the revolutionary aspects that surrounded the invention of the printing press, little changed as far as libraries were concerned. Essentially, it was more of the same. Items were physical, they could be housed within four walls so boundaries were seen clearly and managers could 'manage' accordingly. Planning took into account bigger buildings and more staff. This formula was a simple one and widely understood.

The Industrial Age that began after 1700 allowed an increasingly fixed and predictable management model that was autocratic and methodical. Assembly line thinking could be directly applied to item processing and, with every worker in their place and doing their own job, management could be highly organised and efficient.

Given the increase in the volume of material there were early attempts in several parts of the world to provide more rigorous *classification* systems – codes and practices that would improve the ease with which physical materials could be stored and then retrieved as required. One of the more influential systems was that developed by Melvil Dewey in 1876. There have been others, the Library of Congress Classification being among them.

For a significant time, library collections remained physical and finite. Well into the twentieth century it was possible for even major libraries such as the Library of Congress in the US and the British Library in the UK to consider it possible to maintain a physical collection of items in an orderly manner. The size of the collections had changed certainly, but new technologies allowed more convenient means of locating items in these larger collections and users came from a greater variety of classes, places and societies. Larger libraries and card catalogues were an almost universal expectation for the first half of the twentieth century.

In the eastern world, literacy had been a fact for many centuries. However, it was largely the right of the rich and important few rather than the common people. Public service examinations placed a high value on literacy and the competition for success was considerable. But access, generally, to literature was limited. Likewise in the western world reading and writing had been, during the middle ages, the privilege of the richer classes. Before that, they had been largely the prerogative of the clergy. Ordinary 'workers' who made up the majority of the population did not need these skills, it was argued, and so they remained distanced from literature.

This situation changed as industrialisation began to undo some of the traditional values. Mechanics Institutes, libraries in all but name, began the work of 'educating' the masses. Learning, particularly reading, became not only more common but more popular. General *literacy* considerably increased the number of potential users, reading was in demand, and thus libraries became common even in the smaller towns and villages.

The advent of *personal computers* in the later years of the twentieth century brought major change to both the storage of materials in library and the way those materials could be accessed. For the first time there were automated ways of dealing with searches and of controlling storage arrangements. Computers could search millions of items in milli-seconds. Searches that had previously taken years could be completed in a matter of moments. This was of course provided the data had been entered correctly and comprehensively in the first place. Data entry became one of the 'new' roles of library personnel and one more feature of library management.

This new digital development was accompanied a little later by the additional and related task of scanning and the growth of an outsourcing industry to provide these services offsite. All of these technologically driven changes took place over a rather limited time, becoming part of a new climate of change that was set to challenge traditional management models. For the first time, collections and their management began to move beyond the four walls of the traditional library. At the same time the work of library staff began to move beyond the handling of physical items and impinge on the worlds of the information technology and the corporate manager. Even in the smallest of school libraries, the library 'person' quickly became something of a computer guru in the eyes of many people (Lee & Winzenried 2009, p.121).

Figure 2 The library at Alexandria today (reproduced under creative commons licence)

Libraries like the modern one at Alexandria (figure 2), a distant cousin of the one that existed in 50BC, took on a new look but generally fulfilled the same functions in the same way. Instead of users having direct access to physical materials, computers offered a means not only of searching for items but often of viewing them as well. Thus the 'modern' library tended to assume the appearance of a computer laboratory rather than housing shelves of physical items. The change in terms of library appearance, the roles of its staff and the nature of its daily business was enormous.

Hardly had these changes begun to effect library design and operation than the development of the *internet* brought further changes. Almost overnight it seemed an information user did not even need to move from their own chair at home. It was suddenly possible to view items in a library at the other side of the world. The internet brought with it a host of authoring tools that meant absolutely anyone from almost anywhere could now write what they liked and make it available. In order to search the quantities of information that were growing almost too rapidly to calculate, the construction of web search engines had to evolve exponentially. Quality control, however, seemed to become more and more impossible. Shirky's (2008) book title says it all – 'Here comes everybody'!

Within a very short period of time, the rise of mass media outlets such as Wikipedia, Facebook, and Twitter have become information (or misinformation) sources of absolutely massive proportions. The ease with which information can be circulated and the extent to which it can be circulated is the major 'new' feature of the present information landscape. With the best presses in the world, publishing and printing a book takes time. There are a finite number of copies in circulation and transporting them to the user can be a further constraint. No such limits affect Twitter and the like. Access an internet-connected computer and you have it. While internet access and computer ownership are not universal – they are quickly moving down that track. For the information manager, managing something that is self-perpetuating is in itself something of a 'new' and different concept. It provides rather formidable challenges. Again to cite Shirky (2008), it is akin to 'organising without organisations' and bordering on managing the unmanageable (and thus the title of his book).

What happens next?

Today, it is possible to see how almost every individual of almost any age can become immediately involved in the production and use of information for themselves in remarkable ways. Shirky speaks of the 'here comes everybody' situation and of the 'power of organising without organisations'. Many of us can identify precisely with his concepts of the power of individuals within the information context (Shirky 2008, p.6), but what are the implications for future managers? Will they have any role at all?

Quite recently my own son was struck by a car on his way home from work. Fortunately the accident was not totally serious but his leg injury did cause some alarm. Early on the scene was his wife who, as any good wife would do, took a picture of the injury with her mobile phone and emailed it to her mother, an experienced casualty nurse. Mother, SMS-ed back a 'don't worry' and pasted the picture on Facebook so that another medical friend of the family could double check that the wound was repairable. An hour or two later our son's mother rang her brother 1000 kilometres away to give the news, only to be told that uncle had heard of the accident from his own son on the other side of the country who had seen the wound on Facebook some time earlier!

Not only had the news spread into unexpected realms but at lightning speed. 'News' had become old hardly before it had even become news. Information had been created, stored and retrieved more than 4000 kilometres distant without a single cataloguer or librarian being involved and within the space of a couple of hours. A number of 'consultations' had taken place on the basis of one photo shared around the internet.

This sort of public consultation together with rapid and widespread access is the context in which the library of today is functioning. Positioning library for the future in this sort of ever-changing world is an enormous challenge. Shirky talks of 'the power of organising without organisations' and Harkin refers to 'dangerous ideas that are changing how we live and who we are' (Harkin 2009, xiii). Both writers along with so many others struggle to see what the next moves might be in a world that has taken change as a constant and embraced a series of technologies that are forever minimising the distances between people otherwise separated by thousands of kilometres and across all manner of cultural divides.

To consider Shirky's argument for a moment, how is it possible for a manager in a modern library to 'organise' materials in a way that is suitable to people who are constantly operating independently? Further, they are doing this with the help of technology that an organisation finds difficult to use (or that it cannot use on the grounds of its responsibility to a corporate/government ethos)?

Organisation is difficult for libraries in the sense that every move made requires the expending of some limited resource (Shirky 2008, p.30). Each and every meeting, decision, agreement that is made demands a cost. It might be time, attention, money, personnel or materials, but it is a cost. How then can an organisation like a library hope to compete with an individual who can work, it would often appear, independently and at a fraction of the cost.

For example, how does the concept of 'moral purpose' (Fullan 2001a), making a planned difference for the better, deal with a world that prefers to organise itself in its own way regardless of the good of anyone other than the person first creating the 'data' and based on cyberspace mechanisms that allow individuals to create their own versions of organisation?

Organisational challenge

These are just some of the questions facing would be managers of information providing organisations. Complicating matters perhaps further is a growing trend on the part of those holding the purse-strings to conceive of their information provision mechanisms as conventional business entities. In some contexts this works well. The user, either directly or indirectly, pays for the information and that money maintains the information sourcing unit. However, when this type of arrangement is extended to institutions that deal in learning – from kindergartens to higher education, I begin to have serious concerns.

Industry can consider information provided as something of an outcome or as a product in its own right. How does one assess the product of a school or university? It is true that governments tend to assess the product of universities in terms of their research activity, publication and numbers of students – but is this really what the university is 'producing' or is it rather a by-product of another production? Similarly, the product of a school is often seen in terms of league tables and/or formal test results. The product of public libraries is all too often seen only in terms of the number of visits. In each instance, the most important product, that of knowledge creation, is largely ignored.

I am not convinced by current arguments that a library, particularly one based in a learning community (school, university, municipality, or whatever) can be run simply as a business using business modelling. Business has an identifiable and tangible end product. Education in all its aspects has the intangible product of changing the minds of humans – of making a difference, of growing knowledge.

Thus, there is another dimension to learning establishments; one that Michael Fullan might call the *moral purpose* (2001a, p.13ff). This idea of a moral purpose is the first of five key issues that must be considered if the library is to survive into the future. Phillip Hughes takes the idea a little further:

> My own stance is that education is inescapably a moral activity. It is not possible to teach others without conveying a moral message of some sort, consciously or unconsciously, and to do so without

specific thought is either to deceive oneself or to deceive others
(Hughes 17/09/09).

In the field of information provision, it is necessary to keep this direction firmly in mind. We provide information not in order to produce a tangible and physical product but to lead a mind to additional knowledge – the application of information to the daily activity of that mind. The way we provide information and the information that we provide needs to be guided by significant, considered and well defined purposes. This action is perhaps in complete contrast to the lack of organisation faced by people in their daily lives as they interact with digital media in a community setting. I am not advocating a fortress mentality that sees the information professional as fighting to resist the digital revolution, but rather a coaching service that understands the environment but is able to relate closely to the individual and offer tailored solutions for the person.

Shirky (2008) and others (Tapscott & Williams 2006, Harkin 2009, among them) are highlighting the current digital anarchy that exists in society. However, this same anarchy is all too frequently seen by some business managers, including school-based ones, as the solution to their information provision. Shirky, in particular, is highlighting the situation for what it is; an amazing but impersonal construct that allows us to communicate more often but not necessarily more productively and quite often quite destructively for some individuals.

Information provision needs to be firmly based around a defined purpose and it needs to consider the individual in a special way. This is especially true in the formal education sector where the client is young and vulnerable. However, the same issues can all too often exist, though they are usually overlooked, among older learners.

This leads us to the second issue to consider, that there needs to be not only a clear (and clearly advertised) moral purpose but also an equally *clear plan* for fulfilling that purpose. Such a plan needs to include clear and practical ways in which the purpose is to be achieved as regards all the stakeholders concerned. In a highly technical environment, such a plan must take into account the rapidly changing environment and all of the challenges that go with those changes. Change itself needs to be accepted as part of the daily working environment for the information manager of today and no less for those of tomorrow.

Further, that plan needs to be clearly presented in such a way that the whole transaction is transparent. Nothing is quite so damaging to the modern organisation as a perception that it is trying to deceive, mislead or otherwise carry out covert behaviours. Clients in particular need clearly to see that their needs are to be met and how that will take place.

Thus, the third major issue that must be addressed is the need for organisations providing information to be clearly *responsive* to client needs – not the needs assumed by managers in the past, but by the real needs of clients right now (see Warner, chapter 3, in particular on this). If clients are comfortable with their information provision context, not only will they perform better in the present but they will carry a more positive attitude into the future (see Johnson and Healy, chapter 3). For most people, the library is where lifelong learning becomes a reality or otherwise.

This idea leads to a fourth major aspect of the information provision landscape – *relationships*. Fullan (e.g., 2001, p.51ff) spends considerable time with this aspect of management. In this respect he is neither the first nor the last. If information management is to be truly client responsive then there needs to be a close relationship between manager and client. Such a relationship will be built on trust, will be totally transparent, and in it the client will see that their needs are clearly understood and that there is a considerable possibility that those needs will be met.

The final imperative is the need for a stronger *product focus*. In many information organisations, provision seems to end once the client has the data they requested. If our moral purpose only extends as far as leading the horse to water, what have we really achieved? The next step is perhaps the most important of all, making that data so useful to the client that they can use the material in a way that makes a difference to their lives. If libraries were retail outlets the problem for us would go something like this:

> We like what we have in our shop; it is what everyone has always
> bought from a shop like ours. Plus, our shop is bigger than anyone
> else's and has more computers for our staff to use. We 'know' that
> this is what our sort of shop has always sold, that this is what
> people *ought* to want, we 'know' that this is what is *good* for them.
> Yet everyone seems to be buying 'what we have' somewhere else.

So often the managers of libraries have resisted changes to the way they operate or their style of operation on the grounds that – *We have always done it this way.*

On a slightly different tack, consider the way government authorities hand out computers to school students on the assumption that thereby learning will be improved? Research into teacher dynamic and interactive whiteboards in New South Wales government schools currently underway (Winzenried, Dalgarno &

Tinkler 2010) is finding that while these boards are being handed out to schools the teachers themselves are having difficulty using them. While the technology is being provided, there is no associated training and no time provided for staff to learn to use the technology. Product focus in this instance tends to end on this note – 'we have x thousand schools that now have IWB technology rather than we have x thousand teachers who we know are using them effectively and regularly'. Here is another caution for the would-be effective information leader/manager.

Just as many libraries have finally decided that quoting the number of books borrowed is no longer a true measure of library activity, so it is not enough for the information manager to measure success in terms of quantity of data delivered, number of terminals in use or number of hours people are logged in. The end product of obtaining information needs to be more than sales over the counter. It needs to be more along the lines of people now able to seek for themselves, people who are confidently approaching information professionals with their next information need and people who have gone on to write books, teach children, present papers, carry out research, and so on, because their confidence is strong and their needs are being met (see further discussion round this point in Law, Hughes, and Warner, chapter 3).

In summary, then, what is needed if the library is to survive into the future is a fusion of five key issues; moral purpose, clear plans, client focus, solid relationships that can last a life-time and a strong product focus – have we changed lives? Technology, whether it is Web 2.0, Windows 7.0 or Web 4.0, can only go so far. It can provide us with a powerful set of tools but it cannot establish firm personal relationships (not yet at least, though Johnson's 'affection settings' (see chapter 3) lead to some interesting speculation). There does need to be a personal dimension and the library remains the most well-positioned vehicle for this.

The library

In the twenty-first century, library has become a word of many meanings. For the vast majority of people there is usually a clear connection between 'library' and 'books'. For 2000 years, libraries were places where physical items were kept, read and sometimes borrowed. However, increasingly the word has other implications.

Libraries in many countries now feature the use of technology as a key part of their operations. These may be for access to the collection catalogue or as a gateway to the world wide web. Back in 1997, Lawrence Dowler used the then rather adventurous term 'gateways' for libraries as they began to more regularly offer users access to the web as an integral aspect of library services. It is the presence of this technology and its many resources that is changing the way library is now being defined.

However, the latest technology this year is often superseded by another next year. Just when we have begun to talk widely about Web 2.0, several world players, such as the BBC in the UK, is starting up with Web 3.0. The only constant is change (Sanders 2004, p.18, Lee & Winzenried 2009, p.114, and a host of others). Change in libraries, change in the way they operate, change in the nature of the client and change in the time and place that information is required by the client are all critical aspects of contemporary information management and thus critical to library managers.

To some, these changes necessitate a change in name, and thus in some areas there is the tendency to change a name in the hope that somehow this will make the library more acceptable and more permanent (although how frequent name changes can relate to permanency is something of a conundrum). In the 1990s, it was popular in Australia for school libraries to become information centres, resource centres and even information services units (Lee 1996). Changing the name became an end in itself. But the essential work and nature of those institutions rarely changed at the same time. They might have embraced (outwardly) more of the technology but the nature of the back offices remained, many staff rarely appeared in public and the managers continued to tell clients, as well as their own managers, what was needed. The client was just as regularly disenfranchised as they had been since the early twentieth century when libraries, subsidised by public money, had come to be expected to be institutions for democracy and social equity following the demise of the user-driven and purpose-built libraries of the Mechanics Institute era. Name changing was a largely rhetorical issue and has remained that way.

The difficult area of managerial mindset has remained very constant despite the frequent name changing. One writer and library teacher at higher education level recently postulated that the 'current leaders in power [in libraries] are those that have risen through the ranks, very often people-phobic and staff-distrusting, resentful and divorced from the ethic and grounding of relatedness and relationship' (Giovenco 14/11/09). This might be a little extreme, but it does relate well to the growing number of teachers who decide to retrain as teacher librarians in order to 'escape the stresses of the classroom' (Elyse Taylor interview 02/05/09). Over many years as both a library administrator and then as a teacher of teacher librarians at higher education level, I have heard this comment numerous times. What exactly is it that they are escaping and what attitudes are they thus bringing to library management?

Warner draws attention to similar attitudes in chapter 3, when he notes a 'sometimes traditional view that if you couldn't relate with people you became a librarian or teacher librarian'. While the media have at times done little to change this general perception of library staff (c/f. the Australian television comedy/drama, *The Librarians*, ABC, 2009).

Let us not become too discouraged. This book is about library futures. It is not necessarily all about change. However, we cannot avoid change altogether. Just as libraries have encountered considerable change in the past, so they will in the future. This book therefore will involve itself with change management as well as with management more generally. We argue that if information managers keep an open mind, one that has client needs as its primary focus, then they will be in a better position to ensure their library, whether school-based or otherwise, will have a healthy future. All too often at present, managers have a mindset that belongs to another age and one that does not necessarily meet the needs of clients – present or future.

Consider ...

How often have you been in a school library where the order has rolled across the floor space '**No food and drink in the library!**'

This is often a rule applied to all forms of library, yet we live in a time when many, perhaps most, of the more successful book shops are allocating precious sale space to integrate coffee shops. Why? You might think that food and drink among new books is a problem greater than mixing it with old books, yet commercially it is seen as a sound move.

At home our clients, if they read at all, frequently do so with a drink or a snack of some sort in hand. They might even be reading 'our' books in this fashion. Why then can't they do it in the library?

Where have our rules come from? Are they relevant now? How do they contribute (or otherwise) to building a secure client base for the future?

Talking of library futures often conjures up the expectation of some vivid description of what a library of the future may look like – perhaps we can do a little crystal ball gazing on this one. However, the greater concern here is the question 'Does library have a future?'

Many years ago in 1985, Robert Heller made the point that 'real business … is to manage the affairs of the company so that everybody involved (employees, stockholders, customers, communities) has good cause to be profoundly thankful for management's work' (Heller, p.9). This summary of management role is masterly and comes perilously close to the moral purpose and relationships of Fullan and others ten years later. Management of library is no different. Quality management tends to be somewhat invisible but effects in a major way each of the complex relationships that exist as part of that library community. Success or failure in this regard relates to survival of your business – the library.

My key argument is that libraries will only have a future if it is directly relevant to users and this requires visionary leadership. The way library and its leaders recognise and then respond to users will be crucial. If library does not seriously take this into consideration, it is likely to become redundant, irrelevant, and be cast aside in the same way as the horse and cart. Managers' decisions need to reflect this reality, to be adaptable and flexible in their approach rather than the set in concrete model that has often followed from Industrial Age thinking about learning (Eisner 2004, Warner 2006).

For example, in the university world there are some major places of learning that are cutting down on library staff, reducing the hours of operation and resizing their operations on the assumption that this represents a responsible reaction to digital libraries and economic conditions. At the same time, those establishments are often building 'learning commons' and finding that their students use such facilities at all hours and in large numbers. The commons become a focus for socialising, and also for learning, study and reading – traditional roles of library. Why are learning commons separate from library? Why are they growing when 'library' is often shrinking?

Consider another situation, becoming more frequently the case on a daily basis. In the formal schooling sector, libraries have had an established place for many years. Increasingly technology has become critical. However, economic restraints and limited management vision quite often means that large numbers of computers are provided with limited infrastructure to support them. Library users are very regularly faced with 'computers not working' or 'internet is down' signs at times of need. Further, the increased use of technology gives many school accounting managers the impression that print materials are no longer really necessary. As a result library staff and hours are reduced to save money. Library skills involving reading and material management are seen as less important. So teacher librarians are replaced by technicians. Result – fewer students visit the library because there are no longer friendly and helpful people who understand their curriculum needs and so management finds it an easy matter to reduce budgets, staff and hours yet further.

The key in these examples rests with a management mindset that has become particularly prevalent in developed countries. Starting with general access to the internet in the mid 1990s, more and more managers have questioned the need for library and for intermediaries between users and information (Allen 1996, p.29, Barberá 1996, p.187ff). In the late 1990s, a large number of businesses that had maintained information mechanisms for their employees decided to save money, eliminate their libraries and the library staff and connect workers directly to the internet. It was the way to go. Five years later many of those same companies were reinstating their information centers after major falls in productivity showed the inefficiency of this approach to information (Rowse 1999, p.63, Dowler 1997, p.93ff). Despite all the technology, people at the 'coal face' still needed some interpretation, collection or management of the information they needed in order to work efficiently. In this regard, visionary leadership is critical.

With the arrival of the interactive web, some of these old ideas have resurfaced. We can get it all on the web and it responds immediately to us. Wonderful, but a certain level of self-discipline is needed if navigating around the web is to produce useful results. Significantly, one of the underlying concepts of Web 2.0 technology is the social interaction it produces. Thus the new technology is beginning to acknowledge the truth that so very many teachers in all sectors have known for many years – learning is most essentially a social construction.

Yes, the current generation demands instant gratification, but equally certain is their new and huge desire to communicate. A generation ago, parents were hard pressed to have their children write a letter to grandma. Today, the children of those children send dozens, even hundreds of messages each day. They build up massive mobile phone bills and spend hours with Facebook, YouTube, Twitter, Second Life, and the rest. Interaction with others is a part of their life and an important one.

These are the clients of our libraries now. How are our libraries dealing with this client? They too often use practices born in the Industrial Age – 'sit down still, read on your own and *silently*'. How relevant is this practice to the present generation? How relevant will it be to the next?

Leaders in libraries

For intending or existing leaders in libraries and information provision generally, all of these factors tend to paint a complex almost chaotic picture. Rather than an information environment, we might speak of an information *ecology* where a host of different, 'living' issues interrelate with each other in complex ways. The humans in this ecology are both the product of the situation as well as a potentially powerful influence on it.

Once, long ago, leading in information could well mean buying large quantities of print materials and cataloguing them effectively such that motivated and skilled searchers could locate the items for themselves (less skilled users had to have the items located for them). Leaders were authoritarian figures who had control of the information, that is, they controlled access to the collection. In an industrial age where order and system were vitally important and universally accepted, this was a sustainable arrangement.

In the modern age the ecology has become more complex. Not only are resources multiplying faster than any attempts to organise them, but the clients have changed out of recognition. They are more demanding, have far more focused needs (mostly), and generally far less patience. Technology has introduced new ways of accessing information and so the leader may never in fact meet the user in a physical way. New styles of leadership are needed and often a complex combination of these styles is required (see, for example, the work of Fullan, 2001). No longer can one individual 'control' access, so new systems of teamwork and collaboration are required.

In some cases, just as in a botanical ecology, the information ecology has developed some of these systems quite organically (see, for example, Shirky 2008). These transitions are clearly seen in the way that organisational theories have changed and adapted over the past hundred years or so (see chapter 1). But for the leader or would be leader in the field of information the new situation calls for great flexibility. In a constantly changing and increasingly complex ecology one who wishes to lead needs to be aware of many variables, and most of all, quite unlike their predecessors, to be able to maintain relationships with both technology and people. Collaboration and interaction have become increasingly critical for future success.

One other aspect of 'management' in the field needs to be considered because of its vital relationship with the information ecology – the nature of leadership. Not only are different styles required to meet increasingly complex needs, but so too is the hierarchical structure being challenged. Leaders are no longer necessarily those officially designated as leaders in an organisation and those paid accordingly. Today it is possible, even helpful, to speak of 'leading from the middle'. In an ecology where relationships are critical, it is possible for many people in that ecology to exercise considerable influence even when not having a recognised or official leadership role. The teacher librarian is one very considerable case in point. All too often these people are not given significant recognition for leadership in their learning communities. Despite this, the pivotal nature of their daily function places them in powerful positions where they can influence much of what happens in the classroom as well as maintain, should they so chose, strong influence with recognised management. As key providers of resources for learning, the potential that they have for influencing the learning of the community and the shape of its outcomes is huge though not always recognised.

The potential of this leading from the middle situation is yet to be fully exploited or studied, but a growing number of cases being cited clearly indicate the way that individuals are grasping the opportunities being offered and making 'their' libraries and themselves vitally important to their respective learning communities.

And so to the present work

This work sets out to challenge some of the frequently witnessed concepts of library – there is nothing new in this, library is being questioned almost daily in real life. Working from a premise that if library today does not clearly identify and work around the real needs of clients it does not have a sustainable future, this work looks at some of the challenges to be faced and offers some food for thought as to how transitions might be managed.

Chapter 1 then moves into a discussion of the potential being offered to the post-modern, even post-literate library. Our excursions into the future highlight a number of areas for action. Effective leading and managing in the modern information context must recognise increased responsibility for the development of citizens who will occupy, quite probably, a very different world. The Industrial Age tended to concern itself with producing clones suitable for repetitive industrial production. In the current age, whatever it might be called, the application of information to the client should aim to produce increasingly flexible and capable decision-makers. Outcomes for libraries now need to reflect social and ethical responsibility as well as the more usual economic outcomes. Additionally, there is a clear indication that environmental issues can no longer be ignored. Future library management involves what has sometimes been called, the 'triple bottom line' (Elkington 2004).

To succeed in the task of better managing information for our clients we need a plan, preferably a plan that is based on some sound principles and tested theories. Organisational theory has been discussed for many years. Fullan in particular has done much to offer insights into this area. We need to consider what sort of framework is offered that will assist development of lasting information management.

In chapter 2 more attention is drawn to the 'person' in the equation – the actual human element of library and their potential for leading and managing. Moving from the theory of management we explore the practical issues; the actual nature of leadership and management as well as the role that is possible within an organisation. In what ways is it possible for library and information managers to actually 'manage' that information provision? Is it possible in the future to realistically take 'control'? We consider aspects of the role of library staff, particularly managers or teacher librarians, as leaders. Leadership is not necessarily a tagged position but comes about somewhat organically because of a unique relationship with the information on the one hand and the client on the other. The intermediary role carries with it a certain 'power' and 'privilege' as well as responsibility. It can be very much a case of which staff at what levels and in what contexts. To some extent it is in the hands of each teacher librarian or library staff member to act as a leader in their work of providing space and resources to their clients as, when and where they are needed. Vision needs to be clear and appropriate and leaders need to by finely tuned to their clients as well as to the living ecology in which they function.

That being said, formalised management, as one of the key stakeholders in the whole information transaction, is largely responsible for much of the devolution, empowerment and managerial construction that shape the client interface. Managers who devolve away from practitioner models and support more managerial constructs can devalue the relatedness as well as the user understanding focus. The more that management divorces itself from the grounded process of people management, facilitation and valuing, the more the value of 'library' will be reduced. The more the focus is on ICT and its related issues, the more difficult it becomes to keep client awareness. Yet this is an easy and rather common position. It is very much a reflection of the past library management stance that focused on collection management and processes as the *reason d'être* for library, leaving the borrowers as something of a hindrance to 'good management'.

To get started with the more practical aspects of the issues involved, seven highly active and imaginative professionals provide us in chapter 3 with their personal visions of the 'library of the future'. Selected from among many, they represent a variety of locations, sectors and professional involvements. These are personal views based on many years of experience in each case. They may or may not be prophetic, but each has a story to tell.

The scenarios raise a wide range of issues and considerations. One immediate standout though is the dramatic similarity between the work of Healy and Johnson. Though working half a world apart and in different roles, there are many of the same issues being raised and the same sort of future being considered. To these two visions of what lies in store for our children and grandchildren is a significant reminder by Warner of the importance of humans in the library equation. Technology is a huge issue now and not at all likely to get less so in the future. There is, however, a real need for human intermediaries within the whole information transfer transaction.

A rather topical reminder from Hannan highlights the green footprint of the future library. Not yet being given all the consideration it deserves, despite considerable spin from the world's politicians, in the increasingly concerning climate control debate, this is one issue that should be seriously tackled by all library managers. Rounding out the debate, Law introduces the theme of responsible action by libraries in the higher education sector and Hughes places school libraries in the current context of Australian Federal Government policy; Where is the 'Education Revolution' without the school library?

Together these essays provide food for thought. In each case there are serious considerations for the way future libraries are being shaped right now. For information managers and those aspiring to that role, whether in schools, the public sector or higher education, a number of important management issues appear.

In chapter 4, the common threads in these scenarios begin to be 'unpacked'. What ideas and observations can be drawn from them regarding library management, client focus and physical plant/property? What are some of the key questions being asked? Despite the different views and sectors represented by the contributors, there are many issues common to all information managers; one of the clearest of those being a high level of client service.

Back in 1996, a study into library staff for the future (2006) using Delphi methodology suggested that client service was going to quickly overtake library cataloguing as a more time-consuming task for teacher librarians in schools (Winzenried 1996). A repeat study in 2006 showed that not only had this been the case, but the rate of the change had been significantly faster than predicted by the earlier study (Winzenried 2009). Linked to the service issue is the importance of determining what the client needs actually are. Do they involve, as several contributors suggest, coffee shops and sleeping arrangements, personalised spaces and flexible furniture with moveable walls?

Besides the service aspect are other critical concerns for the manager and prospective manager. These include the technology involved, environmental responsibilities, interaction with government policy and a host of related issues.

The sum total of all these issues is the need for effective and planned management. Too often in the past planning has followed technology, for example, rather than leading it. Effective information management and secure futures for library appear to be highly dependant on sound organisational theory and practice. There need to be clear goals and purposes providing direction in challenging times.

Chapter 5 closes on the thought that, although we cannot predict any library future with specific physical detail, we can advise that if library is to have any future at all it must start now with a clear recognition of the client it is serving and by addressing their very specific needs. Among serious considerations here is the aspect of information literacy. Seen by many at the present time as one aspect where the teacher librarian has influence as they present classes in information skills, I would argue that by doing so we are not putting the client first. Developing skill and confidence in sourcing the information they need is an intensely personal arrangement. Instead of planning classes, the staff of libraries need to be building relationships one by one – slower and perhaps more challenging, but in the end the only way to ensure the client will find what they need when they need it and also to ensure they come back next time.

In many cases these needs are not currently being recognised or met. These needs may in fact be seriously challenging to current library management practice and policy. Managers basing their practice on specific budgetary or business models are often the ones closing down services, reducing staff numbers, curtailing opening hours and seeing their client numbers decline. There is a connection between these factors. The growth of the learning commons in a number of higher education locations indicates one specific client need. As library professionals we need to review management frameworks and respond to the need as a matter of urgency. Closing down library services and times is not the appropriate reaction.

Further, meeting client needs is most likely to call in to question many of our past management policies and practices. Changing situations in a highly technical world where users are far less likely to organise in the way they once did, will make such changes necessary for survival as far as information provision is concerned.

If they are to survive, libraries must be totally relevant to their users. Their future will be determined by whether they foresee these needs correctly and proactively act on them *now*. It is likely that such action may call into question the long-held beliefs and practices that currently form the basis of library leadership and management.

This book represents the accumulated experience in the field of information provision over many years by the author and his contributors. It offers insights into the living ecology that is the current information provision context. The book does not aim to provide 'solutions' to information problems. In the current context solutions are not a real possibility. Rather its aim is to provide clues and ideas that can form the basis for action, collaboration, and ultimately a sustainable, successful future for information provision within organisations. The future is uncertain in that it cannot be predicted with any accuracy – change is the only constant – but we can clearly see that relationships and vision hold the key to the future survival of library and the future of successful information leadership. Visionary leaders are needed who will not be tied to the practices of the past, who will be totally focused, not on set organisational rules, but on the needs of their clients and the perhaps more abstract need for global survival. We are all on this planet together, our ability to deal with each other is critical, especially when it comes to effective information provision. Sharing will be a hallmark of the future, not hording. *The library of the future begins now.*

References

Allen, G. (1996). Disintermediation: a disaster or a discipline? In Raitt, D. & Jeapes, B. (1996). 20th International Online Meeting, *Proceedings*, London 3-5 December, Learner Information Europe Ltd. UK.

Barberá, J. (1996). The intranet: a new concept for corporate information handling. In Raitt, D. & Jeapes, B. (1996). 20th International Online Meeting, *Proceedings*, London 3-5 December, Learner Information Europe Ltd. UK.

Bodde, D. (1986). The state and empire of Ch'in. In Twitchett, D. & Loewe, M. (Eds.), *The Cambridge History of China: Volume I: the Ch'in and Han Empires, 221 B.C. – A.D. 220*. Cambridge: Cambridge University Press.

Dowler, L. (1997). *Gateways to knowledge*. Cambridge, MT: MIT Press.

Eisner, E. (2004). Preparing for today and tomorrow. *Educational Leadership*, December 2003/January 2004.

Elkington, J. (2004). Enter the Triple Bottom line. Available online at http://www.johnelkington.com/TBL-elkington-chapter.pdf on 11/8/09.

Fullan, M. (2001), *Leading in a culture of change*. San Fransisco, CA: Jossey-Bass.

Giovenco, G. email, 14.11.09.

Harkin, J. (2009). *Cyburbia; the dangerous idea that's changing how we live and who we are*. London: Little, Brown.

Heller, R. (1985). *The new naked manager*. London: Hodder and Stoughton.

Lee, M. (1996). Tech talk. *The Practicing Administrator*, 18/4.

Lee, M. & Winzenried, A. (2009). *The use of instructional technology in schools: Lessons to be learned*. Melbourne: ACER.

Polastron, Lucien X (2007). *Books on fire: the tumultuous story of the world's great libraries*. London: Thames & Hudson Ltd.

Rowse, M. (1999). Only connect: the role of linkage in information search and retrieval. In Raitt, D. (1999). 23rd International Online Meeting, Proceedings, London 7-9 December, Learner Information Europe Ltd. UK.

Sanders, R. (2004). *Australian library supervision and management* (2nd ed.). Wagga Wagga, NSW: Centre for Information Studies.

Shirky, C. (2008). *Here comes everybody: the power of organising without organisations*, London: Penguin.

Stueart, R.D. & Moran, B. (1998). *Customer service charter*. Perth: State Library of WA.

Tapscott, D. & Williams, A.D. (2006). *Wikinomics: how mass collaboration changes everything*. New York: Portfolio.

Taylor, E. Interview, 2 May 2009.

Turner, T, (2005). *Writers and their tall tails*. London: Scholastic.

Warner, D. (2006). *Schooling for the knowledge era*. Melbourne: ACER.

Winzenried, A. (2009). Libraries of the future – serving them better. SLAV Berwick regional meeting, St Francis Xavier College, Berwick Campus, February 2009.

Winzenried, A. (1996). Information managers/librarians in the year 2006: prophets, princes or poohbahs? Online Information Meeting, London.

Winzenried, A.; Dalgarno, B. & Tinkler, J. Interactive whiteboards and teaching dynamic. To be published 2010.

CHAPTER 1
Towards an organisational theory for information professionals

Effective leading and managing in the modern information context must recognise increased responsibility for the development of citizens who will occupy, quite probably, a very different world to our own. If scenarios such as those proposed by Healy and Johnson (chapter 3) in particular are realistic possibilities, then the future will be exceptionally challenging. Preparing our clients for that sort of future, or any sort of future for that matter, is a serious task. There needs to be a plan. For organisations dealing with information, and there are not many that do not do so in some way, there is a growing concern about the cost and cost effectiveness of information provision. Organisational theories that underpin and help to explain these concerns need to include an understanding of the ways in which information is harvested, processed and delivered to the end user.

The Industrial Age tended to concern itself with producing human clones suitable for repetitive industrial production. Factory work styles, mass production, assembly lines and like-alike products encouraged information providers to think in terms of storehouses (Dowler 1997, pp.97-98; Raitt 1997, p.10; Beck 1998, p.13). The same storehouse model tended to dominate education (Warner, chapter 3; Beare 2001, p.42). Learners were containers waiting to be filled with a finite set of facts so that they would be fit for 'assembly line' type operations. This might well be termed the 'Gradgrind approach' made notorious by Charles Dickens in the nineteenth century (Dickens 1996, p.17). Neither education nor information provision was seen in any but an exceptionally utilitarian and finite form. Print was the only format of value, and even then was usually confined to those works considered 'uplifting'. Current social and economic conditions regulated both education and information provision quite rigidly and the end product of both was predictable, safe and universally recognisable. The process towards that end was inflexible.

Dickens was writing from the perspective of the Industrial Age – the age of machines. Humanity was in many respects just another set of machines that needed correct programming. Poor programming would lead to poverty and revolution; correct programming would lead to wealth and prosperity. As Giovenco reminds us, the present world has very different expectations and considerations.

> The issue being presented today is not one of relevance or capacity
> of libraries to service or survive but is one of leadership and
> considered, service-based, and people-focused management.

In the current age, whatever it might be called, the application of information to the client's needs must result in increasingly flexible and capable decision-making. Outcomes for libraries now need to reflect social and ethical responsibility as well as the more traditional economic outcomes. There is a clear indication, for example, that environmental issues can no longer be ignored. Future library management appears to involve even more than what has sometimes been called the 'triple bottom line' (Elkington 2004) and certainly a heightened appreciation for the global environment.

Collectively the outcomes of new learning and new information provisioning require a unifying goal – what Michael Fullan has named a moral purpose. This concept encompasses a clearly stated and outcome-related understanding of the principle driving force of the organisation. It is more than a goal and more than a mission statement although both of those would reflect it. Moral purpose is about both ends and means (Fullan 2001a, p.13). It is a clear statement of intent that shapes what an organisation does as well as what it intends to produce. In the ecology of information provision, moral purpose provides a statement of how a given organisation intends to make a distinct difference by its intentions, processes and products. As the general product is one of improved learning or a more 'informed' client, moral purpose often involved a value statement relating to the ways the organisation will 'improve life' – will make people better.

While it may appear to be simply a replacement for the Industrial Age expectation of factory clones, in fact the contemporary goal must produce a far more complex and flexible worker – one for whom the only constant is change, not repetition. There does need to be serious thought given by all managers and intending managers as to what their moral purpose is as well as the moral purpose that guides their organisation.

To succeed in the task of better managing information for our clients we need a plan, preferably a plan that is based on some sound principles and tested theories. Organisational theory has been discussed for many years. Fullan, in particular, has done much to offer insights into this area. If we are to ensure libraries exist in the future we do need to avoid the smaller and perhaps transitory issues like technologies or formats and set out to provide ourselves with a firm basis for operation, one that will be flexible and effective, just as we wish our 'product' to be. We need a basis for operation that will nurture change and reject repetition. Our 'products' must be able to change freely, just as we do. They need to do this on the basis of quality information and considered decisions, so do we. Far too often though, we are attempting to build flexibility based on a selection of very out-of-date past management folklore. We need to ask ourselves, what process do we set up, what theoretical framework do we accept as a basis for action that will build the future that Shelby and Miles (our clients of the future, see chapter 3), will inhabit?

Some years ago, David Raitt wrote of the need for a sound organisational framework if libraries were to survive in this 'brave new world'.

> Many people .... have attempted to define the electronic library and written about what it might be like – but it is evident that there is much more to be considered than the library itself. There is the whole organisational framework, the policies and the strategies, the technologies available, the staff and users and the social and economic milieu in which the library will operate (Raitt 1997, p.8).

Nothing has changed since then, except that the whole context for information provision has become more chaotic and complex (Fullan 2001b, pp.13-4). Those managing or intending to manage libraries, now, more than ever before, need to have a firm idea of where they are going and what they need to set in place in order to achieve it. In the scenario presented by Johnson in chapter 3, Miles quotes his grandfather as saying:

> the tools librarians use change, the importance of certain tasks that librarians perform changes, and even the services libraries offer to support their schools and communities change. But some things, like the librarian's mission and values, remain constant.

Management and organisational theory

In essence, what is management?

Johnson drops the comment 'Good thing I'm in management where I don't need many technology skills', into his scenario. This might be a tongue in cheek comment but it does raise a few questions. Do managers, in order to be respected and influential, have to exhibit all the skills of their workplace? Do they need to be that 'one step ahead'? What is a manager?

The Industrial Age manager was a controller. Control and imposition were the general themes with fear, scarcity and self-interest being used to get people to work (Wheatley 2009). Power was hierarchical with a carefully structured chain of command that was made clear to everyone involved. Success in management was measured most usually in terms of profits. If profits were made then management was deemed to be successful. In 1985 Heller made the comment:

> A manager is good and a company efficient only because others
> consider the results of their work good: their so-called goodness
> endures only as long as this good opinion holds (Heller, p.18).

I will return to this comment on a few occasions in chapter 4 as it constitutes something of a wake-up call to information professionals across the world and to school librarians in particular. Meanwhile, it is important to note that Heller at least offers a very fluid idea of what management is all about – whatever it is, it is measured by success. Profit was the usual measure of organisation performance and consequently of management performance.

Shirky points out the high levels of accountability that a networked population expects. His 2002 example of public scrutiny highlights new pressures on leaders and managers everywhere as their activities are more open to public comment, and that public scrutiny can be far-reaching (Shirky, p.143ff). Wheatley observes:

> The world has changed … Chaos and global connectedness are
> part of our daily lives … No matter what we do, stability and
> lasting solutions elude us (Wheatley 2006, p.ix).

The work of being a manager is changing with the changes in the way organisations are functioning. As the world becomes more complex, so also do organisations and their internal functions. Management is not what it used to be, and old methods are no longer working as they once did.

Too often the practicing information professional and manager tends to assume a traditional role and bases activity on past practice with little question, building practices and policies on that basis. The result of this is clearly seen in our past and even in much of the present. All round the world information managers whether they be in school libraries, academic libraries, public libraries or in private enterprise, frequently work according to a series of unquestioned traditions. This happens in many walks of life, but it is particularly unhelpful in the hugely changing and challenging world of information. The changes that Wheatley, Shirky, Auletta and others have identified are often ignored. Rather like one or two of the characters in a story by Spencer Johnson, instead of going in search of their cheese they wait at the old cheese station for the cheese they are used to but which will never come (Johnson 1999, p.25ff).

Two very obvious examples of this may be seen in the concern in many libraries over the decline in print usage and the stress on quietness (a lovely old Victorian notion). All too often these are 'rules' that are not questioned – they go with the territory. But why?

There does need to be a new questioning of old practices, practices that are all too easy for the media to identify and ridicule, as well as practices that far too often do not suit the current and future client. This questioning though needs to be directed in a very positive way and organisational theory holds one key to this.

To help counter this background of what might be described as a collection of almost arbitrary and isolated management decisions over many years and to facilitate a shift into the modern, unpredictable and changing world, there needs to be some consideration of information fundamentals as well as of the organisational context for them. We all participate in organisations – schools, corporations, government, hospitals, and so on. Each of us wants to make a recognised contribution to our organisation. We want, if possible, to make an *effective* contribution not just a contribution. When we make decisions or act in certain ways, we want those ideas and actions to count, to make a difference, and to be seen to make a difference. The more we know about how organisations operate, then the more we can adjust our activity so as to ensure that we do make a difference. Theories of organisation are all about giving us this knowledge.

Definitions of theory and organisation

Before starting out on our theoretical explorations, some basic clarifications may well avoid confusion as to what is being explored. Theory is often equated with impracticability and imprecision. However, it is more helpful to approach it as a set of generalisations based on observable practice and in turn used to inform subsequent practice. Official dictionary meanings tend to support this approach. For example:

> a plan or scheme existing in the mind only, but based on principles verifiable by experiment or observation (*Funk & Wagnalls*, p.1302).

> Supposition explaining something, esp. one based on principles independent of the phenomena, etc. To be explained (*Concise Oxford*, p.1344).

A theory it appears is concerned to describe a situation or function in general principle terms that are not necessarily linked directly to the phenomenon itself.

What then of organisational theory? Organisational theory is the explanation and discussion of the broad principles of how organisations work and why. What is an organisation?

> Organisations are social entities that are goal-oriented; are designed as deliberately structured and coordinated activity systems, and are linked to the external environment (Daft 2004).

What is organisational theory?

Organisational theory is the name given to a set of propositions that are constructed within the field of organisation science. It includes a study of organisations in practice, and from observation and research develops a body of knowledge that seeks to generalise on the way elements of an organisation interact as well as the way the organisation interacts with its environment.

Organisational theory is the study of the behaviour and nature of organisations and their environments (Miner 2005, p.4). It is not in itself strategic management, economics or a philosophy – though there are elements of all these and more as it relates to the different interactions of groups, individuals, corporate structures and context issues. Most of all it is concerned with the involvement of personal goals within organisations – the relationship between the individual and the group.

One of the more critical aspects of organisational theory is that it makes an attempt both to describe management styles and structures as well as forming generalisations that will help to further inform management. This means that in its character, organisational theory is an applied science – it scientifically investigates and describes organisational behaviours and then makes the resulting knowledge available for problem-solving and decision-making in the ongoing practice of enterprises or institutions.

The conceptualising of organisational theory is not new. In recent decades though it has gone through something of a refining process as terms like organisational behaviour, organisational science, business theory, and many others were debated and, where possible, delineated. The distinctions though, remain blurred. Writing specifically as regards organisational behaviour, Miner notes:

> Although the exact boundaries of the discipline are somewhat fuzzy ... organisational behaviour's focus is clearly on the world of organisations. The concern is first with the behaviour and nature

of people within organisations, and second with the behaviour and nature of organisations within their environments (Miner 2005, p.3).

Throughout this book, my main concern is to examine both of these issues – behaviour within organisations and the relationship of organisations to their external contexts. Before going further though, there is an issue of terminology. Miner uses the term organisational behaviour. He explains his choice in this way:

> Several other terms have become intertwined with organisational behaviour over the years, although none has achieved the same level of acceptance. One is organisational theory, which has come to refer almost exclusively to the study of behaviour and nature of organisations in their environments. A second is organisation(al) science, which appears to cover essentially the same ground as organisational behaviour … However, right now organisational behaviour has won the day (Miner 2005, p.4).

For me the jury is still out as to which term is the most appropriate and current. In this book I will use the term organisational theory to explore both of the issues listed above – behaviour within and connection to context – as regards organisational function and composition.

Though fuzzy around the edges perhaps, organisational theories form a valuable framework for action and policy construction. They enable operators to have a clearer view of the interconnectedness of the different relationships within the organisation. Organisational theory helps to explain how organisations work and how we think about them, and offers advice on how we regulate our relationships within our own organisation, and ideas on more effective ways of contributing to the organisation.

Theory and practice

The question needs to be asked 'Why start on organisational theory at this point in a work such as this'? This book is intended to be a rather practical collection of observations on the future of information provision. In a work that sets itself the task of exploring library management issues for the future, why then make a sudden side trip into theory? The answer lies in the pivotal nature of organisational theory as it relates to future information provision.

Theory is not necessarily the speculative, 'ivory tower' dreaming it is often seen to be. Quite often a major divide is accepted between theory and practice (Das 2003; Donaldson 2002). Theory is seen as the philosophising, fuzzy and impractical day-dreaming of academics that bears little resemblance to 'real world' practical issues. Miner explores this division briefly in his introduction to the work *Organisational behaviour I.* However, the point he makes is that the two are very much related. He cites several studies of human relations professionals carried out by Rynes, Brown and Colbert. These showed that of the professionals who devoted time to research literature – the theory behind their work – most were employed by more financially successful organisations. Arguably, they were better informed by research and this impacted on their organisation (Miner 2005, p.5). It would seem then that while studies are still few and far between the evidence suggests that theory informs practice. I believe the reverse is also true. Theory and practice are in fact mutually supportive.

Amid the increasingly complex and almost chaotic world of information, both elements are of vital concern. In the past it was possible to build quite rigid structures, both theoretical and practical, and keep them for long periods of time with little modification. Old ideas and theories are being challenged by current conditions. Recent technical advances and increasing individual interactivity has contributed significantly to a new information ecology. New frameworks for analysing organisation need to be made and new ways of doing things need to be built around this analysis and changed understanding.

Shirky speaks with considerable accuracy when he writes of 'the power of organising without organisations' (2008). He is not suggesting that organisational theory is impossible in the current situation, but rather that the world of the individual empowered by current technologies is seriously challenging all of our past notions of organisation as well as of what might be termed 'traditional' organisational theory. In essence, the old theories are no longer helpful. Work practices and organisational structures based on them are no longer appropriate. Concepts and theories ideal for the Industrial Age are now failing to meet the needs of current organisations and their clients.

Evolution of management thought

1880s – systematic management

Rather as its name might suggest, systematic management theory revolved around organisational rules. These rules or systems were developed as contributing directly to 'the [only] way' to make a given product. The systems were independent of people including both management and workers either of whom might otherwise derail the system and cause inefficiency or nonproduction. It argued directly against other theory that suggested power/control should rest with superintendants and foremen. Placing power in their hands would risk 'non-systematic' behaviour and thus prejudice production and efficiency. Human error was considered to be highly likely, human beings were after all rather failure prone, and so a system was needed to prevent it.

One of the more enthusiastic supporters of this theory, Goss (as cited by Yates 1993, p.170) relied heavily on communication to enable a systemic approach. For the purposes of dissemination and implementation Goss wanted new regulations carefully and fully written up such that 'there could be no chance of misunderstanding due to changes of one sort or another' (Yates 1993, p.171). One of the real weaknesses of the theory was its inability to accept change. As time moved on, change became more common and so the 'system' would begin to fail.

1900 – scientific management
When around 1900 scientific methods began to be applied to the study of how organisations functioned, efficiency was one of the critical goals for all corporations. Four important considerations regulated this analysis of industry:

1. Apply a scientific approach to the investigation of each element of the workers task.
2. Scientifically select, train, teach and develop each individual worker.
3. Reconcile workers with jobs so as to match principles and plans.
4. Keep a clear and appropriate division of labour, scientifically balanced.

With science seen as providing every answer, there was a clear focus on using scientific principles in order to determine 'the one best way'. This scientific focus was applied to theoretical considerations as well as to the shop floor. Tasks were carefully analysed, workers closely watched in terms of time and motion, and management skills identified by scientific deduction that would maximise output.

Frederick Taylor is recognised as one of the key writers around the theme of scientific management theory and practice.

1905 – bureaucracy
The importance of bureaucracy was first studied shortly after the start of the new century. This involved the study of networking and relationship among specialised positions. In an area of standardisation, organisations were considered in terms of standard positions and clear divisions of labour. Routine operations were subjected to regulation in terms of standardised behaviours and a clear hierarchy. Tasks were best compartmentalised and emphasis was on position rather than person. These views quickly metamorphosed into administrative theory before being challenged a

little later by a new emphasis on individuals with the rise of human relations considerations in the 1920s.

Efficiency was one of the guiding principles shaping a bureaucratic view of organisations with trained staff following strict rules under close supervision. Subjective judgement of employees was unnecessary, as performance was the critical issue rather than people. One of the considerable limitations with the bureaucratic view of organisations was its tendency to ignore the critical considerations of personality. Individuals were operatives rather than personalities.

1910 – administrative management

While scientific management concentrated on the management of work and workers, administrative management addressed issues concerning the overall structure of an organisation. This concept is position focused with executives seen as formulating the organisation's purpose, regulating employees and maintaining communications. Managers respond to change, rather than organisations or employees. They are seen as professionals who can be trained and developed. Max Weber, a notable promoter of administrative management, saw structure as striving to achieve a 'calculability of rational results, precision, stability, discipline and reliability' (Weber 1947, p.332).

It was this concern for stability and discipline that marked out the way for theorists who supported bureaucratic and administrative forms of management structures. While espousing rational legal authority (the predominant form of authority today), Weber saw it as being attained through the most efficient form of organisation, bureaucracy. While we might seriously question this in the modern environment, at that time of political and cultural instability before the First World War, stability, discipline and 'rationality' were much sought after. Occasionally, the same ideas can be seen in some organisations, schools and libraries at the present time as they attempt to build their own 'security fence' around themselves in a constantly changing world. In 1991 Ken Johnson presented a challenging paper to a state conference in Florida, USA, in which he decried the growing bureaucracy of schooling and suggested in its place a more student-centred approach (Johnson 1991). That paper was not 'very well received' at the time giving an indication that the bureaucratic theories propounded by Weber and his contemporaries still exert considerable influence in schooling into the present era – something that Hughes, Johnson and Warner (in chapter 3) would be concerned about, but not necessarily surprised at.

In addition to Weber, the works of Henri Fayol and Luther Gulick are significant in terms of their contributions to administrative management theory and practice.

1920 – human relations

Human relations developed as a specific study in the 1920s. Amid the general rise in interest for matters psychological, human scientists began to consider in more detail the relationship between the psychological and social issues, and the performance of workers. Personality types helped define people, as more emphasis was placed on employee welfare, motivation and communication. For the first time employees generally began to be seen as people rather than 'operatives'. As a corollary of this it was noted how employee behaviour was influenced by the informal work group. Within these groups, cohesion, status and group norms influenced behaviour and determined output.

Maslow (1943) constructed a 'hierarchy of need' which suggested that social needs had precedence over systematic needs.

As part of human relations research, the 'Hawthorne effect' was first noted – the suggestion that workers performed differently when under observation by researchers. Although the term itself was coined much later in 1955 by Henry Landsberger (1958), the effect was first noted in a study at the Hawthorne Works of Western Electric near Chicago in 1924-32. Although the study was investigating the effect of light conditions on workers, itself a rather administrative concept, the net result of the tests was that productivity rose during the investigation and fell again once the research was completed. The conclusion reached was that productivity improved where there was notice taken of the employees (Mayo 1949). While they were being considered, they worked better.

1930 – quantitative management

As a rather 'natural' consequence of bureaucratic and administrative views of organisation, quantitative considerations became more critical as organisations grew. As organisations grow, they become more complex and one way of responding to this is to quantify their operations. Management saw relief in mathematical constructs that reduced issues to formulae. Quantitative analysis became a popular way of assessing company performance, with the emphasis swinging back to output rather than people. Reducing issues to such regular 'rules' helped managers make decisions that appeared to be based on 'fact' and gave them more clear and precise management tools.

However, the quantitative approach tended to ignore more personal issues that had been raised with the growth in human relations thinking. The two ideas did not sit well together. Further, mathematical understandings were less appropriate in the case of non-routine issues. Management unpredictability or individuality challenged such explanations. There could be exceptions and these were not well covered by quantitative explanations.

Quantitative considerations were well suited to the years that immediately followed the Great Depression and those that led into the early years of the Second World War. Output quantities, production targets and the like were measurable and important. However, as war tolls mounted, individuals tended to grow in importance.

1935 – organisation behaviour

Partly in reaction to the conflict between human relations explanations and the more dogmatic quantitative theories, organisational theorists in the later and immediate post-war years once more turned to considering organisations as units. Employee effectiveness became more of a consideration than simple output figures and the overall health of the organisation become an important issue.

Organisational behaviour investigated the nature of individual, group and organisation processes and their inter-relationships. Behaviourists tended to start from one of two possible understandings. Either workers were lazy, irresponsible and required constant supervision, or they wanted to work and to control their activities for themselves. Either way, relationships as Fullan and others more recently understand them, began to increase in importance. The relationships between employees and managers were seen to also influence the work performed – both its quantity and its quality. By understanding the individual and the way they saw themselves in the organisation, it was possible to assess and promote effective work and improve productivity.

Among the changes to organisational thinking contributed by the behaviourists were the concepts of participation, greater autonomy for employees, and the importance of initiative in the organisation. For perhaps the first time there was philosophical support for the importance on individual action even in large operations. Bureaucracy was seriously challenged and the power of the individual defended. However, a shortfall occurred in a lack of consideration to situational factors such as environment and technology.

1940 – systems theory

To somehow wed the unlikely bedfellows of bureaucracy and organisational behaviour, theorists began to view organisations as systems. In an age of scientific advance, corporations were perceived as well-ordered systems and subsystems. The more order in the corporation the better its organisation, the better its output, and the happier its employees. To achieve this ideal outcome, management needed to work in harmony with its environment (as in contextual, not natural) and goals needed to emphasise efficiency and orderliness. For the first time, theory began to blur the edges a little as it was 'discovered' that there were more ways than one of achieving the ideal outcome.

While systems theory allowed the whole to be more than the sum of its parts, it did not provide specific guidance to managers. Their role was left somewhat nebulous and severely generalised. Organisations were encouraged to adapt to context in order to be more effective but how this might be achieved was left largely unexplored. Certainly the systems theorists exploded the 'one way' approach but did not construct a viable alternative in its place.

1950s – contingency theory

Owing most of its formulation to Fred Feilder during the 1960s, this theory – or perhaps more correctly model – first appeared around 1951 (Miner 2005, p.238). Contingency theory suggests a substantial role for the manager. Power was a function of legitimate authority, itself a result of the sanctions (positive or negative) that the manager could call on in their role. Loyalty to the leader was an important aspect of corporate power and the extent to which a leader could command this loyalty was in itself a measure of the success or otherwise of the leader. Relationships are important in this interaction, but only so far as the leader can command obedience.

1980-2010 – Current re-evaluations

Organisational theory during the past two or three decades has been considerably shaped by the various different propositions put by theorists over many years. One of the most critical concerns of the new era though is that of environmental response – a combination of human considerations and green issues. In an age where social networking allows employees greater access to the workings of their organisation and the general public a greater scrutiny of corporation performance and operation, management has a host of new priorities.

One aspect of this is total quality management (TQM). Drawing from many of the past considerations and theories, TQM considers organisation particularly in terms of customer satisfaction while keeping track of performance as a total organisational entity. It is perhaps characterised by a strong orientation to both internal customers (usually employees) and external customers – the consumers and the context/environment. In many ways it is theoretically a combination of key factors of organisation behaviour, human relations and scientific management. It is a fusion of past thinking with current context.

Modern organisations are seen to operate within their environment, both human and natural. There is a complex set of relationships that shape this interaction. Organisations not only employ people and produce goods; they also contribute to human activity and natural change. Increasingly they are seen as needing to be responsible for and to their environment. The context for organisations is increasingly complex and so the relationships between them and their context are necessarily more complex.

Driven by evidence of the growing complexity of society, Fullan (2001a) suggested, quite firmly, that leadership in all areas needed to become equally sophisticated. The old order of 'do what I say' is not sufficiently robust to offer the foundation for practice needed in the new millennium. Wheatley echoes this when she says:

> If organisations are machines, the control makes sense. If organisations are process structures, then seeking to impose control through permanent structure is suicide (Wheatley 2006, p.23).

Suggesting that leaders needed to change their leadership style and perhaps even more importantly their focus, Fullan suggests a concentration on a small number of 'key dimensions' (Fullan 2001a, p.2). Provided these key dimensions are correctly identified and then become a definite focus, he argues that leaders will more effectively deal with the complex and often apparently chaotic society in which they lead. Citing Heifetz (1994) he notes that whereas in the past leaders when faced with the unexpected had called for a saviour or guide, in the modern climate, where there is often no clear way ahead, 'no simple, painless solutions' – problems require us to 'learn new ways' (Heifetz, p.21). For Fullan, the key to sound leadership in these times is to have a clear moral purpose and to build leadership around that purpose (Fullan 2001a, p.3).

If the past few decades have been notable for anything it has been for change. Wheatley notes 'the world has changed … chaos and global connectedness are part of our daily lives' (Wheatley 2006, p.ix). As this book is written, the first decade of the new millennium is drawing to its close. The national media here in Australia are running with two significant topics; the time spent by teenagers on their social networking and the way history over the past ten years has shown clearly that 'we don't know what is ahead in the next ten'.

One survey suggests that twenty hours each week are regularly spent by Americans in social networking (Bly 24/3/09). Thelwall (2008) suggests that for students, much of this interconnectivity occurs interlaced with study. At the time learners are learning they are actively interacting on a social level. This connectedness seems to be a key feature of most people's lives – regardless of demographics. Surprisingly, some studies are finding that use of the new technologies may well be higher for non-net generation age groups (Kennedy, Dalgarno, et.al. 2007). Whatever the outcome of current research there can be little doubt that we are presently in an age of greater connectedness that ever before. Shirky, Auletta, and Fullan, among others, make the assumption that this is now a part of life. All the indications would suggest that this is not a passing phase, but rather a permanent state of affairs. Johnson and Healy base their future scenarios in chapter 3 firmly on this premise.

This connectedness in itself is a considerable change. But it is only one of many. Quite a few of these changes are being driven by technology or are a result of it. Spencer Johnson recognised this when he wrote his rather famous little book *Who moved my cheese?* Fullan has written widely about the implications of change on organisations. His premise of the inevitability of change echoes the theme of Johnson's story.

> The more complex society gets, the more sophisticated leadership must become. Complexity means change, but specifically it means rapidly occurring, non-linear change (Fullan 2001a, p.v).

The inevitability of change brings new challenges to organisations and to the way they function. It brings a host of challenges for those who would see their role in an organisation as leader. It thrusts some who would rather avoid leadership into positions that are pivotal to the organisation and where leading is no longer avoidable. Today, despite the history of change now behind us, it is still possible to identify many of the characters in the Johnson story – those who wait for their cheese to appear back at the same place, and those who starve while doing so; those who leave the old feeding station to find where the cheese now is, and so on.

The level of change – and particularly its non-linear nature – makes older concepts of organisation redundant. It is not possible to impose systematic or scientific models onto a moving and changing operation. Connectedness threatens and fragments the bureaucratic and administrative theories of the past. Examples like that cited by Shirky (2008, p.1ff) in the case of the missing phone, show how quickly modern connectedness can challenge hierarchies and established bureaucracies.

Further, the speed of these changes is nothing short of breathtaking. For a baby-boomer like me, the uptake of the mobile phone, for example, has been just one more in a whole range of technologies that have radically changed the way we do things. Many teacher librarians will recall the advent of the internet and email. It changed the way we worked dramatically. Library automation is now the 'norm' but it is within the living memory of some of us at least that schools based their libraries on card catalogues. James Gleick generalises on the pace of change in his works *Chaos* (1987) and *Faster* (1999) (subtitled; 'The acceleration of just about everything').

What is needed at this time is an organisational theory (and there may be more than one alternative) that allows for constant change, that considers the individual and the new power that they now wield, that embraces connectedness and that gives direction in a chaotic and complex environment. With the connectedness, comes a new level of transparency, one aspect of organisation that many earlier attempts to theorise did not include. Thus, the 'new' organisational theory needs to be characterised by openness and flexibility.

> Organisations can be seen as open systems, like organisms which
> constantly adapt to their internal and external environment (Miner
> 2005, p.4).

The theory regarding modern organisations needs to reflect this constantly adapting nature and also to consider in new ways the relevance of environment – the context in which the organisation functions.

The field of information is changing just as is the more general context of organisation. It is an aspect of human endeavour that is under extreme pressure. Those who get it right will prosper. Get it wrong and you are history.

> Already, we see increased requirements for better knowledge in
> the workplace to deliver competitive knowledge-intensive work ...
> Globalisation pressures have changed business – and
> correspondingly work – worldwide (Wiig 1999, p.155).

There is considerable urgency and the stakes are high. In the specific field of library services there are already organisations that are going to the wall. Hughes notes above the changes in school library over the past forty years – the decline in the skilled school library personnel as seen through the eyes of the government that pays for them. Both in theory and practice there is an urgent need to adopt concepts that will support the needs of users quite specifically as well as be responsive to the changing environment in which they function.

One of the key factors in this fight for survival has to be the concept of moral purpose that Fullan sees as so important. Without a clear and appropriate purpose, existence in such a challenging context will be impossible. To this key aspect of organisation Fullan adds four other components:

> leaders will increase their effectiveness if they continually work on
> the five components of leadership – if they pursue moral purpose,
> understand the change process, develop relationships, foster
> knowledge building and strive for coherence – with energy,
> enthusiasm and hopefulness (Fullan 2001a, p.11).

I would suggest that to these five might be added a sixth – continuous product review. It seems totally appropriate, even essential, that the end product of leadership needs to be constantly reviewed so as to ensure that the original moral purpose is the correct one, and that it remains constantly relevant in a changing environment.

In summary, current organisational theory takes into account many years of discussion and study. In terms of information organisation the important aspects to consider revolve around purpose, relationships and desired outcome (product review). The driving force and primary concern is purpose. Having a clear, concise and well understood (by everyone involved) purpose will be pivotal to any organisation delivering the appropriate service to the appropriate client. Information organisations need to keep their guiding purpose clear to all, particularly given the increasingly transparent environment in which they function.

Moral purpose

In the mid 1990s, Michael Fullan introduced moral purpose to organisational theory. It was perhaps nothing new to those involved in the 'business' of learning. There has always been a strong element of moral purpose, of making a difference, in learning and in its more formal context, education. 'In education, an important end is to make a difference in the lives of students' (Fullan 2001a, p.13, c/f.; Hughes, 17/9/09 quoted above in the introduction). In a fundamental sense, this has been the case for at least two thousand years, though how that difference was to be brought about and exactly what that difference was has been changing the whole time, and continues to change as we move into the future.

For those in the public library sector, a basic moral purpose might be to encourage the public to read more. Reading as empowerment (as against the process of reading itself) has perhaps been one of the more overt reasons for libraries within the western world. It was this purpose that drove the establishment of the Mechanics Institute – one early form of public libraries. Following that line of thought, the encouragement of reading in the nineteenth century context may not be quite so far removed from that in the twenty-first. Fundamentally, it is the vehicle for self improvement – a key to independence and economic security. In fact, it could well be put into current terms as lifelong learning.

In either case, the basic concern is to 'make a difference'. This idea is common to most organisations that are organised – the reason they have been organised is to bring some change about even if it is only 'to make a better mousetrap'. They are even likely to exist among the organisations that Shirky sees clearly as spontaneous and unstructured.

Organisations in all areas of human activity have in the past few years become concerned with 'mission statements'. Effectively these are the organisational statements of moral purpose. They serve to focus attention on the significant goal of the organisation in a clear and communicable way.

The more clearly these goals or mission statements or moral purposes are stated, the more likely the organisation is to achieve them. Further, the more successful any organisation is in communicating these the more likely it is that the organisation will succeed. Generating enthusiasm for those purposes among members of the organisation will see that success achieved faster.

Having a purpose and then building a clear strategy to bring that purpose about is one of the cornerstones of library management, perhaps of any organisational management. It is not enough to simply define your purpose. There needs to be a clearly marked pathway towards its achievement as well as a process that treats all stakeholders fairly. If educational managers are to achieve their purposes effectively, their staff must know the direction they are heading and be supported to make the necessary changes.

This is all well and good but there is a danger, a very considerable danger, that users and stakeholders tend in this view to be seen rather as artefacts themselves and treated in similar ways to the books or periodicals. They are seen and 'managed' as isolated elements rather than as parts of a dynamic and interactive whole.

One difficulty with this concept is that it is often seen by library and information leaders/managers within the rather narrow view of reading process as an access to text. The moral purpose in this instance needs to be somewhat de-contextualised, so as to move away from emphasis on the 'artefact' of text (the actual reading taking place) and into the realm of accessibility to information as a wealth, mobility and social determinant tool (the information that the reading makes accessible). Many libraries are still focused on books – on the physical items themselves. All too often library use is measured in books borrowed just as reading ability is still occasionally measured by the number of books read (regardless of linguistic challenge or lack of it).

Reading – for instance – is not a matter of the number of books borrowed or books read but of building the ability to connect information, to identify its connectedness and its relationship to information already accumulated. This view is rather artificial, and in the current context frequently damaging to the long-term survival of libraries. There needs to be a shift in emphasis towards a more socio-anthropological framework and context of relevance, meaning and relationships (see, for example, Giovenco in chapter 3).

Viewing items as artefacts (and sometime even the borrowers themselves as such) is to some extent the result of generations of library evolution. For many years, with libraries used as storehouses, the emphasis has been on the item perhaps more than the client. Moral purpose goes much deeper than numbers of items or borrowers. It considers the ways in which human behaviour can be modified by the library over a long period of time. Warner speaks of lifelong learning and the 'disposition to learn'. These are more valuable concepts in terms of moral purpose. They move beyond the artefact level and into the long-term moral dimension. They also contribute more clearly to the concept of information as an ecology – reading, knowledge, resources (of all varieties, human and non-human) and technology are all factors that busily interact with each other, the leader and the client in a wonderful living world of information assimilation.

Giovenco has a serious point when he speaks of both empowerment and development in terms of the 'application, manipulation and maximisation' of a client's information capacities as an essential element of moral purpose. Moral purposes that are based on information as a wealth, mobility and social tool needs to give way to those that place information in a far more individual light where relationships between people, as well as relationships with information, are actively considered. Information in the modern context must be far more human focused. Management needs to direct itself more than at any time in the past towards the very specific needs of its clients – both individually and collectively.

Miles, Shelby and their contemporaries (see chapter 3) are real people. As they become increasingly enmeshed in technology, so the relationships with real people will become more critical as a context, a reality check, for the technical. Aspects of human dynamic, motivation and practice all need to be part of the moral purpose that their information professionals use to guide the future of information provision. Relationships are constructed around moral purpose, are guided by it, and are essential for the effective outworking of that purpose.

Relationships

As noted above, the nature of relationships is a critical factor in terms of knowledge transfer. What Hughes and others have discovered in regards to education, Fullan and friends have found for managing and leading. Building relationships is critical for success. Their views hark back over many years of thinking on control in organisation and general organisational function as well. Between 1918 and 1932, Mary Parker Follett published two books and two papers underlining the importance of relationships in organisational function. Her work was largely ignored until much more recently (Ryan & Rutherford 2000, p.220). In her 1918 work, *The new state*, she noted:

> We cannot put the individual on the one side and society on the
> other; we must understand the complete interrelation of the two.
> Each has no value; no existence without the other ... There is no
> such thing as a self-made man (Follett 1924, pp.61-2).

The importance of Follett, and others who followed such as Metcalf & Urwick and Weick, for instance, is a clear indication that discussion on individuality and collectivisation has a long history. Early in that history it was noted that the organisation does not control the individual but that organisation members both shape and are shaped by their organisation. Follett exercised considerable influence in the US during the first half of the twentieth century perhaps because she was among the first to suggest that 'neither worker nor organisation, neither individual nor collective, holds all the power in a work relationship' (Ryan & Rutherford 2000, p.221).

For Fullan, the first two tasks of a promising manager are to identify a clear moral purpose and then to establish strong relationships with the people he/she has to deal with (Fullan 2001a, p.51). Raitt refers to this when he speaks of the 'social ... milieu' in which library operates (Raitt 1997, p.8). The two major management tasks are the same for business as they are for education. Giovenco puts this a little differently when he challenges:

> The whole basis of humans even as a species is the social contexts
> of our existence and interplay. As soon as we start creating
> externalised concepts of stakeholders/users as artefacts we run the
> risk of losing relevance, validity, connectedness and
> meaningfulness ... i.e., care. As soon as we start putting systems,
> structures and technologies between and around the
> users/stakeholders we then start seeing the users as the other and

potentially the distracter. The systems become the 'cared' or loved ones (Giovenco 14/11/09).

The notion of 'power'

Power is quite often seen as closely related to management – managers have the 'power' to make things happen. In a hierarchical system, power is seen in the form of domination and manipulation. For many centuries our history told the story of power by the sword. This tended to translate directly into the early business organisations, either in terms of those with money dominating or those with position. On the factory floor or in the front office, management was closely related to control. Decision-making was a variation on the theme of wheeling and dealing and those decisions were quite regularly kept rather private, with the majority of people in the organisation largely kept 'in the dark' as to what had been decided, except for the part of it that directly affected them.

In the 1950s, Robert Dahl began to develop his pluralist view of democracy. As a part of that development he reinvestigated the notion of power. His definition of power can best be summed up as the ability to get another person to do something that they would not otherwise have done. His six forms of power ranged from 'best to worst' through:

1. Rational persuasion – truthfulness and explanation to win someone to action.
2. Manipulative persuasion – lying or misleading others into action.
3. Inducement – reward or punishment used to create action.
4. Power – major threats, often physical.
5. Coercion – no alternative given, this level rather presupposes a position of domination where such a situation can be real.
6. Physical force.

While Dahl applied this thinking to governments, it is of considerable value as we consider organisations generally. It is just possible that as you have read the six levels of power above, you have recognised seeing many of them clearly demonstrated in organisations that you have been part of. Dahl argues that the preferred power alternatives are the first few – particularly the first one. In quite important ways Dahl was reworking, probably unconsciously, ideas circulated earlier by Follett. In statements rather ahead of her time Follett had argued in the 1920s that power was a central problem in most aspects of our lives, particularly that of the organisation including industry, politics and international affairs.

Genuine power can only be grown, it will slip from every arbitrary hand that grasps it; for genuine power is not coercive control, but coactive control. Coercive power is the curse of the universe; coactive power, the enrichment and advancement of every human soul (Follett 1924, p.3).

Consider ....

Read Giovenco's note as regards reading.

> Reading ... needs to be unpacked more ... reading as a construct is representative of power and empowerment dynamics ... the process of reading in itself is not and was not the underlying paradigm for the betterment of mankind. It was the tool that represented the power and education constructs. If by some quirk of fate the construct was purely oral-based, then oral illiteracies and processes would be the dominant and defining context.

To what extent do you consider reading to equate to power? Is there a case for the argument that teachers have used the power of reading to control students past or present? How does library relate to this discussion?

Fullan recognises the importance of proper use of power with his six leadership styles. In some ways echoing the power levels of Dahl, Fullan notes the range of options from the coercive to the coaching (Fullan 2001a, p.35). He concludes that two of the styles, coercive and authoritative, had adverse effects on performance while the other four were more positive. While the different styles will be discussed more fully in the next chapter, it is important to note here that the way power transforms into leadership will directly affect the progress and the performance of any organisation.

Since the time of Follett and Dahl many have debated these issues, and the shape of both business and schooling has changed as a consequence. Over the years power in the shape of punishment has been very much a part of education, though not always seen as the desirable part. The intention has always been to develop in learners a perception of 'good and desirable' behaviours so that they will chose to emulate them, rather than a 'do this or I will hit you' approach. The current school bullying debate revolves around these same issues and focuses on the misuse of power. For researchers such as Smith and Brain, bullying is a 'power imbalance' (Smith & Brain 2000, p.1).

In the more structured context of organisations it is sometimes difficult to imagine power without position. What Follett, Dahl and many others are suggesting, however, is that power need not be position-related; hierarchy is not necessarily the power structure of an organisation. Each human being has the power to influence. The extent of that influence will depend on the relationships that we have built with others in our organisation and the level of trust in us that we can develop in others. In the next chapter we discuss 'leading from the middle', a direct outgrowth of this concept of influence as power with a very relevant application to the information provision ecology in the present age.

Consider ....

One of the critical directions on offer to current teacher librarians is potential to ensure that they are part of a learning community, rather than simply a learning program. Building a community where learning is fostered and nurtured is highly beneficial but it frequently requires the application of considerable power and influence in order to develop within each member of the community that ability to relate to each other and actually become a community rather than a collection of independencies.

Consider the organisation that employs you. How is your organisation 'organised'? Does it value people? Does it treat people like adults? Does it develop people? Do managers treat employees as customers? Should they? Is it a community or a company?

The key in all of this is relationships; relationship with other members of the organisational community. In the case of schools this will include everyone from principal to cleaner. Relationships will determine the extent and nature of the influence that can be brought to bear on the organisation by the individual. As mentioned above, this does not relate to hierarchy but rather to the strength which can be brought to bear in terms of relationship, and which can then be used to influence a situation.

It is essential in the postmodern context to maintain connections with all relevant stakeholders. The age when success could depend on secrecy is largely gone. Particularly in the context of information and knowledge – sharing is critical for success. Building relationships with stakeholders as well as critical partners is vital.

Decision-making and problem-solving

Effective communication of moral purpose and of issues facing an organisation will directly impact on the effectiveness of decision-making within that organisation. Decision-making will also be influenced by the relationships between organisation members and how clearly those relationships are perceived.

What Shirky and others are making very clear to us is that there are now far more people actively involved in the decision-making process albeit often very informally. Take for example the classroom teacher. In the Industrial Age, and perhaps well before that, classroom activities focused largely on the teacher as an authority figure in the room who dictated what was to be learned and how it was to be learned. The graphic description by Dickens in *Hard times* again springs to mind:

> Thomas Gradgrind now presented Thomas Gradgrind to the little pitchers before him, who were to be filled so full of facts. Indeed as he eagerly sparkled at them from the cellarage before mentioned he seemed a kind of cannon loaded to the muzzle with facts, and prepared to blow them clean out of the regions of childhood at one discharge. He seemed a galvanising apparatus, too, charged with a grim mechanical substitute for the tender young imaginations that were to be stormed away (p.17).

While moral purpose was perhaps not dissimilar to Fullan's basic educational statement above, it was very much dependent on that one autocratic individual in the most personal way. Decision-making in the classroom was a single person activity by and large.

Enter the computer and the internet (and particularly wireless entry to it in one form or another) and you have a very different scenario. No longer is the teacher out the front unchallenged. An even slightly determined student may choose to ignore the teacher and use their laptop, mobile phone or other device to either interrupt the teacher, or even replace them with another authority. This is not necessarily a bad thing though that may be hotly debated, but it does introduce other stakeholders to the decision-making process. Teachers today have to contend with the competition of online experts as well as the distractions of various 'entertainments' in the classroom that our grandparents never envisaged.

Related to decision-making to some extent – problem-solving is mainly concerned with the ability of each stakeholder to solve immediate 'problems' that occur 'on the job'. These may be as simple as choosing the best boolean search terms, or as complex as selecting the best way of cataloguing a web page so as to be available to the users most likely to need the information it contains.

Teamwork and collaboration

Working with others has its share of excitements. Quite recently, a group of practicing library managers were asked to carry out an online collaborative exercise. They did not know each other until the moment the project began and there was an evaluation of their work afterwards. Here is one comment loaded to a team member's blog:

> This is the most frustrating thing, working with other people. A great exercise in tolerance and remembering other people have lives and lead them. I have texted Beth who has a daughter in hospital and we are not sure what is going on there. Sue has the internet down and no phone service or reception for mobile phone (http://rosehawke.blogspot.com).

Collaboration is not necessarily easy and yet so many teachers, teacher librarians and public librarians when dealing with children love to hand out group tasks. What they tend to overlook is that in any team engagement there are a collection of personalities, all of whom contribute a huge range of social, ethnic and economic backgrounds as well as a fine selection from literally thousands of potential physical and intellectual conditions. Collaboration is exactly what learning to learn is all about (Lee 2006) and leaders are learners too. From an organisational point of view, collaboration is seen by many writers as absolutely essential.

Along with the potential for interaction, the advent of Web 2.0 technologies has provided the information professional with a firm platform for collaboration. Shirky (2008) explores the anarchic nature of the new world order as it impacts on our daily lives, while Tapscott and Williams (2006) note the new levels of interaction and collaboration and the enormous impact that they are having on global economies. Information seekers of all ages are almost automatically turning to either social networks or to google for answers. Auletta subtitled his commentary on the 'googleised' world, 'the end of the world as we know it' (2009). Shirky speaks of a virtual global anarchy brought about by social networking (2008, pp.11-12). His example of the stolen 'sidekick' also illustrates the new power and value of collaboration made possible by new social tools. That a minor issue of a mobile phone being stolen could ignite the curiosity and involvement of millions of Americans and lead to altering the established practice of the New York Police Department, is a powerful case for the effectiveness of collaboration in an instance where there was no formal organisation.

In the teaching and learning world this is equally true. While only small at present, there is a growing body of literature that is exploring the potential for new collaborations as part of the formal learning process (Rollett 2007, Poellhuber et al. 2008, Lee & Winzenried 2009). Web 2.0 tools increasingly are being seen as offering greater potential for the social construction of learning through collaborative operations. These collaborations are not necessarily long-distance ones, and they may be better – but need not be. They can happen within a classroom, a library or a home.

Some years ago I led the development of a student learning management system (SLMS) for a large private school. One of the driving forces was its purchase of several schools located several thousand miles away in a different country with a different culture. Committed to 'sharing' Australian senior schooling abroad, an internet-based system that allowed learners to view and interact both with learning materials and with teachers was considered essential. In the process of development the possibility of extending this access to parents and even grandparents was realised and included. As a result, the students' school reports (updated throughout the year and live online), their worksheets, the full year's curriculum and all the resources that might be needed became available to each learner and their family. Within months it became obvious from the number of parents who began contacting teachers (via the direct email links also provided) that they were, in some cases for the first time, seeing their learner's work and being offered the opportunity to 'help with homework'. A totally unexpected outcome of the program was the considerable number of parents reporting (more than 50 per cent) that their young learner's computer had been shifted voluntarily, from the bedroom to the family room. The learner had ongoing results to show and a pathway for improving results (which was taken more frequently and which did indeed improve results). From this a real interest in collaborating towards further improvement was generated. The results of collaboration were not only improving home interactions but were producing a stronger drive towards improvement.

One totally unlooked for 'side effect' of the arrangement was a sharp decline in both cyber-bullying and also 'inappropriate' social networking. With the learner's computer in a more public eye and more often used for family collaborations, social activities became almost unconsciously more responsible.

In the case of the SLMS, collaboration between family members improved and student results improved. However, the same tools were quickly being used as learners started to interact with each other, with a teacher and even with the wider world. New confidences were gained and even some very young learners were looking for scientists to help with their science, or zoo officials to help with their animal projects.

Collaboration has always been considered a useful tool in learning, thus the almost universal use of group work that has been a part of schooling for many years. However, new technologies have added new dimensions. Similarly, collaboration can assist in the information management field. The scenarios in chapter 3 all tend to assume a considerable level of collaboration, both within a single site and also in the wider cyber community. Johnson's (chapter 3) world databank relies on considerable sharing and collaboration for its establishment, as much as for its ongoing existence. The concept of e-collections suggested by Law (chapter 3) relies heavily on university faculties and schools collaborating to populate them, as well as on inter-university collaboration to share both the work of establishing and of populating them.

Collaboration and team work are just as important in the management area as they are in the learning context. Effective organisation is based solidly on relationships between the constituent individuals. Effective relationships lead to strong teams and more effective collaborations.

In organisations where teams are 'manufactured' (usually in the more hierarchical situations) relationships do need to be carefully fostered, even created. In the library context, the almost universal approach is to create a hierarchy and then go about slotting individuals into that organisation role by role. The teacher librarian, reference librarian, or whatever they are called, then become one individual within a rather rigid framework. What the SLMS experience demonstrates is the power of moving outside such a rigid framework. What is needed is wider visions that reach beyond a single person or a single library and into a learning community. Where library professionals can collaborate on a broader front and offer their clients a share of that collaboration (and the tools for collaborations of their own) the influence and power of those library staff will grow and the success as well as 'repeat custom' of those clients will increase. A broader vision is critical to long-term library survival. Individuals need to be proactive in generating collaboration and teamwork within their own organisation and also beyond it if they are to offer their clients long-term solutions to information needs.

Consider ...

- A regional buying consortia

- The Australian teacher librarian listserv – OZTL_NET

- Membership of the school curriculum committee

- Interlibrary lending

- ALA, ASLA, ALIA membership

- ClickView

- Professional conferences

- Workplace meetings

- Add three of your own suggestions

In what ways are these collaborations? How do they reduce your institutional costs, and thus ensure a future? Reorder the list for your workplace (from most to least valuable). What conclusions have you reached?

Modern technology offers both a huge challenge and a huge benefit to the modern manager. As Shirky puts it:

> Our electronic networks are enabling novel forms of collective action, enabling the creation of collaborative groups that are larger and more distributed than at any other time in history. The scope of work that can be done by non-institutional groups is a profound challenge to the status quo (Shirky 2008, p.48).

Interactions and collaborations using these new technologies are low cost. They are therefore able to offer considerable advantages to the institutions that can best take advantage of them. Information provision is one example of an ideal area for collaboration using these new technologies. Such collaboration can be seen in many different applications. Some of which would have been impossible even ten years ago.

Having considered the importance of an over-arching moral purpose, the necessary relationships that will see it effectively carried out, and their involvement in decision-making and collaboration – it is important to note the place of communication within any organisation. Without clear and complete communication of these purposes and decisions, relationships would breakdown and the purpose of the organisation become less likely of achievement.

Communication/coherence

Having once established a clear moral purpose for the organisation, arguably the next important issue is the clear communication of that purpose to all members of that organisation. For effective action on the part of the organisation those members need in turn to be able to communicate within the organisation and beyond it. If this communication is cost effective, the organisation will survive. If it is not only cost effective but value added, drawing on necessary resources outside the organisation, then there will be growth and future security.

Communication has two key aspects; inclusivity and effectiveness. Communication of purpose needs to reach all areas of the organisation and reach to all of its constituent members regardless of their locations or personal limitations. Communication must be inclusive. It needs to reach everyone.

Effective communication is not simply publishing a directive or sending out a newsletter. Ask any school administrator about the readership of their school newsletters and chances are they will roll their eyes heavenwards. Significant numbers of the parents of school-aged children are possibly not even aware of the existence of a school newsletter. On the odd occasions when a school bag is searched it can yield a fine collection of antique newsletters (together sometimes with a delightful selection of prehistoric lunch items).

Communication needs to reach each organisation member in a way that enables them to receive and react to that communication. Finding the right medium for this can be tricky. A school or library may print a copy of their latest promotion for every member of their organisation, but how can the material be presented in a way that members read it? Perhaps even more importantly, is it presented in a way that will encourage organisation members to become enthusiastic about it and lead to action on their part (and thus to the success of the organisation)?

Case study – a distance education program for trainee teacher librarians

From the student surveys carried out at the end of the teaching session, 57 of the 68 students responding noted that the subject stimulated their learning (for comparison, 3 strongly disagreed). 52 of the 68 considered the support mechanisms to be appropriate and the same number considered that their capacity to communicate effectively had been improved. These survey results were encouraging, and provided some statistical support for the more qualitative material generated during the session in terms of emails and chat from and between students.

As a part of their assessment, each student was required to provide a personal reflection on the collaboration process. These reflections overwhelming featured the voicing of the learners' early concerns at the levels of technology involved, but also their subsequent appreciation for having been pushed into using them. Typical of these was this comment:

> I had no experience of chat-rooms, had never heard of a wiki and knew that MSN was something that my teenage daughter seemed to be obsessed with during study time … I therefore had reservations about my abilities with technology and whether I was capable of 'surviving the steep learning curve' … Once I had a grasp of how to use these digital devices, I also became aware of what a powerful communication tool they can be. The subsequent 'conversations' I engaged in combined with my professional reading also enlightened me to the importance of developing clear, effective communication skills (male student 2008).

In the example above, there appears to be a clear shift from a concern at technology generally to a new perception of the value of that technology in enabling communication. This indicates a considerable skill development as well as a skill transfer from study to workplace. A 'powerful communication tool' was a phrase used in 51 per cent of the reflections as part of the students summing up of their activities.

Experience with interactive technologies in the teaching of information management and teacher librarianship has shown that there is considerable potential for the use of wikis and blogs – particularly in terms of their ability to facilitate collaboration over distance. The technology offers learners the opportunity to collaborate and build team projects, regardless of national or cultural boundaries. Significantly, several students included in their final reflections that they were establishing classroom wikis at their schools as a means of increasing interaction between students, teachers and the library. Another noted that experience with the new (for them) communication tools had 'strengthened my position as leader and negotiator' (male student 2008).

By integrating Web 2.0 tools into a digital hub (Lee & Winzenried 2009, p.151ff), it is possible – perhaps for the first time – to construct a truly global learning program. Such a learning program does not require the expense or dislocation which has been a feature of previous 'global' learning programs requiring learners to be physically located in the one space.

As one key aspect of the internet-borne Web 2.0 technology, meeting in the 'neutral' area of cyberspace while being able to communicate on several levels and actually join in the production of a single product offers solid collaboration and keeps otherwise intrusive 'differences' of nationality, culture, and so on at a minimum.

To a large extent, our intentions for this activity were somewhat echoed and affirmed in these words from a student reflection:

> My learning journey through this subject has been useful not only in my professional life, but it has given me the opportunity to grow as an individual. I now feel more equipped to see problems as opportunities. Most importantly I've decided to try and 'think outside the box', to be creative in how I think and act, and hopefully inspire those around me to feel the same (female student, 2008).

For a subject titled 'The teacher librarian as leader' this is a very satisfactory summary by one of our students. It offers considerable hope that we are awaking the 'visionary leader' in our students.

Technology is a powerful tool in the current information profession. It is an important aspect of the whole ecology of information provision, but it is only one influence within that ecology. It is a given, we cannot avoid it any more than we can avoid change. Visionary leadership is increasingly necessary to exploit the technology as well as to deal effectively and positively with the constant change that is also a vital part of the information ecology.

Innovation and change

I have noted earlier that one characteristic of the modern context is change. It is all about us, it is a constant and it is one of the critical issues to be considered by anyone intending to lead or manage an organisation (or part of one) today. We function within a changing world environment. Chrusciel and Field (2006, p.503) show that the ability to deal effectively with change is critical for the success of any organisation. Within the information provision sector, information is growing exponentially and management has to deal with this. This demands flexibility and agility in terms of all management mechanisms and processes. But can change be 'managed'?

Fullan considers the term 'change management' to be something of a misunderstanding. 'Change', he suggests, 'cannot be 'managed'. It can be understood, and perhaps led, but it cannot be fully controlled' (Fullan 2004, p.42). Change is rapid and non-linear. It creates tensions, but offers great potential for 'creative breakthroughs'. Rather than trying to manage or contain change, he sees the important issue as 'understanding' change. Knowing how it is likely to occur and how it is likely to impact on an organisation offers greater chances of responding positively to the challenges that it brings. Where response to change is reflexive, it is often being mismanaged, and so other problems can result (p.43).

Unsettling feelings about change often surface when people think they are being railroaded into something or they are not sure what the outcome will mean. The way in which change is introduced thus becomes all important. Fullan acknowledges this and suggests that change initiators need to encourage the airing of concerns and discussion to address these concerns (Fullan 2004, pp.97-8). People need to think their opinion is respected and that they will get somewhere by expressing their concerns. The point of these discussions is to identify a moral purpose, to create a cohesive group with a shared direction. In effect, a learning community is being established to support change.

Fundamental to the understanding and the positive coping with change are relationships within an organisation. One of Fullan's key points about change is its likelihood to produce arational factors:

> different individual idiosyncrasies, approaches, and problems;
> Friendships and animosities that affect the functioning of
> subsystems; and political factors, such as power and
> authority, protection of turf, and competition for resources
> (Fullan 2004, p.43).

It is these arational factors that can cause the greatest disruption to efficient organisational progress. Critical to their resolution are the strength of the relationships that exist within the organisation and in particular to the level of trust in those relationships (Fullan 2004, p.100).

Shirky (2008 p.302) cites the example of a sixteenth century Manutius who rather than decry the changes that followed the invention of the printing press took some control of the situation and brought about improvements, among them portable-sized books and new styles of writing. Shirky's point and mine is that we can easily sit down and lament the current context. That would be easy, but all too soon we would find ourselves alone. Alternatively we can choose to play the active role of directing and stride through the changes in information provision with a guiding purpose before us, a purpose that Fullan calls moral purpose (2001a, p.13ff).

By taking the time to vision a future that is purpose driven we do stand a better change of leading our libraries into a secure future. Such visions need to be innovative in the face of change yet closely linked to the real needs of clients. We need to start visioning even in cases where we are not necessarily the 'designated' or 'official' leader. Change does not wait for formal hierarchies. In fact, one of the main points I believe we can find in the work of people like Fullan and Shirky is that change will not wait for us. We have to, if I might use that terrible expression, 'seize the day' and this is what makes for a visionary leader.

Two leadership theories

There are a considerable array of theories as regards what makes a leader and how leaders function (see, for example, Miner, 2005 who surveys eight of the more commonly discussed ones). Two of them are particularly useful to this current work and to information provision particularly. As noted earlier, the position of the information professional in an organisation, the status of the public library within the wider realm of government function, is not always high on any 'official' priority list. Relationships can be used as leverage to develop influence and build an 'unofficial' priority but this suggests a special type of leader. Both charismatic leadership theory and transformational leadership theory offer important insights into future information leadership. Both theories owe much to the early organisational theory of Max Weber (see above) but each has been developed beyond Weber and given a separate existence and value.

Charismatic leadership theory

Arising in the 1970s from ideas first put forward by Robert House, charismatic leadership theory suggests in essence that leaders will be most effective when moral purpose and commitment are given meaning by leaders who exercise a charismatic influence over their followers. This charismatic influence is based around the extent to which individual leaders ('official' or otherwise) can inspire followers with a willingness to cooperate. The more that the follower 'likes' the leader, the more they will follow. Leaders who have charismatic effects are more likely to have followers willing to follow beyond the usual call of duty and who will show their loyalty in more positive attitudes to their work, greater enthusiasm to cooperate and a generally more consistent willingness to work.

In this arrangement, the characteristics of a charismatic leader are such as inspire their followers and usually include both a high level of proficiency at articulating expectations and associated ideological goals as well as having a strong personal appeal based on well-developed relationship-building skills (Miner 2005, p.339). Put simply perhaps, the theory argues that leaders with charisma are more likely to attract commitment in their followers than those who do not have charisma. The level of charisma will directly relate to the loyalty of supporters and their productivity under that leader.

House (in Miner 2005, pp.337-360) later refined this basic theory to allow for socialised charismatic theory where leadership included a basis for egalitarian behaviour and also the collective interests rather than the leaders self-interest (Miner 2005, p.341). By developing a more collaborative and team-based set of charismatic leadership skills, the leader in an organisation may generate very considerable loyalty and commitment to the causes espoused by that leader. They have very considerable power to lead and to achieve.

Transformational leadership theory

The theory of transformational leadership was developed a little later than charismatic leadership theory and also owed much to Weber and the work that he did with behavioural theory in organisations. Presented first by Bernard Bass, transformational theory rests less on the individual personal characteristics of the leader and more on their ability to motivate support by offering followers clearer views on the importance and value of designated outcomes (Bass 1985, p.11). Leaders who are transformational have the ability to take their followers beyond self-interest and to generate enthusiasm for the sake of team, organisation or larger policy (Miner 2005, p.363). They are able to motivate people to do more than they had previously expected to do – to transform themselves and their productivity.

Charismatic and transformational processes are closely related but it is possible for a charismatic leader not to lead to transformational results. Self-interest may interfere or the charismatic leader may have personal goals that do not transform their organisation. Charisma, to some extent, is needed in a transformational leader simply because they are asking their followers to go beyond what is needed – this requires exceptional loyalty and thus some degree of charisma is likely to be required.

For the information professional and leader who may be placed into hierarchical situations that seem powerless, the notions of charismatic leadership and transformational leadership are important considerations. Though powerless in the conventional sense, they may in fact exert considerable influence and thus power by developing strong charismatic and/or transformational characteristics. By taking the opportunity to build relationships through their own personal people-skills, they may well prove to be strong leaders in their organisations and to carry many others within those organisations to greater achievement and recognition. Recognition can often gain increased regard within the organisation, bring more official recognition and in the longer term provide for their own as well as the teams' future security. Perhaps oversimplifying things somewhat, a school library leader who presents their priorities clearly, attractively and persuasively on a regular basis is more likely to have increased budget and increased respect than one who does not. Their level of influence will depend to a considerable extent on charisma (there are other factors as well, but charisma is a critical one) and their ability to transform their organisation and the position of library in that organisation will depend on taking that charisma and combining it with clear, appealing and achievable goals.

To be visionary leaders in information, charismatic characteristics need to be fostered and developed, team-building and communication skills developed and strong relationships forged.

In summary

Organisational theories have been developing over many years. Initially rather simplistic in their concern for productivity, order and hierarchy, more recently it has become common to speak of organisation in terms of a series of relationships. The strength, nature and capacity of those relationships as well as the level of trust within them will help the organisation to achieve its purpose. This purpose needs to be explicit and clear so that all members of the organisation can see the importance, place and role in the organisation. Purpose and relationship will be a formative part of the decisions that are made, and the process for making those decisions. It will also play a key role in developing teams within the organisation; of providing a sense of place for the organisational team.

Change is the greatest challenge of the modern era. It is unavoidable. It can either make or break an organisation. Where relationships are strong and the purpose clear, members of the organisation can be supported through the changes most effectively, generally with dignity and success. Where relationships are poor and communication lacking, dealing with change will be less effective, possibly even terminal.

To make certain that the organisation is constantly heading in the right direction its moral purpose needs to be continuously reviewed against is final product. Keeping the end product in mind, comparing it carefully with the purpose, and maintaining strong communication channels to all members of the organisation will provide the best possible chances for long-term survival.

Within the library industry these issues are totally relevant. Giovenco has noted:

> The inherent artificiality of libraries needs to be attacked and addressed so that it refocusses & sits within a more socio-anthropologic framework & context of relevance, meaning & connectedness (Giovenco 14/11/09).

In the terms of this chapter his warning is clear; actively review your purpose and, if necessary, reframe it for the modern context; keep relationships within the library and with the external context strong and under constant review; stay focused on the end product of learning throughout life; and, above all, keep checking most thoroughly that you are in fact dealing in commodities and services that your clients actually need – not what you think they need or what is good for them – but what they themselves see as their needs.

In essence – a plan needs to be made, and once made needs to be clearly communicated to all stakeholders. These then are the two basics that organisations must begin with. They are both vitally relevant to libraries of any sort. But what is it that should shape any plan that will successfully support a surviving information structure in a chaotic information world? In the next chapter I would like to consider some of the practical outworking of these theoretical considerations as we look to the sort of futures outlined by the contributors in chapter 3.

References

Auletta, K. (2009). Googled: *the end of the world as we know it*. London: Virgin Books.

Bass, B. (1985). *Leadership and performance beyond expectations*. New York: Free Press.

Beare, H. (2001). *Creating the future schools*, London: Routledge.

Beck, T. (1998). The technological future – an overview. In Prytherch, R. (Ed.), *Handbook of library and information management* (pp.10-28). London: Gower.

Bly, B. (2009). Accessed 30/12/09 at: http://bly.com/blog/online-marketing/new-survey-reveals-social-networking-is-too-time-consuming/

Chrusciel, D. & Field, D. (2006). Success factors in dealing with significant change in an organisation. *Business Process Management Journal*, 12(4), 503-516.

Concise Oxford Dictionary. (1964). Clarendon Press, Oxford.

Daft, R.L. (2004). *Organisational theory and design* (8th ed.). Manson, OH: Thomson South-western.

Dahl, R.A. (1989). *Democracy and its critics.* Yale University Press.

Das, T.K. (2003). Managerial perceptions and the essence of the managerial world; What is an interloper business executive to make of the academic-researcher perceptions of managers? *British Journal of Management*, 14, 23-32.

Dickens, C. (1996). *Hard times*, Koln, Germany: Konemann. (Original work published 1854).

Donaldson, L. (2002). Damned by our own theories: Contradictions between theories and management education. *Academy of Management and Learning Education*, 1, 96-106.

Dowler, L. (1997). *Gateways to knowledge; The role of academic libraries in teaching, learning and research.* Cambridge MA: MIT.

Elkington, J. (2004). Enter the triple bottom line. Located at http://www.johnelkington.com/TBL-elkington-chapter.pdf on 11/8/09.

Follett, M.P. (1924). *Creative experience.* Located at http://follettfoundation.org/ceintro.pdf

Fullan, M. (2001a). *Leading in a culture of change.* San Francisco, CA: Jossey-Bass.

Fullan, M. (2001b). *Change forces: the sequel.* London: Falmer Press.

Fullan, M. (2004*). Leading in a culture of change: personal action guide and workbook.* San Francisco, CA: Jossey-Bass.

Funk & Wagnalls (1997). *New encyclopedia*, New York.

Giovenco, G. (14/11/09) Email.

Gleick, J. (1987). *Chaos: making a new science.* New York: Penguin Books.

Gleick, J. (1999). *Faster: the acceleration of just about everything.* New York: Pantheon Books.

Heifetz, R. (1994). *Leadership without easy answers.* Cambridge, MA: Harvard University Press.

Heller, R. (1985). *The new naked manager.* London: Hodder and Stoughton.

Johnson, K. (1991). Stop the increasing bureaucratisation of schools. Accessed 28/12/09 at: http://www.busting-bureaucracy.com/top_right/education.htm

Johnson, S. (1999). *Who moved my cheese?* London: Vermillion.

Kennedy, G., Dalgarno, B., Gray, K., Bennett, S., Maton, K., Krause, K., Bishop, A., Chang, R. & Chruchward, A. (2007). The net generation are not big users of web 2.0 technologies: preliminary findings, presented to ASCILITE, Singapore, 2007 and found at http://ascilite.org.au/conferences/singapore07/procs/kennedy.pdf visited 30/12/09.

Landsberger, H. (1958). *Hawthorne revisited*. New York: Ithaca.

Lee, M. (2006) Managing the school's digital teaching resources and assets *Australian Educational Leader*, 28(3), 36-7.

Lee, M. & Winzenried, A. (2009). *The use of instructional technology in schools: lessons to be learned*. Melbourne: ACER.

Mayo, E. (1949). *Hawthorne and the Western Electric Company: the social problems of an industrial civilisation*, New York: Routledge.

Maslow, A.H. (1943) A theory of human motivation. *Psychology Review*, 50, 370-396.

Metcalf, H.C. & Urwick, L. (1942). *Dynamic administration: the collected papers of Mary Parker Follett*, New York: Harper & Bros.

Miner, J. (2005). *Organisational behaviour 1: essential theories of motivation and leadership*. Armonk, New York: M.E. Sharpe.

Poellhuber, B., Chomienne, M. & Karsenti, T. (2008). The effect of peer collaboration and collaborative learning on self-efficacy and persistence in a learner-paced conditions intake model. *Journal of Distance Education*, 22/3, 41-62.

Raitt, D. (1997). *Libraries for the new millennium: implications for managers*. London: Library Association Publishing.

Rollett, H., Lux, M., Strohmaier, M., Dösinger, G. & Tochtermann, K. (2007). The web 2.0 way of learning with technologies. *International Journal of Learning Technology*, 3(1), 87–107.

Ryan, L.V. & Rutherford, M.A. (2000). Mary Parker Follett: individualist or collectivist? Or both? *Journal of Management History*, 5(6), 207-223.

Shirky, C. (2008). *Here comes everybody: the power of organising without organisations*. London: Penguin.

Smith, P. & Brain, P. (2000). Bullying in schools: lessons from two decades of research. *Aggressive Behavior*, 26, 1-9.

Tapscott, D. & Williams, A.D. (2006). *Wikinomics: how mass collaboration changes everything*. New York: Portfolio.

Thelwall, M. (2008). Myspace, Facebook, Bebo: Social networking students. Accessed 30/12/09 at http://newsweaver.co.uk/alt/e_article000993849.cfm.

Weber, M. (1947). *The theory of social and economic organisation* (Trans. A.M. Henderson & T. Parsons). London: Collier Macmillan.

Weik, K. (1993). Review of leadership and information processing. *Leadership Quarterly*, 4, 109-13.

Wheatley, M. (2006). *Leadership and the new science: discovering order in a chaotic world* (3rd Ed.). New York: Berrett-Koehler Publishers.

Wheatley, M. (2009). Website at http://www.margaretwheatley.com/findingourway.html 23/12/09

Wiig, K. (1999). What future knowledge management users may expect. *Journal of Knowledge Management*, 3(2), 155-165.

Yates, J. (1993). *Control through communication: the rise of system in American management*. Baltimore, MA: John Hopkins University Press.

CHAPTER 2
Manager or leader?

Having considered some of the theoretical aspects of organisational theory and its implications, where then does that leave the 'leader' or 'manager', the person held responsible for providing information to users in an organisation? What makes a leader and why is visionary leadership a goal?

Towards the close of the last chapter the theory of charismatic and transformational leadership was briefly presented. In essence this view of leadership sums up much of the theoretical material in that chapter and provides the basis for the more practical considerations in this one.

Information provision in the present and for the future has many unknowns. Managers who were previously expected to find quick solutions to problems as they arose, and were often measured by their ability to do so, are increasingly finding that this is no longer the case. And it may well be that solutions will never be found to many of the problems arising. Fullan notes:

> The big problems of the day are complex, rife with paradoxes and dilemmas. For these there are no once-and-for-all solutions. Yet we expect our leaders to provide solutions (Fullan 2001a, p.2).

He moves on in the same work to note the conclusion reached by Heifetz in 1994 that leadership can be seen as the ability, not of mobilising others to solve problems but of 'mobilising people to tackle tough problems' – to confront problems that have never before been successfully addressed (Fullan 2001a, p.3). While this might sound daunting, the reality is that many of the issues facing information provision today are new. The constant state of change that surrounds virtually every aspect of life in the current age means new problems have to be addressed almost faster than we can identify them. This is partly the phenomena that Fullan has identified as a 'culture of change'.

In what ways is it possible for library and information managers and leaders to actually 'manage' or 'lead' that information provision? Is it possible in the future to realistically take 'control'? We consider aspects of the role of library staff, particularly managers or teacher librarians, as leaders. Leadership is not necessarily a tagged position but comes about somewhat organically because of a unique relationship with the information on the one hand and the client on the other. The intermediary role carries with it a certain 'power' and 'privilege' as well as responsibility. It can be very much in the hands of each teacher librarian or public library staff member to act as a leader in their work of providing space and resources to their clients as, when and where they are needed.

More recently and particularly since the global downturn in 2008, older concepts of leadership have begun to be seriously questioned. Twenty years before the downturn, Heller questioned the high rates paid to American executives (Heller 1985, p.9). In 2008-2009 this became an international concern with governments in the US and the UK in particular reviewing the situation as they were forced to bail out their larger corporations. The year 2010 opened with considerable public debate as banks in the UK moved to pay their top executives huge bonuses for having helped the banks out of recession, despite the fact that those same banks had been bailed out of trouble with taxpayers' money (BBC news). Management is perhaps set to become more removed (a little) from money and an element of responsibility and accountability seems to be expected, both by governments and by the general public. We have yet to see where this increased concern for accountability will lead, but it certainly has increased the scrutiny of leaders and gives non-traditional leaders greater scope to take initiatives previously not on offer to them. For libraries and their leaders, there are new opportunities as well as new responsibilities.

In the current climate, the digital world, the socially networked world, responsibility and accountability are increasingly critical. Traditional reward systems no longer work as effectively as they did in the industrial paradigm. Patterson, et.al., note that the rather traditional reward system no longer can be relied upon to bring change or improve profitability:

> Stories of well intended rewards that inadvertently backfire are legion. The primary cause of most of these debacles is that individuals attempt to influence behaviours using rewards as their first motivational strategy. In a well balanced effort, rewards come third (Patterson et al. 2009, p.108).

Into this debate then can be brought the principles of charismatic and transformational theory; the concept that a difference can be made, even despite the complexity and near chaos, and that a difference ought to be made with clear moral purpose directing activities. All that is required are visionary leaders; leaders who will see what can be done and who will make a commitment to at least try and achieve higher levels of client service.

To do or not to do? (with apologies to Shakespeare)

In an invitation on her website, author and speaker, Margaret Wheatley makes a considerable point:

> Western cultural views of how best to organise and lead (now the methods most used in the world) are contrary to what life teaches. Leaders use control and imposition rather than participative, self-organising processes. They react to uncertainty and chaos by tightening already feeble controls, rather than engaging people's best capacities to learn and adapt. In doing so, they only create more chaos. Leaders incite primitive emotions of fear, scarcity, and self-interest to get people to do their work, rather than the more noble human traits of cooperation, caring, and generosity (Wheatley 2009).

There are so many issues raised in this short quotation and many of them could be directly applied to present information provision organisations from school libraries to academic, from regional libraries to national archives. Libraries have been one of the many targets of government cost-cutting in recent times. Schools have regularly replaced teacher librarians with technicians in order to reduce spending. The result has not usually been to the advantage either of the industry or of the client. Visionary leaders are needed to take the initiative and provide new ways of improving service in a very sparse economic climate.

As noted briefly in the last chapter, Fullan suggests that to do nothing in this constantly changing minefield of leading and managing can be fatal. He is equally certain that quick decisions under pressure can be just as fatal (Fullan 2001a, p.v). Doing nothing is not an option. Further, effectively dealing with and 'managing' the current situations that face organisations generally, and information ones in particular, can mean the difference between success and failure, between survival and terminal decay.

Fullan would respond that any plan needs to be firmly based on moral purpose (Fullan 2001a, p.3). To have a plan and to make a difference he suggests require that we basically intend to set out and do something that is 'good', something that will improve our clients in terms of their access to knowledge and their ability to deal successfully with information.

In education generally it has been understood for some time that having a moral purpose and also establishing significant relationships between learner and facilitator are two of the most important factors for success (e.g., Hughes and Warner, chapter 3). Studies over many years have shown a clear connection between success in learning and a strong teacher–learner bond (Abbott-Chapman & Hughes 1990). While this connection is common to all teaching and learning, it becomes particularly noticeable in cases where learners have a disadvantaged background. Teachers who made a difference to their less privileged learners were able to break the cycle of disadvantage because of the strong relationship of respect between themselves and their students.

These teachers were quite varied, showing considerable individuality but did show two common factors: their conviction that all students could succeed and their capacity to use a wide range of teaching approaches. These teachers could not be placed under any of the common classifications: progressive, constructivist, traditional, progressive or learner-centred. Rather they had a great range of teaching approaches, covering all these different categories but with the capacity to adapt their approaches to different circumstances and individuals (Abbott-Chapman & Hughes 1990, p.1). The contention here is that the same is true of information provision. Now, more than ever before, information provision needs leaders who will pay closer attention to the individual client and be increasingly more experimental, flexible and persistent in their approach to circumstances.

Dowler notes that, reflecting the educational institutions that they are often attached to, libraries need to focus on the key areas of promoting teaching, learning and research (Dowler 1997, p.xiii). With so many things in common, it is not surprising that libraries have the same needs as do schools – staff that form firm and significant relationships with each other and with their clients as well as a strong sense of moral purpose.

Clearly action is not an option, it is an imperative. Action that is to cope with the increasing complexity of information delivery and management needs to be carefully planned and based on a solid theoretical foundation. If provision is to be client-focused as our scenarios all stress, then a considerable understanding of the needs and the psychology of those clients is critical to the planning. With the cost of technology ever increasing, strategic planning and rigorous review of the worth of specific technologies is also important.

Fullan and others point to the two aspects of moral purpose and relationships as being at the heart of all successful leading and managing. But perhaps equally important is product review – ensuring that goals are met and differences made. In the field of information there does need to be more emphasis on checking to see if we have made a difference and if the difference made is the right outcome. Rather than simply provide a book or a resource, we need also to follow that up to see if the resource was used and whether our information aims were met in the client response. For all of this to occur, we need proactivity and we need visionary leaders who will be proactive. Hartzell has suggested that proactive people look for change opportunities. They anticipate and prevent problems and take action (cited in Donham 2005, p.297). Hartzell in turn cites the psychologist Crant as saying:

> The notion of proactivity argues that we can intentionally and directly influence these and other elements and by doing so influence and enhance our chances of being successful in our jobs (cited in Hartzell 2000, p.15).

To sit back and do nothing is a formula for disaster. We need to be proactive, visionary and leading if we are to ensure our own and our organisations survival in the future – whatever that future might be.

Leading and managing

The term 'manager' is often seen as a title, generally associated with a specific wage or salary structure, that entails telling others what to do and when to do it. Management was in the past most clearly seen in terms of autocratic processes and clearly defined hierarchical structures. That type of management is not the primary concern of this present work. Consider the following thoughts about management.

> Management is about coping with complexity. Leadership, by contrast, is about coping with change (Kotter 2001, p.4).

> I have never been fond of distinguishing between leadership and management; they overlap and you need both qualities (Fullan 2001a, p.2).

> Leadership in business and in education increasingly have more in common (Fullan 2001a, p.vii).

The suggestion here is that management needs to be seen in a different way than in the past. It is more complex, involved with change and central to all our activities whether in business or education – to all learning situations.

Steven Covey (1990) speaks of a circle of influence – those things that a person can control. Donham extends this notion to a 'locus of control' (2005, p.296). For myself I am wary of the word 'control'. Given the earlier discussion, control is too reminiscent of the Industrial Age simplicity of precision and discipline. The modern era is too complex and changing for control to be an ideal term. While Kotter (above) sees different jurisdictions for manager and leader, I tend to think that Fullan has a more helpful understanding. It is no longer easy to clearly define the boundaries between management and leadership, particularly in the field of information management and perhaps even more particularly as one drills down into the work of, for example, the teacher librarian.

Most commonly, the teacher librarian works alone in their school – the sole link between information and their organisation. Their role necessarily carries with it all the qualities of both a manager and a leader. The job is a combination of both, and further includes all the knowledge transfer, coaching and mentoring skills of a teacher at the same time.

Modern management is more usually concerned with best use of resources and sustaining those resources. We each can become efficient and well qualified managers of the energy resources within our own homes for example. We are perhaps best placed in this regard because it is our own home that is involved and we generally have significant control in terms of what technology we use there, what energy needs we have and what decisions can be made to most effectively conserve energy and thus to manage the available resources. Decisions are made on the basis of effect (economy) rather than on the directions of someone else who does not live in our house.

This form of management does not involve a system of hierarchies where we respond to directives from above and then issue edicts to those eagerly waiting our directions on the rung below. It is rather a system of balances, comparisons and trade-offs that are aimed not only at producing the outcomes needed but also conserving the resources and respecting the people involved. Much of the management is devolved and as such sees more management decisions being made by 'non-management designated' people in the organisation.

In short, management may be a role not a position. Our potential for management may be a balancing act rather than a hierarchical directing one. While management concerns itself with resources, leadership is generally a person-orientated activity. Donham (2005, p.296) lists his suggested attributes of a leader as including: 1) technical competence, 2) conceptual skills, 3) people skills, 4) judgement, and 5) character.

These are rather more ethereal than the ability to move physical resources around the chessboard of an organisation. They involve transfer of skills and knowledge, the dealing in intangibles rather than tangibles. Attributes such as these provide a foundation on which the leader may build strong relationships and exercise considerable influence. Fullan speaks of leaders as producing 'leaders of leaders' – a perpetual transfer of skills and confidences to other members of the organisation regardless of their 'position' in the organisation (Fullan 2001a, p.vi). Cohen and Bradford (2005) speak of leaders as exercising influence without authority. In direct contrast to the Industrial Age of hierarchies, Donham, Fullan, Cohen and Bradford see, much as does Shirky (2008), that with the organisational world becoming more complex, leadership is influence regardless of position.

> You need to influence those in other departments, and divisions,
> that is, people you can't order and control. You need to influence
> your managers and others above you, and you certainly can't order
> and control them! (Cohen & Bradford 2005, p.3).

If we consider then that leading and managing are a single task that faces the current and future information professional we can see them as both allocating/managing resources and as exercising influence on others. This influence can be very strong. Knowledge has often been seen as power. In the modern context the word power may have different meaning to what it did in past ages but, none-the-less, there is a real power in leading others to information, helping them to assimilate that information and providing them with skills or skill development opportunities that might help them assimilate further information in the future. All this is part of the important work of the information professional.

Leading from the middle

In the world of library many staff perceive themselves as powerless – they don't have a position, there is no recognition from above in terms of job description or earning that designates them as managers. However, there is always the potential for exercising the power of influence. This potential is considerable, it can be life changing, but it is very often totally unrealised.

In the school library context a teacher librarian, for example, necessarily must have a reasonably deep understanding of curriculum at every level. Weakness in this area can lead to serious shortfalls in resourcing the curriculum, gaps in the collection, and a perception by clients of inadequate resources. Because of the wide knowledge – one that is rarely shared by any other member of staff – the teacher librarian is in an ideal position to make recommendations to the whole staff as well as to the recognised, hierarchical 'managers'. These recommendations might involve avoiding curriculum replication, providing a new section of resources, providing new 'spaces' for the different approaches to curriculum that might be needed, and so on. Their position carries considerable responsibility, with the potential to change whole school processes and environments. They have, in effect, very considerable power to affect the learning that is taking place.

In essence this is opportunity for leadership. Visionary leaders can take advantage of this unique position and influence all areas of their learning community even if they are never named or paid or otherwise 'officially' recognised as leaders. Developing both the opportunity to influence and the ability to do so should be a key intention for any information professional and for the teacher librarian particularly.

Cohan and Bradford introduce their 'influence model' with the following quotation from the UBS Investment Bank.

> One of the biggest challenges facing us in UBS-IB is the ability to influence others over whom we have no direct authority. Flatter structures, globalisation, and cross-functional teams have brought fresh challenges and having to influence people who have different styles or views makes the task even harder.

> Being able to influence one's boss, peers, or top management is often quoted as being a key reason for the success or failure of individuals (cited in Cohan & Bradford 2005, p.3).

By building sound relationships that extend their influence, even the 'ordinary' (as in unofficial) people in any organisation are in a position of quite significant influence and power. While relationships will be discussed further below, it is significant that Cohen and Bradford, as do Fullan and others, emphasise the critical importance of relationships to the success or failure of the ability to lead (Cohen & Bradford 2005, p.96ff, compare Fullan 2004, p.77ff). The extent to which each of us can establish and maintain relationships will determine our ability to influence. In the information profession, all of the same characteristics of organisation mentioned by the UBS above exist and so our success is going to similarly depend on how well we can influence those about us – our bosses, our overarching organisations, our peers, our clients, even our governments. In most cases we need to do this in an almost total absence of 'official' power position.

Donham speaks of this influence as 'leading from the middle' (2005, p.299). His work is eminently practical. Among the insights he offers are two gleaned from

Jim Collins' work, *Good to great* (2001). First, leaders who wish to be effective from the middle of their organisations do well, Collins suggests, to keep a clear view of what they can be best at as well as what they cannot be best at. They need to know their strengths and weaknesses and work around them. Second, they need to be passionate about what they do (Donham 2005, pp.297-8). Passion can have interesting connotations, but as enthusiasm and vitality for a cause it can rarely be bettered as a way of motivating others and developing respect for a role or task.

Knowing ones limits (and staying within them) is vital for the modern leader. There are distractions aplenty in the information ecology and these can be a danger to leading effectively from the middle. Quality relationships with official authority are most helpful and these can be more effectively created and maintained where boundaries of expertise are clearly identified. Similarly, being passionate about the areas that are your strengths and your responsibility can help create relationships as well as help to take others with you as you lead out in your area. Positive action based on your skills and passionately presented has a powerful influence.

Avoiding the power on offer, not accepting this position and its responsibilities can all too often lead to a denigration of library influence. Folding one's hands and saying 'I'm not paid to do that' is often an excellent way of signing your own death warrant as well as that of your library. Other people will move in to fill the vacuum and, before long, the library becomes somewhat redundant, as does the position. Leadership needs to be pro-active or all too often it vanishes.

Leadership styles

Quality leadership, that is effective and valued leadership, requires a considerable array of skills. This is especially true in cases where there might not be the 'authority' of formal position to support the leadership. One of the key skills is the style of leadership applied to each situation. If leadership requires purpose, relationship and clearly defined outcomes, as the theory suggests, then leading involves application of these in a 'real people' situation. Past theories have seen a shift from authoritarian approaches and the realisation that productivity grows as people are more clearly valued. The choice of leadership style thus becomes critical to success or failure as a leader and, by extension, success or failure of the organisation.

Based on research with the consulting firm of Hay/McBer in 2000, Goleman (1998) identified six leadership styles that are relevant to the information industry. Fullan in his work on leading in a culture of change (2001a) notes these and then uses them as part of his design for organisational leadership. They are significant and bear repeating.

1. Coercive – the leader demands compliance. ('Do what I tell you.')
2. Authoritative – the leader mobilises people towards a vision. ('Come with me.')
3. Affiliative – the leader creates harmony and builds emotional bonds. ('People come first.')
4. Democratic – the leader forges consensus through participation. ('What do you think.')
5. Pacesetting – the leader sets high standards for performance. ('Do as I do, now.')
6. Coaching – the leader develops people for the future. ('Try this.') (Fullan 2001a, p.35).

In the Industrial Age there were few choices in this area. Authority and coercion were the hallmarks of the time. Anything else was quickly eliminated. People were expendable and volume of output was all that mattered. Leadership in all areas was authoritarian and hierarchical. This had some benefits for the industrial model perhaps but in an age of more 'people power' a simple stand on authority has significant limits especially when seen, as it so often is, in the historical light of dictatorships in the twentieth century.

Despite this, Fullan notes that of the six styles the two that negatively affect performance are the coercive and pacesetting options (not the authoritative). In his discussion of these styles, Fullan notes that best results are usually achieved when a combination are used – a combination that may well change rather constantly depending on the situations within the organisation. Pacesetters and coercers, for example, do not help in the process of innovation implementation (Fullan 2004, p.51). These styles tend to lack the empathy for people that adopting changes most needs. They are, however, vital to visionary planning. There are times, he suggests, when direction might need to be on the pre-emptory side and thus there is value in the authoritarian style on occasion. However, the best approach is usually a mixed approach.

People don't follow others by accident. They follow those who they respect. Their respect is not generally won by being told what to do in an authoritarian way. Sometimes the fear factor works, but more often the relationship between worker and leader, client and librarian lacks respect. There are times for strong leadership.

Maxwell speaks of the leadership 'law of respect' in terms of followers being willing to follow the strong leader (Maxwell 2007, p.76) but this is only one of his 'laws' – all twenty-one of those he identifies are equally critical. His laws are suggesting much the same concepts as the leadership styles of Goleman and Fullan. For leadership to be successful there needs to be a sympathetic and skilled use of many different approaches – a combination of many different leadership laws.

Pacesetting leaders, for example, can often end up isolated by taking too much decision-making on their own shoulders. Pacesetting may help innovation begin, but unless it is followed up with some real recognition of how the innovation is affecting people (affiliative style) and how convinced workers are that the innovation is necessary (coaching style) it is very possible that the leader will find themselves out on a limb with their followers somewhere else altogether. Being an effective leader will depend on the way you choose your style of approach to each situation. This will then relate to what your overall leadership intentions are – your moral purpose and your effective relationship building.

Frances Hesselbein, president of the Drucker Foundation in the US, sums up the needs of the future leader in terms of the 'how to be' leader rather than the 'how to do it' one of the past (Lauer 2009, p.237). The transition she recognises in these leader titles shows how much she and other leaders have recognised the move from authority to collaboration. It is no longer sufficient to say 'do this or else'. Effective leadership in the modern world requires far more than raw power.

The 'how to be' leader Hesselbein envisages as a 'leader for the future'. They will be leaders who recognise people as the most important part of an organisation, who banish hierarchy and build for flexibility (Lauer 2009, p.237).

> 'Leadership is a matter of how to be, not how to do,' she said.
> 'You and I spend most of our lives learning how to do and teaching others how to do. And yet we know that, in the end, it is the quality and character of the leader that determines the performance, the results' (Reardon 2009).

For Hesselbein, leaders are those who offer their followers a vision. 'They hold a vision before us, a vision beyond what is, to what could be' (Reardon 2009). This vision comes about through a combination of seeing the importance of people, mobilising those around them and around the vision and keeping very aware of what their customers need and value (Lauer 2009, p.237).This is a powerful combination and one that needs a range of leadership styles as well as considerable awareness of the needs of the client/customer. Leaders need to reflect in their style of leadership the attributes and results that clients want to see in their organisation

(Hesselbein & Goldsmith 2006, p.144). Knowing those client needs is a key to leading effectively into the future. Identifying them and keeping them in focus is a critical aspect of leading for the future.

Identifying needs

Information provision is currently being challenged as never before. Google has becoming almost a synonym for library. Information is quite frequently seen as being 'all on the net' so why employ information professionals? One cause for this, and it is by no means a simple matter, is that libraries have failed to correctly and adequately identify their clients' needs and to meet them personally. Heller noted this issue as regards business generally among established corporations in the 1980s.

> For instance, eight of the Fourteen Flops didn't stay close to the customer – companies like Avon, Disney, Revlon, Tupperware and Levi-Strauss .... Take the last named. ... As long as the worldwide jeans market was booming, Levi's management could afford, paradoxically, to ignore it. ... 'We were internationally orientated'. As for customers, 'we let the relationship with our retailers fall into a sad state of disrepair; the company completely missed the powerful (and profitable) trend towards fashion jeans'. Direct, in-the-home sellers Avon and Tupperware similarly failed to react to the blatant consequences of more women going out to work. Disney went on flogging clean and decent entertainment into an increasingly less wholesome market-place (Heller 1985, p.22).

These examples are among many that could be named. Quite a few became almost infamous in the recent global downturn. Many of the failures, if not all, could attribute at least a part of their problems to poor relationships with their clients. In so many cases, they had felt themselves invincible, ignored their client needs and the realities of the world around them and kept to the old products that had been their staple in the past.

The message to current and future information professionals is clear. Library in the past has enjoyed a certain amount of stability and respect providing a print-based storehouse of information and waiting for the customers to arrive. However, the world has changed. Customers need to be encouraged, satisfied and even enticed. They also need to be offered different services more appropriate to their needs. Identifying these needs is step one. Step two is modifying the library to suit these new needs.

Relationships are the foundation on which improved client satisfaction is built. As Giovenco (chapter 3) notes:

> If you deconstruct or destroy that relationship then you create inevitable negative outcomes & more complicated problems which the profession & service models are now experiencing but not understanding.

In an age when digital information is vastly outgrowing the print industry, why does there need to be the level of desperation often displayed as regards print materials? Surely, they can remain a choice but the professional effort needs to lie with the majority of material. Relationships with the clients and with other members of the organisation up and down the hierarchical scale are surely more important. Library leader purpose needs to be focused on the far greater issues of building trust with staff and students, creating a relationship between user and information that will stand the test of time (and truly lead to lifelong learning). The need for print materials as a matter of priority is not a sufficient moral purpose. (The need for silence in libraries also eludes me other than as a relic of the Industrial Age axiom of 'children should be seen and not heard'.)

What is critical in the debate that Giovenco initiates is that whatever the intention for particular materials, modes of library behaviour, or whatever, the guiding principle need to be not 'What do we want for the library?' but 'What do our clients want the library to be?'

As far as the future of library is concerned, if there is no adequate service to clients, if they do not see the value in what is being provided, then library will not have a future. Clients need to have their needs met and met on their territory not the artificial one of the past. It is imperative then for libraries to establish routines and practices that continuously monitor the needs of their clients and react to those needs. The trick though is that if library simply reacts then it is always going to be bringing up the rear and be following the clients.

Satisfaction surveys are fine and have value. However, measuring the past is not an adequate way of moving into the future. More needs to be done to assess needs before they become critical and preparing accordingly. Identifying client needs is vital.

Welch notes that promoting the library involves 'making the client paramount in our considerations' (Welch 2006, p.184). This requires analysis on the part of the leader and their organisation. 'What is it (exactly) that the client wants?' and

'Can we be certain that we have it correctly?' These are critical questions. They require a certain amount of serious research. To build library policy and practice on a false notion of client needs is to spell doom for the future of your library and quite possibly create problems or limitations on your entire learning organisation.

A SWOT (strengths, weaknesses, opportunities and threats) analysis is one means of analysing library performance. It is a method that is fairly straightforward to use and involves staff 'brainstorming' the value of what they are doing. The problem with this approach is that it is difficult to include client views in such an analysis. Further, while considering the threats, there may be some discussion of possible changes or innovations, and SWOT analysis tends to look at present/past rather than future. With a marketing hat very firmly on, Welch helps out by offering a further two possible analytical tools suitable to the occasion.

In the 1990s, Peter Balan developed a notion of core benefits – 'the benefits consumers expect to receive' (1991, p.97). To these he added further tangible and intangible benefits. By analysing these in a systematic way Welch suggests we come closer to understanding exactly which are the benefits most valued and required by our clients. Tangible and intangible benefits flow from core benefits and all three are required in order to be sure our clients will return.

The benefit analysis developed by Balan and suggested by Welch is one approach to identifying needs. It is perhaps best suited to analysis by staff of libraries rather than by their clients. As such it may miss some of the critical factors of client need. One of its major strengths, however, is that it offers an excellent means of building stronger staff teams and developing relationships between library management and library employees. It also offers strong potential for maintaining a focus on existing direction as well as identifying areas for future development. What it is less able to do is to identify those innovations and changes that are so much a part of the current information ecology. These may sometimes result from analysis that shows a particular weakness but not necessarily.

Welch also offers a priority action matrix method for analysing library performance. Using this tool, the various different services offered are prioritised by clients (and staff ideally) (Welch 2006, p.193ff). This method has the advantage of gaining useful feedback directly from clients. Existing library practices are ranked by importance and performance to provide a picture of what is being done well and how important clients see it as being.

Again, this method tends to consider existing processes rather than future ones. By measuring the current practices and processes it is possible to see which are client needs and which are not. This leads to the problem with any attempt to measure library services – what happens when the survey, analysis or whatever, shows a service currently being offered is not considered by the client as necessary or relevant?

The importance in these various tools lies in two areas; they need to be regularly and frequently undertaken; and they need to be carefully acted on. All too often a survey is taken, set aside until someone has time to look at it and then finally interpreted as 'we are OK', all without too much serious analysis.

There are of course a wide range of performance analysis tools on the market and suited for library applications. However, it should be noted that many of these are essentially financial in their analysis. A quick google of 'corporate performance tools' yielded some 172,000 possibilities, with many offers of software tools to assist analysis. This is obviously only one search of many that could be done – which brings me to an important point. One of the most valuable ways of assessing your performance is through relationships with other professionals in your sector. Maintain connections with library operations in your vicinity – make it a priority. Find out what is working for them and ask yourself if it could work for your clients. Add possible future services to your analysis tools to check for potential winning moves. It is with this in mind that I introduce in chapter 3 some scenarios from various leaders in the information field. Each has an important story to tell and while every point from every scenario has its merit, some aspects will be more suitable to some situations than to others. Again, the needs of your clients will help decide which points are worth considering as you move into the future. Each of us does well though to keep an open mind on what those who have travelled the road before us are suggesting. Experience is valuable. We don't need to make the same mistakes twice and there is much to learn beyond our own immediate placement.

Finally, it is important when considering analysis of your performance and of client needs to check regularly and act on the results. Best practice suggests that a variety of approaches is better than single one. Do more than just hand out survey slips. Also keep in mind the nature, location and disposition of your clients. One client often overlooked is the 'non-presenter'. Use your relationships, connections, parent organisation, or whatever, to try and learn about the clients who could be but are not using your resources. Why are all students in the school not coming to the library? Why is only a small percentage of the population making use of your municipal library? What might be done to increase the number of clients that arrive at your door or link to your web page?

Leadership in library needs to be proactive, not reactive or reactionary. Visionary leadership is essential. Frequently management pauses at the 'we have never done this before' or 'that's not what library is about'.

This involves risk-taking but survival depends on it. Budget constraints are a fact of life. Spending money on print materials (for example) if your clients want non-print materials, is not going to ensure your long term survival. Forecasting is necessary and risks will need to be taken. Policies will need to be revised constantly and old established ideas replaced with new ones.

Consider ...

At home in the evenings most families actively engage in a variety of 'activities' within the limits of the home and sometimes or often within the same room. These may include watching television, playing computer or Wii games, reading, cooking, eating, drinking, talking, and so on. Quite regularly a number of these will be happening in the same space at the same time yet everyone allows for and even expects this behaviour. However, when some of those same individuals go to school next day they enter the school or university library only to be told to be quiet. They may not take their snack in, they may not talk, they may not watch TV, use their mobile phone or listen to their iPod, and so on. Why?

What is different? Why is it different? What are rules like these doing for learners? Who wants these rules? Who wants to enforce them? What is the end product they are designed to achieve and is it valid?

When identifying the needs of your clients, having your goals in mind is critical. However, that is not necessarily what it seems. If clients show that their goals do not match with yours it is going to be necessary to overhaul the goals rather than scrap the clients. At this stage a reminder of earlier discussion regarding change might be useful. Change is a way of life in the current and future age(s). Flexible management is essential. Innovations will be needed and thus goals and objectives – the detail of your moral purpose – will need to be flexible also. This will be easier if you have considerable freedom to set your own goals, but often library and information provision more generally is embedded within larger parent organisations. These will have moral purpose, goals and objectives of their own. Hopefully all of these will match your own but sometimes this is not the case. Moral purpose being that very inclusive general direction that provides overall guidance should be able to remain consistent if it has been effectively defined.

Schools will always have a powerful moral purpose to improve the learning of their students. However, one only need to look briefly at the history of schooling or the plethora of educational theories to see that there is not a definite agreement as to how this moral purpose is to be carried out.

Once identified, client needs must be reflected in clear goals for the organisation – goals that are well known and 'shared' by all members of the organisation. One particular organisation I was involved with posted their critical goals behind the door in every toilet cubicle in the building. They made sure, in quite an interesting way, that employees contemplated these on a fairy regular basis. It was one of the few organisations that I have been involved in where all the team knew exactly why they were there and what it was that they did on a daily basis.

As a case in point, consider the public aim of Google; 'to organise the world's information and make it universally accessible and useful' (Auletta, p.5). While the ambition is perhaps rather on the grand side, and one could argue regarding the reality of such an aim, there is none-the-less a clear indication of what the organisation is all about. Having formulated this aim in the way they have it has become possible to start systematically analysing the success of the company as it attempts to meet the aim. Constant monitoring and analysis will keep the organisation on target (or alternatively, demand a change in the aim itself if it is found to be untenable).

Mission statements are often decried by their detractors as management 'hocus pocus' (Welch 2006, p.187). However, they do serve to focus attention on 'the main game' to keep members of the organisation clearly focused on what it is that they are trying to achieve. Having identified client needs effectively, these are ideally bedded into mission statements, objectives and the other daily management policies that regulate practice and hopefully inspire working teams. Nothing is achieved by wildly impractical statements of intention. I can vividly remember the reaction of a London conference floor to an announcement by an American CEO that his company would by 2000 own 'all human knowledge'. I don't think he actually achieved that goal and I am fairly certain that his organisation no longer exists – swallowed up no doubt by an organisation with more achievable intentions. Alternatively, a succinct, 'real' statement can provide a powerful force for motivation (Welch 2006, p.187).

The important issue as regards identifying needs is, having identified them, converting those findings into clear and accepted common goals and directions. Organisations to be most effective need to have all their people rowing the same boat in the same direction. A simple but inclusive mission statement supported by clear, unambiguous goals that clearly reflect the present and future needs of the client will help the organisation achieve its best potential. If the mission statement holds strong moral purpose, then the outcomes are likely to be further advanced.

Mobilising your followers

While there might be every incentive to lead from the middle, a sound knowledge of leadership styles and a clear view of end results desired, there can still remain the problem of knowing where and how to start.

> We all know what we want to achieve, yet are often unsure how to
> go about it or even who are the key people needing to be
> influenced (cited in Cohan & Bradford 2005, p.3).

Most of us are individuals working within organisations. As one operative in a larger environment we can sometimes feel out of our depth and/or under appreciated. There are times when you ask yourself the question 'what am I doing here?' and perhaps, 'will I still be doing it ten years from now?'

The answer to the second question is perhaps the easiest to answer – probably not! The one thing we can be assured of is that situations will change. The one constant is change. There still remains the question of purpose and this is why Fullan, Hughes and others are so convinced that moral purpose, clearly defined and clearly understood, is vital for organisational success. We are part of a team and in that team relationships are critical as we head towards our purpose together. There does need to be agreement or at least consensus on the direction we take. Askew in the Streeton Primary School book *Q is for quality* has a neat illustration for this:

> When someone says, 'Hey Look!' and doesn't point, everyone
> gazes in a different direction. They soon become disenchanted and
> walk off. On the other hand, if you stand on the corner of a busy
> street and point up, those passing by will look up (2000, p.13).

The visionary leader needs to be able to point clearly and often. They need also to be able to point with conviction and in the complete confidence that they are pointing the right direction. Clearly defined objectives, outcomes, mission statements, and so on, are a first important step along this pathway. Defining the parameters for action is vital. The next big step is taking everyone else along with you. Influence is the power to get your work done, your goals reached. The information leader has a lot of people to influence, some of them at a considerable distance perhaps. In chapter 3, Healy and Johnson in particular highlight the extent of reach that may well be involved in the not too distant future. As leaders our influence needs to be extensive as well as effective. How is this achieved?

Relationships are at the heart of effective influence. Team building, collaboration, decision-making, and more, are aspects of the relationship landscape that are vital to effective and visionary leadership. Anyone who has been asked to coordinate the efforts of others will appreciate the importance of influence, and 'how maddening it can be to need others to get work done' (Cohen & Bradford 2005, p.4). In a children's story called *The little red hen,* the hen asks for assistance time and again. No one helped her and she had to do everything herself – until it came to handing out treats, that is. Along similar lines is the story by Spencer Johnson, *Who moved my cheese* (1998), where his 'little people' find their cheese no longer in the usual place. Rather than go and find it elsewhere, they choose to face starvation. Getting some folk to change their habits or to join in a task that requires effort is not always easy. Leaders need to be able to construct relationships that give them the influence needed to achieve their goals.

Consider ...

The quality management guide in education can be applied to the teacher librarian job in the library. Quality management is a different way to organise the efforts of people. This article says that leadership provides people with PD and growth. Win/win situations are sought after and problems will be prevented when people see how they fit in, e.g., if you train up the office staff, they will see themselves as being beneficial to the library and will see their place in the niche that is the library. Reward staff, library monitors and parent helpers. Have a vision for the future. Collaborate to help and improve processes and work as a team. Share and make known your values and beliefs, mission and purpose. Surveys can be used to assess needs and successes can be advertised in the newsletter. The only good competition is seen as competing to get better at pleasing the customer or helping the environment thru recycling. The wooing of the customer is never complete and thus the library needs to be constantly reinvented and new products, processes and the features of the environment are constantly improved upon. In the library we can discuss with the students what it is that they need to do well. How can we enable that to happen? Attention needs to be placed on the teaching learning process and above all students participating in creative team (BLOOMS) activities learn to set goals, work together and develop social skills. Rose Hawke (source: http://rosehawke.blogspot.com)

Effective influence relies on a leader's ability to build relationships of respect, inclusion, communication, sympathy, and listening, personal support as well as a considerable level of skill in your particular field. Each of these involves an element of risk on the leader's part, but together they build a platform from which it is usually successful to influence those around you and together achieve considerable productivity. But wait, there's more. These are what Cohen and Bradford term relationship-related 'currencies' – aspects of relationship that are recognised by corporations as building influence. They further include:

- inspiration-related currencies (vision, excellence, moral/ethical correctness);
- task-related currencies (new resources, challenge, assistance, organisational support, rapid response, information);
- position-related currencies (official recognition, visibility to higher-ups, reputation, insider-ness, importance, contacts); and
- personal currencies (gratitude, ownership, self-concept, comfort) (Cohen & Bradford 2005, pp.39-45).

It is quite an impressive list and yet it is one that so many current information leaders and workers could relate to.

Each of the aspects in their list is, I suggest, on almost daily display in the teacher librarian or municipal library staff member. The extent to which these currencies are available to the individual will relate directly to the ability of that individual to influence those around them and to make a lasting difference to their workplace and the wider information ecology.

As a general rule those who use their influence clearly towards the moral purpose of the organisation and in an unselfish way, find that they are more successful and that they receive more positive attention from those about them. Organisations of all types are frequently unforgiving of the selfish use of power. They are usually most forgiving where corporate goals are the focus rather than personal ones. The way they use their influence will have an effect on their future and the future of their operation. There is always the danger of manipulating rather than influencing. Cohen and Bradford (2005, p.284) offer the following summary of the fine line between influence and manipulation.

Is it manipulation to:	**Answer**
Be aware of what you are doing to gain influence?	No
Fit your arguments and language to other party's interests?	No
Not mention your ultimate goal if not asked?	No

Exaggerate your costs to make trade seem better?	No
Push yourself to become interested in and concerned for the other person?	No
Do a favour you wouldn't do for everyone?	No
Paint the most favourable picture of the benefits?	No
Fake caring and interests for the other?	Yes
Lie about your intentions?	Yes
Lie about your costs?	Yes
Lie about the benefits?	Yes
Commit to a payment you do not intend to make?	Yes
Seek weakness and vulnerability in others to get them indebted in ways that violate their integrity?	Yes

They sum up with the conclusion that 'influence attempts are not manipulative if you can tell your potential ally your intentions with no loss of influence' (p.284). This is a significant ending and one of significance to the information leader. Within the information profession few would argue against those in the workplace acting as a team. Teambuilding, even in more isolated establishments (in terms of number of staff, rather than geographically), is one more of the vital challenges faced by information providers.

Teamwork has not been altogether popular in western cultures in the past. The fierce individualism that seemed to be an outgrowth of the Industrial Revolution within those cultures predominated into the 1990s, with people in the workplace more likely to compete with each other for a promotion than to work together to keep their corporation alive in order to provide promotions. There has been much more consideration and effort expended on the concept and reality of teams since that time. As noted in our excursion into organisational theory, there is now a dominant teambuilding aspect to organisational structures. Flatter management systems and the breakdown of traditional hierarchies have contributed to this.

In essence, teams will work most effectively if they share a general focus and commitment to a clearly defined and relevant goal and if they can freely and frequently interact. To use a classroom example, five children together are likely to complete a jigsaw faster that five individuals – and possibly with a great deal more enthusiasm. In the organisational context, providing clients with information how and when they need it is more likely to be effective where there is an efficient team of information personnel sharing their skills and time. Making such teams possible though is where the 'rubber hits the road'.

There are also many situations where teams might not be relevant. Many school teacher librarians work in isolation. Teaming for them is perhaps rather meaningless at first. However, in developing a more effective learning community – part of the intention of many school authorities across the world at the present time – there are new opportunities for these previously isolated workers to become part of highly motivated teams that extend library influence out into the school and even the community. Many of these opportunities are quite new. They offer huge potential for extending the value and influence of the information profession and provide opportunities for leadership previously not available. Teams are best suited to complete tasks beyond the limits of the individual. Schooling, lifelong learning, and community education are all currently moving well beyond the abilities of individuals. Technological changes have made this more the case than ever before. They are also offering a number of new ways of 'completing' the task that were not previously available. Not until recent times, for example, could the 'team' of learner, information professional and remotely located scientist join together to provide a young learner with direct access to science happening in the Antarctic.

However, building and maintaining teams takes effort and organisation. For a group to work effectively it needs to have at least a defined membership, interdependence and a perception of group identity (see, for example, Law & Glover 2000, p.69). It is this last point that welds a group of individuals into a team. Until there is a clear perception of cohesion in the group, the team cannot function as a team – at best it is a group of individuals. For the potential team builder then the challenge is to create a feeling of 'teamness'.

Tuckman in 1965 addressed some of the key issues of team forming. He identified four different phases (a fifth was later added) that together result in an efficiently working group:

> *Forming* – characterised by uncertainty and anxiety.

> *Storming* – characterised by conflict and internal dissent.

> *Norming* – characterised by development of cohesion and satisfaction as 'team' members.

> *Performing* – characterised by central focus on task completion, with interpersonal difficulties involved.

The fifth added later was;

> *Adjourning* – disbanding of the team with the task completed (Law & Glover 2000, p.72).

Consider ...

Forming new relationships by Tracy Avery

When forced into a new relationship with colleagues, there are many steps to be taken along the path to fostering a relationship that sees no one person as the dominant figure. The steps can be defined and relate closely to the similarity of courting a beau. As an individual, one must ascertain the degree to which they wish to contribute and the personality type they wish to portray within these relationships/groups in the workplace. When placed in a group for a group assignment, much time is spent setting up the relationship with the other people forced into this situation. There is much to-ing and fro-ing to firstly introduce oneself and enquire about the personal background of each person, as well as setting up compatible talking times. This is the 'Getting to know you' stage. One then can move onto the 'Relating and being friends/or not' stage, whereby the decision can be made as to whether you like the personality of the people you have met. These two stages may take a considerable amount of time and development of trust from each person. Within this stage a degree of caring and sharing can develop between the group members. Sympathy and empathy can develop and foster to help with trust building. Now that you have built a rapport with your group you can begin to work cohesively. Each personality should be known, including limitations. Each person's leadership qualities, or lack of, will be shining through as will the commitment level they portray be easily seen. The 'Check my personality' stage begins. As an individual within this group, you need to decide upon the leadership role you wish to take on. How are you going to portray yourself? How will decisions be made, autocratic, democratic or collaborative? With all these important factors sorted, it becomes time to knuckle down and start on the project at hand, thus begins the 'Let's get moving' stage. During this time, the initial 3 stages will be constantly revisited. Oh, but wait! There's more! One more person to add to the mix, coming in 2 weeks behind the completed stages. Now come the many questions, What if she doesn't like what we've started? What if I can't appreciate her personality? Will she be willing to accept all that we have done and pick up from there? Will she contribute, plus more, as she has been absent? Do I resent her for not being here in the beginning? Or more to the point ... Can I continue to develop my qualities as a leader and continue the great role that I have undertaken within my group? The story unfolds (source: http://rosehawke.blogspot.com).

One of the critical aspects of the theoretical considerations discussed in chapter 1 is the level of interaction and collaboration between individuals. That same importance is reflected in the scenarios of chapter 3. In the field, the ecology of information, there is considerable agreement that teams and collaboration are the best way to deal with the ever-more quickly developing wealth of information available. For the individual there is much less hope than for the team that they can effectively work through the important information. Building a personal knowledge tends to be seen as more possible in the social context of groups and teams.

While for the most part it is personal human-to-human relationships that are being considered, the limits themselves are theoretical. These interactions might be with avatars, academics, teachers, peers, computers or environments.

The concern is to keep the relationships human. Warner is correct as he emphasises repeatedly the relationship of the school library with its students rather than its systems. He speaks of dialogue as a critical factor in the whole information interaction. Learners may be self directed but they need relationships that can transfer to them the confidence and skill that will ensure lifelong learning. Shelby reflects (Healy, chapter 3) on the importance of information specialists 'always on hand' in her Centre. This is an important focus for her and one that gives confidence.

In 1997 De Gues reported on a study of companies that had been successful over several decades or more. He found that the 'living company' was characterised by a greater sensitivity 'to the chemistry of people within the organisation and to the evolution of and relationships with its external environment' (cited by Fullan 2001b, p.13). Fullan himself notes that 'If moral purpose is job one, relationships are job two, as you can't get anywhere without them' (Fullan 2001a, p.51). Kouzes and Posner (2000, p.149) conclude that the difference between the ineffective and effective leaders is that the latter 'really care about the people [they] lead'. Relationships help to motivate the people you want and need to influence. The success of your leadership will depend on the extent to which you can mobilise them in the directions that you want to take them. These relationships will extend from your senior administrators to the least frequent of your clients. Significantly, these relationships appear as givens in all of the scenarios in chapter 3 below, and the theme of connection with the environment in which we work is also a regular aspect.

Strategic planning

Logically, once you have established your reasons for existence, your moral purpose, the next step is to decide by what means you are going to achieve that purpose. Checking on client needs helps fine tune the purpose and give it some specific directions. Motivating those around you helps make the progress towards the purpose and its goals more likely to be successful. Strategic planning is all about splitting your goals and objectives into manageable portions and setting in place methods by which they can be achieved. These methods quite usually have much to do with marketing strategies.

Strategic planning in the modern context is not about accepting every innovation that appears on the horizon (see Fullan 2004, p.44ff). It is rarely wise to run with every innovation to be found that might in some way interact with your purpose. However, the converse is equally true. To ignore innovation will usually lead to stagnation and eventual death. Strategic planning is something of a reality filter. It needs to consider the potential futures and plan for change before that change is forced on the unprepared organisation but it also needs to consider the ability of the organisation to cope with any change. Goals may be identified as ideal that are well beyond the reality of what can be achieved by the organisation (Hamel & Prahalad 1996, p.158). These need to be identified in the strategic planning stage and either abandoned as impractical or made the subject of long-term planning that will make them possible. What is feasible is often more to the point than what is 'desirable'.

Strategic planning requires leaders who can think and plan strategically. This requires the identification and development of some specific skills. Davies and Davies speak of the importance of 'strategic leadership'. Strategic characteristics in a leader will help that leader become the visionary one so necessary to the information field today. Strategic leaders are different from other leaders in that they have a dissatisfaction or restlessness with present situations and a large capacity to absorb and adapt their role as leader (Davies & Davies 2005, p.8).

To be an 'effective influencer' requires versatility in selection and use of a range of strategies. Just as no single solution can be found to the dilemmas of the modern information ecology, just as truly there is no single strategy that will be sufficient to make a difference to it.

Cohen and Bradford (2005, p.123) suggest four categories of strategy that the leader should consider: 1) straightforward trades, 2) show how cooperation helps achieve allies' goals, 3) uncover hidden value, and 4) compensate for costs.

When making plans to effect a change, followers are more likely to accept and work towards that change if there are some clearly definable 'trade-offs'. If it leads to less time on unloved tasks, for example, you can be sure of some considerable support. If it leads to fatter pay packets, even more support is likely. In the information ecology, the second of these is less likely than the first perhaps. Automation of library catalogues was initially seen by some as excessive work and high cost. However, once benefits of self-search, search times and decline in client questions (that usually meant staff work) became visible, then the attitudes changed. Trade-offs helped make the change more acceptable to the point where acceptance was almost universal.

Uncovering hidden values is one strategy that can be useful to the information leader. The information community, rather like the education community, can be mysterious. Unlike the factory that makes bricks or the bank that makes profits, the information 'business' deals in more ethereal materials. What quantity of information does each client need? How do we know when they have enough?, What is enough?, and so on. Cohen and Bradford suggest a number of measures that reveal hidden benefits and can be readily applied to the information situation. They include:

> The cost of employee turnover (and knowledge loss).
> Costs involved in excess inventory.
> The link between satisfied employees and increased sales (client numbers/visits).
> The value of customer loyalty.
> The cost of bottlenecks or service delays (Cohen & Bradford 2005, p.124).

Internet in the library was, and in some places still is, somewhat controversial. Client demands have pushed the change forward, at some speed. The costs though are considerable. To plan for this new technology, libraries have had to compensate for the cost in various ways. The cost does remain an issue but the needs of the client are clearly recognised and so some form of innovation or at least adaptation has had to take place. In some cases in the past this has been more reactionary than strategic. More recently, though, strategic planning has seen a greater number of libraries taking the initiative to provide more and better services as part of their long-term planning. By planning strategically (rather than reactively), they can minimise financial disruption or compensate for it more effectively.

Once the planning is complete (if it ever can be considered in that way), the strategy needs to be put into action. Once the plan is formed, each element of it needs to be converted into operational steps (Davies & Davies 2005, p.9). Tichy and Sharman (1993) suggest that strategic action planning has three stages:

Awakening,

Envisioning, and

Rearchitecturing (cited in Davies & Davies, p.9).

The awakening stage is where the organisation realises that it needs to change in order to stay competitive; current practice is identified as needing improvement and new directions need to be found as a basis for a more secure future. Envisioning takes place as the plans are made that will take the organisation forward to its new position. Rearchitecturing is the stage where changes will affect the organisation and where goals are achieved and new ones considered.

Perhaps somewhat on the simplistic side, these steps can help the visionary information leader get started along the strategic planning pathway. The problem is, of course, that nothing is quite that simple. More than one strategic direction is likely to be 'in progress' at any one time and quite frequently directions need to be modified along the way. Goals can change and so a highly flexible plan needs to be in place. This is where the importance of strategic leadership skills lies; particularly in a leader's ability to understand in detail the potential discontinuities, competitor intentions, and evolving customer needs (Hamel & Prahalad 1996, p.158).

Time and time again, success with strategic planning will come back to rest on the ability that you have as leader to listen to your peers, clients and administrators, to relate positively with them and to take them where you need them to go. As Fullan notes, it all comes back to 'relationships, relationships, relationships' (2001a, p.51ff). Failure to effectively maintain your relationships with those most involved in the change will lead to their disaffection and will derail your plans for change.

When working through major change, plan for personalised support – listening and talking – with each of the stakeholders concerned. Returning to the interesting case of the student learning management system (SLMS) mentioned in chapter 1, one of the most critical strategies in that development, one that changed so much of how learning was displayed and monitored, was a listening strategy. Perhaps most closely aligned to the second of Cohen and Bradford's strategies above, considerable time was spent showing just how the changes were actually meeting needs in a better way than before. More practically, this took the form of a small team of 'facilitators' being set up in the short term to talk with each of the stakeholder groups affected by the change. For parents, one individual particularly was identified and established in a mini 'call centre'. Chosen especially for their initial lack of technical knowledge but identified as having huge potential for flexibility, parents in particular related well to the 'I am one of you' type approach. Having a listener who did not try and blind them with technology but who spoke 'their language' brought the focus more quickly to the benefits of what was being offered rather than that of the new, technical way of doing things.

Similarly in the case of teachers who were faced with placing courses, including worksheets, assessment items, and so on, online and visible to students and parents at the start of each year, such a level of transparency was both new and concerning. For them a small office was provided for the manager (perpetrator) of the concept where they could directly, and candidly, air their concerns. While it had its moments for the manager concerned, provision for 'letting off steam' and then talking through the issues directly with the person who could modify the system had huge advantages. Online and live reporting directly to students and parents throughout the year was quite an innovation. It was a very different process for teachers and made their work more public and open to far greater scrutiny than ever before. However, the combined strategies of listening management (in confidence) and emphasis on the straightforward trades (no more frantic report writing at end of year/term, less actual report writing time, fewer issues at parent interview time, happier relationships with parents and students over reports and progress, and so on) proved critical to complete staff take-up within the first year of the project. For each stakeholder group, specific client needs were met as precisely as could be managed.

Motivating people is one aspect of good management and leadership. It is even more vital to the strategic leader. Having your followers prepared to follow into the less known is the challenge, but it is vital in the ever changing and increasingly complex ecology of information provision. The ability to influence, to motive those around you and to take them where they have never gone before – is the very essence of visionary information leadership. Balancing resources against future needs and goals remains a constant preoccupation with most of those working in libraries today.

Money matters

Hughes notes the important link between adequate financial resourcing and quality educational outcomes in his contribution to chapter 3.

> This is why effective school libraries, well resourced, are vital in
> the task of achieving a successful basic education for all students,

an essential in a world where education is so crucial to life opportunities.

The connection is a critical one.

While most agree that money needs to be expended on resourcing libraries, there is a danger that considerations of client need and quality outcomes may fall foul of unsympathetic business practices. Money managers basing their practice on specific budgetary or business models are often the ones closing down services, reducing staff numbers, curtailing opening hours and seeing their client numbers decline. There is a connection between these factors. The growth of the learning commons in universities, for example, indicates a clear client need. As library professionals we need to review our management frameworks at all levels and respond to the need as a matter of urgency. Closing down library services and times is not the appropriate reaction.

It is a rather common modern practice to see education as simply another business form, and school business managers are very right to control spending, balance budgets and so on. When they start to involve themselves directly with the classroom, however, library professionals should be sceptical and concerned.

Business in the first instance deals essentially with tangible end products – these might be building a better mousetrap or creating a high interest return on an investors' money. The product is real, finite and generally predictable. Education, the formal process of encouraging learning is very different. While 'base material' – human beings – might be in a sense finite and real, they are not always predictable. Further, the real material being dealt with is mind activity, not simply neural activity, but rather the infinitely more complex and unpredictable internalisation of information. It is this internalisation that is at the basis of information provision in all its aspects, but particularly so in the areas of formal education. An intangible, unpredictable and highly volatile product should not be regulated on the same basis as more commercial outcomes might be. Put crudely, the number of books borrowed does not necessarily equal the number of books read or the amount of information absorbed.

Adding to the mixture is that there are relatively few clear dividing lines between the formal curriculum and the informal one. What an individual 'absorbs' in the formal context may only make its appearance in the informal context of play or evening activity, and vice versa. Very often we make the mistake of measuring our product with scores, tests and tally sheets. Governments in particular are very keen to look at league tables, compare like schools and so on. But what is really being measured?

Respected educator Brian Caldwell (2004) recently reviewed the Australian federal government's 'Education Revolution' policy. While he found that government were very concerned to compare schools in terms of their national testing program and publish results publicly (so that parents 'could make informed choices', top performing countries had 'no mandatory system of national tests' (O'Keeffe, Viscusi & Zeckhauser, p.34).

Information may well be presented to an individual today and yet not actually become a part of their knowledge until years later when other influences may suddenly make it relevant to them. One of the simplest examples of this is in the field of history. How often do students say 'Why do we have to know this?' (a usual response – 'for the test'!). In reality, they may never actually relate to that 'vitally important' piece of history, date or whatever. But once in a while, somewhere along the way, one or two of them may well say, 'So that's why this building looks like this'. Suddenly their history teacher is seen in a far more flattering light. All too often this is not much good to the responsible history teacher because they have become history themselves.

Teachers of mathematics are similarly burdened. If all the math teachers who have had students say to them 'Why do we have to do this?' were placed end to end, it is certain that Pythagoras would have had a rule for it.

Hughes lays responsibility for the change in learning priority not on the school or library, but on the government that makes the policy regulating budgets to a large extent.

> The priority of a successful basic education through the national curriculum has been accepted by the Australian Government, noting our failure in recent years to provide an effective education for all students. This priority will be difficult to achieve and provides a challenge to the process of developing the national curriculum. Such a task is much more than a matter of design of courses, important as is that process. It requires that there are sufficient trained teachers and that these are supported by quality learning resources which are properly staffed and organised.

His comments are timely. At the present time, federal government is placing considerable emphasis on their so called 'Education Revolution'. Question is, to what extent are they, or any other western economy government for that matter, in real touch with their 'clients'. Past history suggests that governments in western democracies are more interested in a quick vote than in an educational revolution. Current practice in terms of the federal government tends to be focused on 'free laptops'. The laptop has long since been discredited as an actual aid to real, lifelong learning (see, for example, Lee & Winzenried 2009). So, to what extent are governments actually aware of real client needs? Of real learning? And of real information provision?

Again, Hughes makes an important point when he notes the shortfall between practice and rhetoric as regards school libraries.

> A related area of need is to provide good quality teaching and learning resources for those teachers and for their students. For the latter this takes on additional benefit where their access to good learning resources is limited at home. Urgent attention needs to be re-directed to school libraries, high on the list of national priorities in the decade 1965-1975, but neglected in the years since.

In an area where internet and social networking is increasingly seen as an imperative for public libraries (as well as those almost everywhere else) public spending on libraries does not seem to be considering this cost.

This leads in to one of the more troublesome areas of leadership and strategic planning – the priority allocation of resources. It is unlikely that many information operations face their task with unlimited budgets; all the best to those who do. More commonly, resources have to be allocated on a priority basis. Finance, staff, time and technology are among the primary resources available for information leaders. These often have to be juggled rather acidulously because supply is short and quite often the levels of resource can change mid-task. This process needs to be done once goals and objectives are established. Welch reminds us that identifying a top priority and not allocating sufficient to it is a recipe for problems (Welch 2006, p.41). Using whatever tools are available the priorities need to be weighed up in the balance of real client needs rather than organisational past practice or present wishes. Make certain there are sufficient resources (and a small allowance for contingencies) to complete that task or goal, whatever the decided priority.

On the face of it, all of this might be somewhat discouraging. However, what it does point out clearly is that if ever the information industry has needed visionary leaders, now is the time. Leaders who can fine tune their skills at motivating their own organisations and providing more of what the clients need will see their organisations grow in terms of customer satisfaction as well as potential for making a difference in the economy and with influencing government policy. Strategic information leaders need to address not only their local needs but also those of the wider community all the way through to national government levels.

Product review

If any consideration tends to sum up all of the previous discussion it is the theme of product review. Throughout all of the planning and motivating stages there needs to be a clear vision of what is being aimed at – the moral purpose – and whether it is being achieved – product review.

The critical aspects for survival into the future could be summed up as: Identify client needs, keep management responsive, remain open minded and constantly look for opportunities to change rather than chances to reinforce the past. Clear goals that are both realistic and challenging will help keep the focus on the organisation's moral purpose. Relationships are vital as a key part of understanding client needs and of becoming more influential in all aspects of your organisation. Vision of where we should and could be is essential as it informs strategic planning and keeps it on track. Above all, be prepared to change.

In this age, perhaps more than in any other, it has become an imperative for informational professionals to actively promote their libraries and the services that they offer to their clients. It is no longer viable for a library to sit and wait patiently for clients to come to them. Those days are gone.

In the next chapter we will look at the visions of seven quite different information professionals and consider what they see as the future of their industry. Each has a story to tell. The accumulated years of wisdom that they encapsulate are quite considerable. What the future holds for them, as with all others working and living with them in the information ecology, is uncertain. They do have a vision though, some perhaps more immediate than others. That vision is what is guiding their planning, the relationships that they are building and maintaining as well as the goals they have set for their libraries and organisations.

While each is facing their own particular situation, there are some rather important common threads and these will be explored in chapter 4 following on from the scenarios.

References

Abbott-Chapman, J. & Hughes, P. (1990). *Identifying the qualities and characteristics of the 'effective teacher'* (pp.1-95). Hobart: Youth Education Studies Centre, University of Tasmania.

Askew, G., (Ed.). (2000). The 12 quality principles. In *Q is for quality*, Yallambie, Vic.: Streeton Primary School.

Auletta, K. (2009). *Googled; the end of life as we know it*. London: Virgin Books.

Balan, P. (1991). *Creating achievable marketing plans*, Adelaide: Polyglot Enterprises.

Caldwell, B. (2004). Reimaging the self-managing school. Specialist Schools Trust. Available at http://www.sst-inet.com.au/files/Brian_Caldwell_-_Re-Imaging_the_Self-Managed_School.pdf

Cohen, A. & Bradford, D. (2005). *Influence without authority*, New York: John Wiley & Sons.

Collins, J. (2001). *Good to great: why some companies make the leap – and other don't.* New York: Harper Business.

Covey, S. (1990). *The seven habits of highly effective people.* New York: Simon and Schuster.

Davies, B.J. & Davies, B. (2005). The strategic dimensions of leadership. In Davies, B., Ellison, L. & Bowring-Carr, C. (Eds.). *School leadership in the 21st century: developing a strategic approach* (pp.7-16). London & New York: Routledge Falmer.

Donham, J. (2005). *Enhancing teaching and Learning* (2nd Ed.). New York: Neal-Schuman.

Dowler, L. (1997). *Gateways to knowledge.* Cambridge, MT: MIT Press.

Fullan, M. (2001a) *Leading in a culture of change.* San Francisco, CA: Jossey-Bass.

Fullan, M. (2001b). *Change forces, the sequel.* London: Falmer Press.

Fullan, M. (2004). *Leading in a culture of change: personal action guide and workbook.* San Francisco, CA: Jossey-Bass.

Goleman, D. (1995). *Emotional intelligence.* New York: Bantam Books.

Hamel, G. & Prahalad, C.K. (1996). *Competing for the future.* Boston, MA: Harvard Business School.

Hartzell, G. (2000). Being proactive. *Book Report* 18(5), 14-19.

Heifetz, R. (1994). *Leadership without any answers.* Cambridge, MA., Harvard University Press.

Heller, R. (1985). *The new naked manager.* London: Hodder and Stoughton.

Hesselbein, F. & Goldsmith, M. (2006). *The leader of the future.* San Francisco, CA: Josey-Bass.

Kotter, J. (2001). What leaders really do. *Harvard Business Review*, Harvard, CT. December 2001.

Kouzes, J.M. & Posner, B.Z. (2000). *The soul at work* New York: Simon & Schuster.

Lauer, C. (Ed.). (2009). *The management gurus: lessons from the best management books of all time.* London: Atlantic Books.

Law, S. & Glover, D. (2000). Leading effective teams. In *Educational leadership and learning: Practice, policy and research* (pp.71-86). Buckingham, UK: Open University Press.

Lee, M. & Winzenried, A. (2009). *The use of instructional technology in schools: lessons to be learned*. Melbourne: ACER.

Maxwell, J. (2007). *The 21 irrefutable laws of leadership*. London: Thomas Nelson.

O'Keeffe, M., Viscusi, W.K. & Zeckhauser, R.J. (1984). Economic contests: comparative reward schemes. *Journal of Labour Economics*, 2(1). 27-56.

Patterson, K., Grenny, J., Maxfield, D., McMillan, R. & Switzler, A. (2009). Influencer. In Lauer, C. (Ed.). *The management gurus: lessons from the best management books of all time*. London: Atlantic Books.

Reardon, V. (2009). Frances Hesselbein: 'Leadership is being, not doing'. Accessed 26 January 2010 at: http://vincereardon.wordpress.com/2009/06/01/frances-hesselbein-leadership-is-being-not-doing

Shirky, C. (2008). *Here comes everybody: the power of organising without organisations*. London: Penguin.

Tichy & Sharman (1993) in Davies, B.J. & Davies, B. (2004). Strategic leadership. *School Leadership and Management*, 24(1), 29-38.

Tuckman, B. (1965). Developmental sequence in small groups. *Psychological Bulletin*, 63(3), June 1965, 384-399.

Welch, L. (2006). Groundwork: the situation analysis. In *The other 51 weeks: a marketing handbook for librarians*, Wagga Wagga, NSW: Centre for Information Studies, Charles Sturt University.

Wheatley, M. (2009). Website accessed 23 December 2009 at: http://www.margaretwheatley.com/findingourway.html

3

CHAPTER 3
The scenarios

Scenario 1 Miles' library – annotated

Doug Johnson

7:00 AM

'Miles … Miles, honey, time to get up,' the librarian's voice whispered softly in the still dark bedroom. Miles, a senior in the graduating high school class of 2025[1], slowly came awake.

'OK, OK, I'm awake, Marian. Schedule, please,' Miles requested using the auditory interface to his school library portal[2], accessed through a small device on his nightstand.

'You are meeting with your ecological science team F2F in Learning Space 17, Main Library at 8:45. Carlotta will be fifteen minutes late. You've registered for 'Advanced Semantic Web Searching' with Head Librarian Baxter from 9:30-11:00 in Seminar Room B of the Main Library. Your IEP[3] Advisor, Dr Li, wants to meet with you in her office at 1:00 about your senior project. And I have finalised the MUVE meeting schedule with Professor Shahada in Amman for 4:15 SLT this afternoon. Your lacrosse team practice has been cancelled, but time has been reserved in the simulation area of the gymnasium for team members wanting virtual practice[4].'

'Gee, that's all?'

'No, Miles, dear. Your report on theologian Reinhold Niebuhr is due tomorrow. Would you like me to reserve a video rendering terminal in the library for you?'

'Marian, you are a slave driver!' Miles cried, slowly crawling out of bed.

---

[1] 2025 is the approximate year my youngest grandson, Miles, will graduate from high school assuming children are still attending thirteen years of schooling beginning at the age of five or six – a big assumption.

[2] Customisable portals are common, although still text-based, as of today. iGoogle is a popular example. 'Add-on's' in the Firefox browser also exemplify the extensibility that users are being to require of any information accessing/processing tool.

[3] An individualised education plan is required by law for US children having been identified with special needs today. By 2025, these will be required for all students and created with the help of sophisticated assessments and data-mining tools.

[4] The Nintendo Wii gaming device currently allows users to participate in simulated sports and exercise.

8:30 AM

'Looks like almost a full day in the library for me,' Miles tells his girlfriend Jennie as they walk from the bus stop up to the school. Jennie is one of the main reasons that Miles still goes to his neighbourhood bricks and mortar school at least three days a week.[5] 'Let's grab a cup of coffee there while we have time.'

'Seems like you've been living in the library this year,' observed Jennie. 'They should be charging you rent!'

'Well my senior project, 'Can sims be programmed to exhibit free will?' has really been more involving than I thought. I mean, it's the perfect combination between my interest in religion and computer programming, but it's been a lot more work than I thought. And the library has been my primary resource for this project.' Miles was embarrassed to admit that his presence in the school's physical library was only a fraction of the time he spent in the library's virtual spaces. 'Just stamp 'nerd' on my forehead, I guess,' Miles sighed.

The library Miles and Jennie enter might look cavernous were it not for the low ceilings and dividers filled with green plants that break up the space into small, intimate work areas. A combination of soft seating and small, easily rearranged worktables in coordinated colours make the library look both work-like but comfortable. There is a low hum of conversation, especially near the entrance to the library where a small coffee shop is located, but noise-cancellation technologies keep the main part of the library surprisingly quiet – considering there are over 200 students working here. The perimeter of the library has doorways leading to small conference and seminar rooms, faculty offices (this location is in high demand), and technology labs filled with powerful, specialised computers. Student work is silently displayed throughout the library space on monitors of various sizes with small signs indicating the channel on which the audio is being broadcast.[6]

---

[5] Physical schools will still exist in 2025 since the societal charges placed on education of socialisation and child containment will still exist. Inexpensive childcare will continue to be demanded by working parents – even if more are working from home.

[6] David Loetscher and others have envisioned a 'learning commons' that is user-centred with workspaces for a variety of groups with a variety of purposes. See: Loertscher, Koechlin & Zwaan (2008). *The new learning commons: where learners win.* Salt Lake City, UH: Hi Willow.

Students and teaching staff alike carry a variety of small portable computing devices that automatically connect to the data network via the library's portal interface.[7]

Miles says goodbye to Jennie and heads toward Learning Space 17 for his meeting with his team.

8:45 AM

'Hey, Juan. Hey, Liz,' Miles says with a wave as he plops down on one of the sofas occupied by his learning team. 'Any word from Carlotta?'

'She's having an emergency with some stuff at home and will be audio conferencing with us[8],' Juan reports.

'Sounds like the emergency is a bad hair day.' And with that, Carlotta's voice says, 'I heard that. And just for your information, I never have a bad hair day! But I do have a little sister with the sniffles.'

'OK, OK, I've got lots to do today,' Liz chides. 'I think at the last meeting we decided that our project was going to be looking at creating self-reporting devices for the green plants here in the library powered by the small voltage they themselves actually produce. Are we still agreed?' Heads nod. (85 per cent of all energy needed to power the school is generated by projects designed by the students themselves over the past fifteen years.)

'So, Miles, what did your search on similar projects turn up?'

'Yeah, your creepy Marian avatar dig anything up?' asked Juan. 'Do you still have her affection module running so she calls you sweetie, sweetie?'

'She's not creepy, just twentieth century,' Miles replied. 'She looks and sounds just like Shirley Jones's character Marian in *The Music Man*. If you weren't such a cultural Neanderthal, you'd appreciate the reference. As for her obvious and well-placed fondness for me, I'd say you're just jealous[9].'

Carlotta laughed, saying, 'Miles and Juan, if you weren't such good friends, I'd say you couldn't get along.'

---

[7] Today's netbooks and smartphones using 802.11x and EVDO wireless networks are early versions of those being used by Miles and his contemporaries.

[8] Built in laptop cameras and microphones along with simple programs like Skype are already making video conferencing commonplace in schools. The trend of more ubiquitous cameras and microphones, simple conferencing tools, and greater broadband connectivity will continue to grow.

[9] Customisability in both ability and appearance are common in both MUVE (MutliUser Virtual Environments) such as Second Life and MMORPG (massively multiplayer online role-playing games) such as World of Warcraft avatars today.

Miles is the acknowledged expert at data acquisition in the group. Liz's strength is in leadership, organisation and historical knowledge; Juan's visual communication and maths skills are outstanding; and Carlotta's interpersonal abilities keep the team moving and working well together – plus she is the acknowledged science whiz of the team. Miles considers each of these fellow students an integral part of his personal learning network.[10]

Miles himself does not conduct data searches – he programs bots that search for him. Ever since helping his older brother Paul create and modify creatures in the primitive simulation game Spore as a pre-schooler and later learning how to design custom Google search[11] engines in elementary school, Miles has been devising ever more sophisticated programs that help him meet his information needs. The librarians have been instrumental in helping Miles develop these skills, and several thousand other students – and adults – use some of the search bots Miles has created. Lately, he has been giving the bots physical form as avatars and personalities using code from a new bank of twentieth-century entertainer models.

'Marian found about 750 gig of materials related to using plants' own electrical production properties to power sensors. I asked her to condense and audio-synth this data to five, ten and fifteen minute summaries. I've sent the audio files of the three top reports to you. In my view, this project is increasingly doable ...'

Encouraged by Miles's findings, the group discusses next steps, creates a timeline, and debates the format of the final report on the project. Their next meeting on the coming Friday will be virtual, using the library's video portal.

9:25 AM

Miles hurries toward the seminar room on the other side of the library for his class with Librarian Baxter. Cutting around dozens of students working individually or in small groups, Miles glances up at the latest ALA's LISTEN campaign 'poster' being displayed on one of the library's LED monitors. It features Tammy Fox, daughter of first decade hottie Megan Fox, displaying her favourite audio-book cover. Another LED promotes an ALA PLAY poster showing popular cartoonist Brady Johnson with his favourite video game. (The READ campaign was discontinued in 2020, along with the paper versions of the posters.)

Only one thing seems to be missing in Miles's school library – books, magazines or any paper information source. The last print books – school

---

[10] Collaboration and group work skills are a part of every set of '21st Century Skills' being promoted.
[11] Customised search engines can be built now using Google custom search.

yearbooks and some local history publications – were sent to Ghana to be digitised five years earlier. All those materials are now available online.[12]

Nearly 99.9 per cent of intellectual property in all formats – text, visual, audio, and programming code – is in the world IP databank. On submitting work to the databank, a small identifying script is inserted into each work. Each time the creation is accessed, a nominal payment is made to its creator. Content users can pay either a flat monthly fee for unlimited access to the databank or pay per petabyte of data.[13] Miles's school library does not own or lease any information sources. But it has built, using freeware APIs, a powerful portal and guide to the databank.[14] And it allows its staff and students to customise that portal.

Miles enters the seminar room just as Mr Baxter begins to outline the objective of the ninety-minute lecture/demonstration/guided practice session on honing one's understanding of semantic web searching skills[15], specifically dealing with language-specific idioms when doing multi-lingual searching with auto-translation tools. About ten students are attending in person and another fifteen in the library's MUVE conference room. The virtual participants are not just from Miles's school, but from other high schools, a university, and a home school. One participant is simply a retiree with an interest in the topic. The seminar will be recorded and added to the databank.

'Miles, what are you doing here?' Sergey back-channels using a primitive chat program. 'You could be teaching this stuff!'

'Thanks for the vote of confidence, but I heard Baxter just came back from an ALA conference with some beta code on idiom translation. I'm hoping that if I look interested enough, he'll share.'

---

[12] Full-text searching of over seven million books is currently available as part of Google's Search the Book project. Google has reached an agreement with publishers to scan and make available not just out of copyright titles, but out of print titles.

[13] Stanford law professor Lawrence Lessig in his book *Free culture* (New York: Penguin, 2004) advances the idea of such a compensation scheme for intellectual property creators, based on redistributing the proceeds from a tax on recording media to compensate musicians and videographers.

[14] Subscription services to full-text magazine indexes, video collections and e-book collections have been common since the 1990s.

[15] The semantic web, a means of describing data on the internet in ways that make it more easily searched by discriminating among homonyms and other word meaning discrimination techniques (Berners-Lee, T., Hendler, J. & Lassila, O. (2001). The semantic web. *Scientific American Magazine*. May 17.

Mr Baxter coughed. 'Miles, would you google-jockey[16] this seminar, just in case questions arise?' Miles nodded and made a mental note to find the etymology of that strange term.

11:00 AM

Miles uses the time between the end of the seminar and his meeting with Dr Li to grab a sandwich in the school cafeteria with Jennie and then take a quick nap in the library. Research on adolescent sleep needs convinced the library advisory committee that napping is a legitimate use of library resources and that library policies should reflect this. After Marian again awakens Miles, he checks his Twitface account and then listens to two audio reports – one a real-voice podcast and the other a speech-synth conversion – recommended by Mr Baxter in the earlier seminar.[17] He reviews his progress on his senior thesis.

Miles's school is one of several operating in his small community. It is based on a highly individualised, project-based, collaborative learning model that uses performance assessment only. 'Developing creative problem-solvers with a conscience' is the articulated mission of the school. All required classes end when students are twelve and have passed the national reading/writing/math proficiency test. After age 12, each student works according to an IEP, written by the student, his parents, a team of teachers and school librarians, and the other members of his formal personal learning network (PLN).

---

[16] Assigning a class google jockey is a current practice in higher education. See EDUCAUSE Learning Initiative '7 things you should know about google jockeying', May 2006.

[17] Miles's library serves the 'postliterate'. Any number of recent studies are concluding that reading is declining – primarily the reading of novels and longer works of non-fiction. I define the postliterate as those who can read, but choose to meet their primary information and recreational needs through audio, video, graphics and gaming media. Print for the postliterate is relegated to brief personal messages, short informational needs, and other functional, highly pragmatic uses such as instructions, signage and time-management device entries – each often highly supplemented by graphics.
The postliterate person's need for extended works or larger amounts of information is met through visual and/or auditory formats. The term 'postliterate library' may at first glance appear an oxymoron, but it is not. Our best libraries are already postliterate, increasingly meeting the needs of users who communicate, play and learn using media other than print. And the attitudes we as professional librarians adopt toward the postliterate may well determine whether our libraries continue to exist. My article, Libraries for a postliterate society, multimedia & internet @ schools, July/August 2009, further describes these ideas.

Another school in Miles's community is entirely computer-based, with each student using a structured, game-based programmed curriculum designed for his individual educational program. A third school retains the 'traditional' classroom, fifty-minute period, teacher-led, core content model. Neither of these schools have either physical or virtual libraries or librarians. (Miles's first podcast that earned him databank payments was a commentary arguing that sending children to traditional schools should be considered child abuse.) All families are given educational vouchers and are allowed to select which school to attend. Vouchers became politically feasible in 2017 when a law was passed that no school can charge more in tuition than the standard voucher amount and that all students, including those with special needs, are eligible for each school's lottery that selects the incoming class.[18]

1:00 PM

'I'm very pleased with the progress you've been making on your senior project, Miles,' said Dr Li with a smile. 'Explain to me again why you believe that your sims are showing signs of free will.'

'It's their preferences, Dr Li!' Miles reports, 'Kurzweil, one of my oldest sims, is choosing blue clothing at a rate outside statistical probabilities. In fact, even though he has a choice of several dozen coloured garments from which to choose each day, he almost always chooses blue. He also seems to like anchovies on his pizza.'

'And you are sure this is not a programming bug?' asked Dr Li.

'I've gone over the selection routines about twenty times and asked three others in my PLN to do independent audits of the code. Everyone agrees that Kurzweil should be making random choices.'

Dr Li and Miles confer for nearly an hour, once bringing in Ms King, a Hong Kong librarian who specialises in science fiction in popular culture and its

---

[18] The societal demand for school 'choice' has led to many different options beyond the traditional public school in the United States. Private schools, parochial schools, magnet schools, charter schools, online schools, open-enrolment – with a demand for government tuition vouchers controlled by parents – are all examples of the diversification of education. The reality is that not every type of school needs a library, even today.

treatment of religious and moral dilemmas. She quickly produces a qualitative list of works in which self-aware technologies are featured.[19]

'Here's one last dimension you might want to consider,' suggests Dr Li. 'What might be the meaning of this discovery on how we as humans view ourselves? That we humans may merely be 'sims' in a great cosmic programming plan?'[20]

Miles checks to make sure his audio note-taker[21] caught this question, before agreeing that this was a good idea.

'Oh, before you go, I also want to check how the composition of your PLN is working for you. I understand that you did not accept my suggestion of dropping your grandfather's membership in favour of adding a second programming expert.'

Miles considered his PLN. The school requires that all students have a 'formal' personal learning network of twelve members. (Like other students, Miles's informal PLN has more than 100 members at any one time accessed by a variety of networking tools.) For their formal PLN, some students create expert groups from specialised fields of high interest; others form a group with as diverse a representation as possible. Librarians are a part of nearly every student's PLN and they take this responsibility seriously.[22]

'With all respect, Dr Li, I did keep Grandpa Doug on my PLN rather than choose another expert. I recognise he knows little about my major areas of study and is hopelessly out of date on anything technology related, but because of his advanced age, he sometimes adds a sense of perspective that I don't get from other students or experts,' Miles maintains. 'He's also good for a joke now and then.'

Dr Li nods. 'Perspective is valuable, I will admit. But I've seen his jokes – pathetic!'

Miles thanks Dr Li, and asks his librarian avatar Marian to send his advisor's last question out to his PLN for input, thankful his senior year and this project are nearly complete. Miles is looking forward to his first year as a North Dakota State University Bison. His older brother Paul, however, has warned him that his first

---

[19] The exponential growth of information will require the specialisation of librarians into areas of interest.

[20] Ray Kurzweil in his book *The singularity is near* (New York: Viking, 2005) suggests this explanation – that we are all part of some cosmic simulation game, for human existence.

[21] A growing body of academic research shows that students who record instructions and classroom lectures get better grades, justifying personal mp3 player/recorders in schools.

[22] Personal learning networks, a self-created set of experts, colleagues and resources that can be relied upon to meet daily learning needs, usually dependent on networked technology, are currently being explored by educators.

year of college will be tough since many professors still lecture. He advises making sure his PDA has a full battery charge for multi-tasking during the core courses.

2:00 PM

Miles uses the next hour putting the finishing touches on his report on Reinhold Niebuhr that's due the next day.

Luckily, Marian was able to schedule Miles a full hour of time in the 3D rendering computer lab.[23] This is one of the few individual projects for which Miles is responsible this term so he has chosen to examine his favourite twentieth century theologian's influence on US government policy. After listening to and viewing over eighty hours of materials on the topic, Miles's final project will be pseudo-discussion with Franklin Roosevelt, Lyndon Johnson and Barak Obama, each discussing major Niebuhrian beliefs in relationship to their administration's social policies.

Miles hopes that this project will be judged to merit inclusion in the school's student research 'virtual museum.' Miles's older brother Paul holds the record number of pieces of student work in the museum with three projects. Miles's goal is to get one more of his projects added this spring – giving him four. The permanent addition of student work to the museum is considered an honour.[24]

Like his fellow students, Miles writes very little, choosing instead to convey his ideas and research using the more natural communication methods of sight and sound. Technology makes it simpler to create audio and video reports than written ones. When a teacher does require a written 'paper,' Miles uses a speech-to-text conversion program to create his first draft and then edits that version. Most video and audio reports can be done using his personal computing device, but now and then Miles likes to explore more sophisticated modes of communication like the 3D rendering software that requires a more powerful processing. The library's labs supply equipment for this purpose. Miles and his fellow students can write very

---

[23] Despite the ubiquity of personal computing devices, cutting edge applications will continue to need very large processing capabilities, unaffordable by individuals, and therefore housed in the library.

[24] Educators have long known that the larger the audience for a student's work, the greater the level of concern by the student about the quality of the work. Permanent collections of student work, organised and managed by the library, should become a part of the school culture and contribution to the world's knowledge base.

well; they simply choose to communicate in what they feel are more powerful ways.[25]

At one point, Miles gets stuck on a highly complex task he asks of the rendering program. In answer to an online call, the support librarian pops up in a window in the lower right corner of the screen and efficiently helps Miles over the rough spot. Visual literacy is considered as important, if not more, than textual literacy for Miles and his classmates in this postliterate work environment, educational system and society. Librarians view the communications portion of information fluency models as a critical part of their curriculum.

Satisfied at last, Miles stores his simulation in his digital warehouse along with all other work he has created since he was in elementary school.[26] He glances at the clock on his screen and decides that he has time to get home and do his MUVE conference with Dr Shahada there.

4:00 PM

As Miles walks in the front door, his dad calls out from his home office, 'Supper's at six – I blocked it off on your calendar. Attendance is not optional. Oh, and when is that lawn going to get mowed? The grass gets any longer you'll not only have to mow, but bale as well.'

Sighing at the hopelessly agrarian reference, Miles acknowledges his dad and heads to the family room. Rather than use the smaller, 54' screen on the computer in his room, he decides to go holographic for his meeting with Dr Shahada. He grabs a cola from the fridge, gets comfortable in one of the big easy chairs, and opens the connection to the University of Jordan. The family room fades and is

---

[25] Education and librarianship have a current bias toward print. This communication/ information format has served civilisation well for several millennia. Most professionals today demonstrate high levels of proficiency in print literacy skills and they can be expected to defend the necessity of such skills. Most educators are competent readers, writers and print analysts, but neophyte video, audio and graphic producers, consumers and critics. It is human nature to be dismissive of those competencies that we ourselves lack. However, postliteracy is a return to more natural forms of multi-sensory communication – speaking, storytelling, dialogue, debate and dramatisation. It is just now that these modes can be captured and stored digitally as easily as writing. Information, emotion and persuasion may be even more powerfully conveyed in multi-media formats. In Miles's school the bias toward print will fade as new generations of media-savvy educators take charge.

[26] Comprehensive portfolios, managed with the help of librarians, will be under lifelong development by all workers of the 'creative class'. Cheap mass storage of materials in digital formats will allow creators to keep all work and never delete a project or file.

replaced by a holographic multi-user virtual environment. Dr Shahada is already at his desk and Miles finds himself sitting across from him. The image is good enough to read the text on the diplomas displayed on the wall behind the professor's desk.

'Salaam lakim, Doctor,' Miles begins, happy to have a chance to practice his Arabic, a language he has studied both formally and informally for ten years. (The rest of the conversation is conducted in Arabic.) One of the reasons Miles's parents chose his current school was that its staff recognise that multi-lingual professionals are at an advantage in the global economy.[27] In 2015 when Miles chose Arabic as one of his 'focus' languages (along with Tagalog), his parents wondered if other languages would have been more beneficial. But the rise in democratic governments and a permanent peace settlement in the Middle East in the 2010s led to the region's growth as a world economic and educational leader.

'The blessings of Allah upon you as well, Miles,' Dr Shahada replies with a smile. 'I've been looking forward to our conversation today. To get to the point, one of the librarians here at UJ spotted some of the avatar-represented search bots you've been creating and also noticed your proficiency in Arabic. Our library in collaboration with the computer science department here at UJ would like to offer you a summer internship with us. You would be working with our librarians to improve our own library portal by adding idiomatic Arabic-speaking avatars.'

'It sounds exciting!' remarked Miles. 'Would I be doing this work in Amman or telecommuting?'[28] He and Dr Shahada continue to discuss this opportunity until nearly six o'clock.

One of Miles's school library's major services is to provide and support 'learning portals'. While text-based portals have been a common library offering for over ten years, the virtual environment interface is relatively new. When Miles logs on to his library portal, he sees a 3D representation of his physical school library. His avatar moves through it easily, looking far more natural than the funky Second Life-like creations of early MUVEs. He can see which members of his PLN network are online, check for messages (audio, video and text), do real-time video/audio communications with those both in and out of the library, and view his

---

[27] Thomas Friedman's book *The world is flat* (New York: Farrar Straus Giroux, 2006) described a world economy and argued that cultural understanding would play an increasing role in successful business.

[28] The continuing increase in fuel costs has led to a growing percentage of home-based workers. Home-based work has led to a greater need for 'dispositions' as outlined in AASL's *Skills for the 21st century learner* (Chicago: American Library Association, 2007).

selected and school-required news feeds. Around the library at various stations are librarian avatars with whom Miles can engage. While one sits behind a general information desk, others are subject-specific, offering guidance in languages, science, mathematics, history, communications and other areas. Virtual doorways lead to teacher, advisor and guidance virtual offices and to the school's virtual museum of permanent student project displays. There is also a doorway to Miles's 'warehouse,' a visual depiction of links to all the projects he has undertaken as a student.[29]

What makes the portal especially valuable to Miles and others in his school is its customisability. Using open source APIs (application programming interfaces) and programming scripts, Miles has rearranged the standard library layout, deleting some components like the annoying electronic posters and adding features like a real-time Arabic translation avatar, a collection of rare Tagalog documents, doorways to several research labs, and a hidden door to a representation of his bedroom at home where he can work on personal tasks.[30]

It is, however, Miles's work in creating custom-search bots represented by avatars that excites him. The library provides a set of tools that allow students to create 'librarians' who will follow carefully composed search parameters, following ever more sophisticated semantic rules.

6:00 PM

During his conference with Dr Shahada, Miles received a message comprised of several ideograms. It was Jennie keying from her phone, asking Miles if he wanted to meet her for a jog. He discretely replied that he was busy, but suggested they meet in the 20th Cent game after supper. After mowing the lawn with a push mower, Miles sits at the kitchen table where his mom, dad and 10-year-old sister Maggie are already engaged in conversation.

Maggie tells about the latest version of Oregon Trail that she and her team are playing in their US history class and about the research she is doing on animal rights of the nineteenth century; Dad shares his day of F2F pastoral visits to his elderly parishioners and how nice it was to get out from behind a computer screen.

---

[29] An online presence has been of growing importance since the 1990s for all institutions, including libraries. The MUVE 3D environment has been predicted to became the standard interface for web navigation.

[30] One of the reasons for the popularity of today's Firefox browser is its extensibility. By using 'add-ons,' one can customise the tool to meet one's personal style of working. The expectation of extensibility will continue to grow.

But it's Miles's mom's reflections about her day as the town's public library director that really interest him.

'I am always surprised at just how popular our 'Edit Yourself, Market Yourself, Support Yourself' workshops are – even after all these years of holding them. It seems it's take some people a long time to realise that the databank and payment plan changed the model of making money from one's intellectual property. While many creators choose to contract with editors and marketers – often people who once worked for large publishing companies – even more people have added editing and marketing to their own job skill-sets. It's really gratifying to see the public library as an effective community and personal development resource.'[31]

While Miles and Maggie visit their public library rarely, they both take advantage of its online presence. Maggie is a part of an active gaming group sponsored by the children's section and relies on its recommendations of new games. Miles attends the public library's online seminars and often consults its resident personal branding guru – 'Purple Cow' Smith.

'I suppose it's time to hit the studies,' Miles says after finishing his last bite of dessert.

'Time to talk mushy to Jennie is more like it,' teases Maggie. 'And don't forget, it's your night to do the dishes.'

7:00 PM

After the last spoon is dried and put away, Miles spends thirty minutes playing virtual lacrosse – the cancellation of his regular athletic practice is making him feel a bit sluggish. He checks his vital stats on the game station after his workout and sends them to his data storage locker in the library.

Back in his room, Miles logs into the MMORPG, 20th Cent. His regular avatar easily moves from one virtual environment to another, quickly morphing when the situation calls for it. Jennie is already online.

'My friend Winslet just finished programming a challenge this afternoon and asked me to beta it.' 20th Cent, like most popular games, relies on users to create

---

[31] Lulu.com and other self-publishing sites are changing the relationship of professional editors and markets and writers.

quests, puzzles and adventures for each other.[32] Both Miles and Jennie prefer 'amateur' created content to that designed by self-designated professionals. 'Think you can survive the sinking of the Titanic this evening?' Jennie asks. 'You know, you look a little like Leo DeCaprio.'

'Let's try it. If I am going down with the ship, I can't think of anyone I would rather have with me.'

Jennie's and Miles's avatars, now looking like Leo and Kate, teleport to the White Star docks where they board the ill-fated ship – Miles playing steerage, Jennie, first class.

Jennie and Miles are capable readers. Due to an early childhood educational programs, both, in fact, could read before entering kindergarten. But like the majority of their peers, they nearly always choose other media for nearly all their information and entertainment needs. Even video and audio are increasingly less popular than gaming. Miles and his peers demand engagement – not just entertainment – and engagement requires interaction.[33]

Games themselves have evolved, becoming an art form and are considered a medium of serious commentary on human nature. The Pulitzer Prize in gaming reflects the respect now paid to the creators of serious games for their plots, characters, settings, tones and themes.[34] And games, of course, are an accepted and effective pedagogical tool – especially for elementary students.

It takes Miles and Jennie almost three hours and a dozen attempts before both are rescued before freezing in the icy North Atlantic waters. Jennie notes several anachronisms that Winslet might want to fix before public release of this scenario. Miles gives Jennie a virtual kiss, logs off and heads off to brush his teeth.

10:30 PM

There is a quiet knock on Miles's bedroom door.

'Hi, Mom. Come in.'

'What are you reading, sweetie?' Miles's mom asks when she sees him propped up in bed with an actual paper book resting on his knees. As an avid

---

[32] The MUVE Second Life is a model of an environment that is almost completely user-generated; the MMORPG World of Warcraft (modelled after the earlier analog Dungeons and Dragons game) relies on user-generated 'quests'.

[33] The 'net' generation is spending more time in front of screens but less watching television – demanding entertainment be interactive rather than passive.

[34] The library helps its patrons discover and understand this still relatively new medium, offering game discussion groups, organising game fan clubs, and arranging game developer talks and seminars.

reader herself, Mom is always a little disheartened by how little her two younger children read for pleasure and is delighted when one actually picks up a book.

'Oh, it's an antique paperback called *The diamond age* by a twentieth-century writer named Stephenson. Pretty interesting how he predicted the OLPC movement that Negroponte and his cult began. Uh, Mom, can we talk a minute?'

'Sure. What's going on?' Mom asks, sitting on the edge of the bed.

'Don't faint, but I think I might major in library science next year instead of computer programming. Jennie was teasing me this morning about how much time I spend in the library and it got me thinking about how much I like working there.'

'Well, that is a surprise, Miles! The field and training has changed so much since I got my MLS twenty-five years ago, and it has really changed since your grandpa got his library degree almost fifty years ago – long before personal computers were commonplace, let alone the internet,' Miles's mom observed. 'My training seems obsolete, now. Good thing I'm in management where I don't need many technology skills.'

'You know I talked to Grandpa just now, bouncing this idea off him. He said about the same thing – that the tools and roles of the librarian have changed so dramatically, especially in the last twenty years or so. But then he added something. He said that the tools librarians use change, the importance of certain tasks that librarians perform changes, and even the services libraries offer to support their schools and communities change. But some things, like the librarian's mission and values, remain constant. Librarians still support intellectual freedom and fight censorship. Librarians are still about open inquiry and access to information and ideas. Librarians are still about helping people find and use information that is reliable and help them use it to improve their lives. And librarians have always been about helping people help themselves by learning how to be lifelong learners and informed decision-makers. And Grandma Annie, who was listening in, added that librarians have always wanted people to find enjoyment, fun and excitement in learning and reading.'

Miles's mom rolled her eyes. 'Did Grandpa also go on about how librarians' people skills, not their technical skills, are the most important?'

'Yup. But you know he also said that he thought I'd make a great librarian and would be proud to have me in 'his' field.'

'Well, that's Grandpa – always trying to recruit the best and the brightest.'

Miles yawned. 'Thanks, Mom. I need to get some sleep. My senior project is one day closer to being due so I need to really get cracking on it tomorrow.'

'Good night, Sweetie.'

As his mom left the room, Miles put down his book, switched off the bedside lamp, and spoke to his avatar,

'Please wake me up at 7, Marian. Goodnight.'

'Goodnight, Miles, my love.'

'I've gotta turn down those affection settings!' Miles thought as he rolled over and closed his eyes.

Scenario 2 Sink or swim: digital dilemma in higher education

Derek Law

Universities began as a need to concentrate resources. A concentration of scholars who worked together; a concentration of students who learned together; a concentration of resources in libraries; a concentration of expensive specialist equipment in laboratories. The need for the university to occupy a coherent single space was central to their development. It was late in the twentieth century before technology began to change that. Film and radio allowed lectures to be delivered off campus; cheap international travel allowed at least some students to study away from the campus at least some of the time. By the 1960s in the United Kingdom, the Open University used a combination of television and summer schools to allow degrees to be taken through technology. But even here the Open University has a major campus and students still have local tutors. Most universities now offer some online programs, while others, such as the University of Phoenix, specialise in that approach. And now the web has completely altered the fundamentals of the concept of the university as a host of institutions rush to create virtual spaces in virtual worlds such as Second Life.

So, for the first time in five hundred years, there is a need to fundamentally review what it is that a university as a place exists for. A recent encouraging report on the so-called 'Edgeless University', sees this as an opportunity. JISC (The Joint Information Systems Committee), which commissioned the report, described it thus:

> Technology is changing universities as they become just one source among many for ideas, knowledge and innovation. But online tools and open access also offer the means for their survival. Their expertise and value is needed more than ever to validate and support learning and research.

> Through their institutional capital, universities can use technology to offer more flexible provision and open more equal routes to higher education and learning. We need the learning and research that higher education provides. But this will take strategic leadership from within, new connections with a growing world of informal learning and a commitment to openness and

collaboration. By exploiting this role, universities can harness technology as a solution and an indispensable tool for shaping their vital role in the future (Bradwell 2009).

Universities both create and consume information and knowledge. The progressive evolution of computing and the internet has both globalised and increased that creation and consumption, while creating quite realistic alternative routes which allow information users to bypass what were previously centrally provided services and seek alternatives at times and in places which are convenient to the user. At the same time, the staff who undertake the provision of information services have found the skill-sets they require on the one hand changing at an impossibly rapid pace and on the other merging and overlapping. Web managers, content management system managers, repository managers, VLE managers and so on can be employed by any or all of the units which constitute these information services.

Within that wider debate there is a need to question what the nature and role of the university library should be and the nature and role of the university librarian. As Campbell (2006) has put it:

> Because of the fundamental role that academic libraries have played in the past century, it is tremendously difficult to imagine a college or university without a library. Considering the extraordinary pace with which knowledge is moving to the web, it is equally difficult to imagine what an academic library will be and do in another decade. *But that is precisely what every college and university should undertake to determine* [my italics]. Given the implications of the outcome, this is not an agenda that librarians can, or should, accomplish alone.

Nor are we alone in facing challenges from the internet and technology. In a recent article in the online forum Cato Unbound, the perceptive commentator Clay Shirky (2009) said of the future of journalism:

> The hard truth about the future of journalism is that nobody knows for sure what will happen; the current system is so brittle, and the alternatives are so speculative, that there's no hope for a simple and orderly transition from State A to State B. Chaos is our lot; the best we can do is identify the various forces at work shaping various possible futures.

These words apply just as certainly to libraries.

The greatest threat comes from the major players such as Google and Microsoft. Microsoft has developed a scholarly communications lifecycle in which everything from research data to research outputs resides in the cloud. Google has developed a model of college life which is entirely web-based, while its digitisation programme Google Books already has more than seven million books available. In other words, its collection is larger than all but the largest university libraries. It then seems inevitable that cash-strapped universities will question whether they need a library at all. This first happened in 2005 in the United Kingdom at the University of Bangor, where a consultation paper claimed that, librarians do not deliver 'value for money' when compared to the internet. It states: 'the process of literature searches is substantially de-skilled by online bibliographic resources'. The report dismisses the support that subject librarians bring to the academic and student communities as 'hard to justify'. This proposal was largely rejected but the sentiments are bound to reappear and even the half-way house of outsourcing may be considered.

The green agenda may also have a profound impact on the concept of libraries as place. It has been very fashionable lately to look at the lifecycle costs of electronic information. One of the striking things about such studies is to demonstrate how little we know about the lifetime costs of existing libraries. A huge amount of effort goes into determining the annual library budget, with rare institutions perhaps looking at a three-year rolling budget. But other major costs are simply ignored. Utilities costs (as with the rest of the university) are typically top-sliced from university income, as are local taxes. Maintenance, building upgrades (perhaps required by legislation or technological advances) and other costs are simply ignored, while the capital cost of building a library every fifty years or so is forgotten. The University of Strathclyde recently reviewed some of these costs. The library has a large but not huge collection of just over a million volumes and serves a student population of 20,000. The cost of utilities (power and water) is some £500,000 a year. The cost of maintenance, taxes and upgrades is unquantified but may well be the same sort of figure again. The cost of a new building with a fifty-year life was estimated at a minimum of £50,000,000. In other words, the overhead of running the library and amortising its capital cost is about £2,000,000 a year. This compares with a book/materials budget of £2,500,000 and a staff budget of £2,700,000. As a very crude rule of thumb then, for every pound the library spends on a book, it spends a pound on staffing and a pound on maintaining the building.

So how might libraries and librarians respond? There are three key areas which need to be addressed. The first is tackling the issue of born-digital material. Hitherto libraries have sadly neglected this, perhaps because it is too complicated. As a profession we have preferred to digitise the material we already possess in paper form and to sit down with publishers to negotiate licenses similar to those already possessed by other consortia. There is no debate about the philosophy of e-collection building and it is doubtful that any university library has an e-collection development policy. Yet the analogy with the paper-based library is clear. In any major research library, the majority of items accessioned each year will be rare books and special collections – the non-commercial materials which lie at the heart of great collections. Yet we have ignored this as we approach digital material. It is very likely (pace the development of institutional repositories) that no university has a proper record of the research outputs it produces each year. It is even less probable that any university knows how much digital material it collects each year, randomly scattered around the hard drives of the university – in truth it is a rare university that knows how many hard drives it has. Yet universities produce huge quantities of born-digital material. A list (probably incomplete) would include:

- Research papers
- Conference presentations
- Theses
- Wikis
- Blogs
- Websites
- Podcasts
- Reusable learning objects
- Research data
- E-lab books

- Streamed lectures
- Images
- Audio files
- Digitised collections
- E-archives
- E-mail
- HR records
- Student/staff records
- Corporate publications
- National heritage artefacts

It is likely that each of these items is being managed and curated, but by different groups and individuals and to different standards. It should be a central task of the library to manage this activity. It may or may not hold the material but it should certainly be seen as the central and expert arbiter of preservation standards and archiving policy. One might go further and consider the area of special collections. A classic example is the University of Texas Human Rights Initiative, which aims to undertake the bulk harvesting of human rights sites from the world wide web, the custom harvesting of human rights themes from the internet and the preservation and disclosure of born-digital documentation. All of this material is fragile, and at high risk as governments attempt to suppress it. But whether Rwanda, Burma or Chile, this initiative will capture and preserve a hugely important set of materials.

All of this material requires two things which only librarians can give. First it needs to be bibliographically secure. It must be definable then accessible. This relies absolutely on work done by the local library. Second it must be aggregated with the resources of other university libraries and value added through creating virtual collections with metadata and tagging which demonstrates links between items in different libraries. Thus one might imagine a definitive collection of David Livingstone papers being created from the resources of thirty or forty libraries in a dozen countries or linked collections of research data coming from grid computing. The beginnings of such aggregation can be seen in the first struggles to build major collections. For example, the recently launched European database aspires to make available ten million cultural heritage objects from hundreds of European libraries, museums and archives by the end of 2010. This proved so popular at its launch in 2009 that it crashed under the weight of ten million hits on the website. In the same vein, Gallica links almost a million French objects. Importantly, both collections are distributed and libraries are using technology to aggregate links rather than objects. Both collections point to the digitised objects of the past rather than born-digital resources. But the methodology and importance are the right ones.

The second key area on which libraries should build is that of the trusted brand and trust metrics. Most of the marks of trust in the paper world simply do not apply on the internet. If a book is published by, say, Oxford University Press we have a set of values associated with that on the level of scholarship and authority for example. If a website is ox.ac.uk, we have little idea of whether this is a Nobel prize-winner or a first-year undergraduate. On the net, only Google seems to have any level of trust. However, even that is beginning to wane as we learn how Google kowtows to the Chinese government and has routinely passed material on usage to the US intelligence services. At the same time it is the American librarians who took a stand against the PATRIOT Act and refused to reveal information to the intelligence services about user behaviour. Libraries and librarians are seen as trustworthy, helpful, neutral, unbiased and objective. The whole area of kite marking, quality assurance, relevance ranking and recommended resources is an area ripe for exploitation.

The third key area is that of training, or user instruction. Prensky's notion of digital natives (2001a, 2001b) was contentious when he first propounded it a decade ago, but, as with climate change, the overwhelming weight of evidence is that the teenagers of today are fundamentally different. More interesting than that debate, however, is the growing weight of evidence that while the net generation are technically competent, they are information illiterate and assume that a Google search exhausts the possibilities of information gathering. It is, almost a definition that publishers sell on difference not similarity. No one closed a sale by claiming their product was the same as a competitors! So there is a need to instruct in how to maximise the benefit from the different search engines, indexes and electronic resources available to the university. This is a much harder challenge than it might appear. OCLC studies have shown that user satisfaction declines when librarians try to help. This is popularly attributed to what is known as the 'eat your spinach' syndrome. That is the librarian will insist on showing the student how to use the tool properly, rather than helping with the quick fudge which will get the student assignment completed on time. Nor should it be seen as purely a student phenomenon. There is growing evidence of young researchers using social networking tools for collaborative research – OpenWetWare is a prime example of this – and again the library has a real possibility of helping promote those tools and services.

Finally, there is one underlying principle that needs to be re-established and that is partnership rather than service. For decades librarians were seen as partners in the life of the academy – minor partners, perhaps, but partners nevertheless. Then, from the 1980s onwards, libraries expanded at a huge rate with rapidly rising budgets, staff numbers and collection sizes. Librarians became managerialist rather than academic. As a result, libraries have never been better run or managed. But as a consequence the library has become just another service department with all the power and status of the Director of Catering and a much smaller budget than the Head of Estates. We – and the burden falls predominantly on professional leaders – need to restore the notion that we are partners and part of the academy.

Conclusion

The keystones of building a library future then are user training, quality assurance of external resources and the building of e-collections aggregated with those of other libraries. Whether librarians will embrace this challenge remains to be seen.

And even if they do, it will be fascinating to see how the concept of the library as place develops or diminishes.

References

Bradwell, P. (2009). *The Edgeless University.* London: Demos.

Campbell, J. (2006). *EDUCAUSE Review*, 41(1) (January/February) 16-31.

Information World Review (2005). Bangor University librarians face job cuts. http://www.computeractive.co.uk/information-world-review/news/2083942/bangor-university-librarians-face-job-cuts

Prensky, M. (2001a). Digital natives, digital immigrants. *On the Horizon.* 9(5), 1-6.

Prensky, M. (2001b). Digital natives, digital immigrants. Part 2: Do they really think differently? *On the Horizon.* 9(6), 1-6.

Shirky, C. (2009). Not an upgrade – an upheaval. *Cato Unbound* (July 13, 2009). http://www.cato-unbound.org/2009/07/13/clay-shirky/not-an-upgrade-an-upheaval/

Scenario 3 Education revolution – a place for the school library?

Phillip Hughes

> ... school libraries can have a positive impact on student achievement – whether such achievement is measured in terms of reading scores, literacy or learning more generally ... (Lonsdale 2003).

What does the revolution include?

This paper puts forward the case for the school library to be included in the massive changes which are involved in an education revolution. Behind the idea of such a revolution is the basic concept of improving education for all students, not just for some. In that search to improve learning, to provide ready access to the wealth of learning the world offers, is a special gift. The gift is even more precious when it is open to those whose opportunities outside school are limited. Through the school library, properly equipped and staffed, schools and teachers can open up new and wide horizons. Any revolution that is worthwhile opens opportunities never before available.

The new Labour government was elected in 2007 with its commitment to the 'Education Revolution'. This returned education to a high point on the list of national priorities after a period of almost twenty years during which it had been notably absent. The commitment raised high hopes in many people who have waited, not always patiently, for some national attention to the many needs of education.

In the period since that election there has been a great deal of soul-searching and of claims for attention. In the massive reconsideration that this 'revolution in education' demands, there are elements in the education world which are easy to overlook but which can play a key role in the ambitious aims that a revolution implies. Teaching and teachers will be at the heart of any successful process of reformation. An element which is crucial to enhancing the role of teachers is to provide support by making available the best information and research processes to support student learning. The school library, or learning resource centre as it is accurately called, can play an important central role in the massive effort to make Australia one of the countries where 'Education for All', the key aim of UNESCO, becomes a reality. This is the aim which is central to the government program 'an excellent education for every child'. It is an aim which experience worldwide has shown can be met and to which Australia is committed.

In 2009 the deputy prime minister Julia Gillard noted what had been achieved in the early period of the national program.

> We went to the election in 2007 arguing that Australian families deserved better. That a global, knowledge-driven economy makes an excellent education for every child a necessity, not an optional extra. That the early years are an essential foundation of a modern, equitable education system, not an afterthought. That it was possible to undertake ambitious, long term reform through collaboration. We're now delivering: our election commitment to start a Digital Education Revolution, under way with two rounds delivered and new computers already in schools around the country; a $2 billion investment in equipping our schools and students for the 21st century. Our $2.5 billion program for Trade Training Centres is also being delivered, with the first two lots of funding already delivered and a new round of funding underway (Gillard 2009).

The 2007 policy was a welcome initiative, but in the period after election government priorities became more difficult to define as the world economic recession affected all countries. Nevertheless, Australia acted to implement significant new initiatives in this new milieu.

> That is why, in the midst of this economic storm, we are undertaking the largest school building program in Australia's history, $14.7 billion: $12.4 billion for a major building project in every primary school across this country and $1.3 billion for a national school pride program, undertaking those maintenance and repair jobs that principals and teachers have struggled to fund in recent years; $1 billion to create new science and language labs in around 500 secondary schools. Take into account the National Education Agreement, National Partnerships on Literacy and Numeracy, Teacher Quality and Low SES Schools, the National Asian Languages and Studies in Schools Program and the Local Schools Working Together program, a total of $62.1 billion will flow to schools from 2009-2012. This is an 85 per cent increase, or getting close to double the $33.5 billion from the previous

> Government in the last four years on recurrent funding and infrastructure. This is a decisive demonstration of the Government's commitment to renewing Australia's schools and to achieving equity and excellence together. The hard work is just beginning. These are the foundations of a new future for public education in Australia (Gillard 2009).

This new priority status was widely welcomed in education where years of neglect for some sectors of education helped to maintain major inequities in Australian society. During the 1990s and early in the 2000s, education was not on the list of Commonwealth priorities and some areas in particular, including higher education and public education, fared badly in the allocation of national funds. This situation is now undergoing rapid change.

> In 2007, through COAG, all Australian Governments committed to the development and implementation of a rigorous and world-class national curriculum from kindergarten to Year 12. The development of a continuum of learning in literacy and numeracy skills, ranging from basic competence in the early years through to the advancement and extension of these skills in the middle and later years of schooling, will be a foundation of the new national curriculum. It will be developed by 2010, and implemented by the States and Territories from 2011 (DEEWR 2009).

The government established the National Curriculum Board (NCB) to oversee the development of the national curriculum. The board will consult with the wider education community and draw upon existing quality curriculum materials from the states and territories and from educationally high-performing countries. The national curriculum will provide the curriculum essentials that all young Australians should have access to, regardless of their background or their school location. The national curriculum is a welcome innovation, but an innovation that will require major support at the school level in addition to significant efforts at national, state and local levels.

To build a successful foundation for this profound change will require substantial support to teachers who will play the key role. In that support school libraries can act as the organiser and site for the information resources which they can muster to add to teachers' effectiveness.

The next few years will be vital for education generally and particularly so for those areas which have been low on the list of national priorities, including public primary and secondary schools and higher education. The building program will be welcome in the primary and secondary schools, particularly in the public sector where it is badly needed to make up for many years of neglect. There is a danger that the necessary attention to the building program may divert attention from the quality of what occurs within the buildings, new and old. The prime need is to provide sufficient teachers and to support them with the best that can be provided in the way of learning resources. This is why effective school libraries, well resourced, are vital in the task of achieving a successful basic education for all students, an essential in a world where education is so crucial to life opportunities.

The priority of a successful basic education through the national curriculum has been accepted by the Australian Government, noting the failure in recent years to provide an effective education for all students. This priority will be difficult to achieve and provides a challenge to the process of developing the national curriculum. Such a task is much more than a matter of design of courses, important as is that process. It requires that there are sufficient trained teachers and that these teachers are supported by quality learning resources which are properly staffed and organised.

An assessment by the Department of Education, Employment and Workplace Relations (DEEWR), which will have a substantial national role in achieving a more effective education indicates the substance of the problem.

> Participation in upper secondary education in Australia is not high by international standards. While other OECD countries have progressively improved school completion rates, these rates in Australia have changed little over the past decade. In 2007, the apparent retention rate of all Australian full-time students from Year 7/8 to Year 12 was 74%, which has remained relatively stable since 1996. The Australian Government aims to lift the rate of students attaining a Year 12 or equivalent outcome to 90% by 2020. This requires big improvements among the most disadvantaged groups (DEEWR 2009).

To increase from 74 per cent of the age-group to 90 per cent in Year 12 is a daunting challenge but it is one that must not only be faced but overcome. This is an urgent issue for Australia as a whole as well as for the early school leavers themselves on whom the effects are drastic. Not only are their employment opportunities limited but their participation more generally in their society is also restricted.

The Business Council of Australia calculates that 35, 000 students each year leave school without an effective education. That group is deeply disadvantaged, not just briefly but over the long term. The effects are very widespread. The director of the Australian Council for Educational Research, Professor Geoff Masters, pointed out some of the cumulative effects when inadequately prepared school leavers join an existing group in the community of those unable to find work.

> It is also where we are failing more than 300,000 young people aged between 15 and 24 who are either unemployed or working part-time and not undertaking full-time education. Currently, the overall level of unemployment is 4.3 per cent; the unemployment rate for 15-to-24-year-olds is more than double that rate at 9.1 per cent. Australia must pursue policies that close and prevent gaps in educational quality, such as gaps between schools in different locations or between private and public schools. All students should receive a high-quality education no matter which school they attend (Masters 2007).

Masters goes on to point out that while Australia's schools do produce high-quality results they compare badly with those countries which had a substantial proportion of high-quality student performances but also manage to achieve reasonable levels of success for almost all students.

The double task of higher achievement for the best students, together with an effective education for all, is one that all nations are pursuing. Few countries manage to succeed at both levels, but Finland, Hong Kong, Canada and Korea feature among the few who come close to achieving a successful basic education for all their students. They perform at high levels in the OECD test programs and also have only a small group of students failing to reach acceptable levels of performance (OECD 2005). These results for the PISA (program for international student assessment) tests have been confirmed by the more recent implementations (Masters 2007).

This situation presents a particular challenge for Australia. In the past it was possible to accept that only some students could achieve an effective education. It was also feasible to suggest that this did not matter deeply as there were plenty of low-skilled jobs available for those who have low levels of education. Those jobs are no longer available in technologically advanced societies. We need to provide an effective education for all students. Some countries are succeeding in this task and the challenge for Australia is clear: we have a responsibility to ensure that all students achieve an effective basic education in the sense defined by the director-general of UNESCO, who sees basic education as the key to effective participation in society.

> Basic education denotes the minimum skills and knowledge
> needed in order to be able to make a full contribution to one's
> environment and to be in control of one's life. In an increasingly
> interdependent world, the contents, and therefore the very notion
> of the 'quality' of basic education are evolving. It can no longer be
> reduced to learning reading, writing and arithmetic. It must also
> teach individuals to be, to do, to learn and to live together
> (UNESCO 2004).

The provision of sufficient qualified teachers and to provide access to the learning resources to support good teaching and learning are necessary steps to achieve an effective basic education for all.

What are the necessary resources? Recent research has shown the value of a properly supported school program using computer systems specially designed for that setting. Successions of major technological developments, all of which owe their source to education, have been tried in schools. Radio, film, television: these successive developments which have revolutionised peoples' homes, their work and their social environment have all featured in substantial attempts to improve education. Previously, their measurable effect on the quality of education has been slight. Now, after a period where they seemed to have the same marginal impact as other technological approaches, there are strong indications of a possible major contribution through computers designed specifically for schools. Two recent books *The use of instructional technology in schools* (Lee & Winzenried 2009) and *The interactive whiteboard revolution* (Betcher & Lee 2009) make a strong case that this new technology, which is specifically designed for schools, can deliver revolutionary changes. The two books report on research which assesses the experiences of teachers using computers in many countries. Betcher and Lee emphasise after their exhaustive research that the point of the new technology is to enhance the work of teachers and not to replace it.

> The international research on interactive whiteboards consistently
> reiterates that the most important variable in improving student
> learning is the quality of the teaching that takes place within the
> school. Although this book has tried to focus on some of the
> technical, pedagogical and logistical issues of implementing IWBs
> successfully, the point remains that none of this matters if these are

not being applied on top of quality teaching practice (Betcher &
Lee 2009).

A related area of need is to provide good quality teaching and learning resources
for those teachers and for their students. For the latter this takes on additional
benefit where their access to good learning resources is limited at home. Urgent
attention needs to be redirected to school libraries, high on the list of national
priorities in the decade 1965 to 1975, but neglected in the years since. In this
pressure for effective universal education we are in danger of neglecting the
key role that properly staffed and equipped school libraries can play in our
current world.

Rise and decline: school libraries

The Commonwealth Secondary Schools Libraries Committee (CSSLC) was set up
by the government to improve the quality and use of school libraries. The
committee recognised that the provision of buildings and equipment was a
necessary beginning, but only a beginning (CSSLC 1969). The committee
emphasised the need for a broad agenda, including provision to make the new
buildings and equipment of major benefit in schools. The committee saw the need
for a holistic program to make sure that the libraries were an integral part of the
schools they served and not just an optional extra.

> the program is not merely concerned with the supply of the
> physical components of buildings, furniture, equipment and
> resources but also with the importance of the library's role in
> education; the education of school librarians to service facilities
> and resources; the education of teachers to use them in teaching;
> the selection, supply and organisation of materials; the
> dissemination of information through publications; the
> evaluation of non-book materials and audio-visual equipment
> (McGrath 1971).

The libraries program operated effectively from 1965 for a decade, involving
secondary schools throughout Australia and, through state governments, extending
to primary schools. This was a very constructive period. Many hundreds of school
libraries were built or upgraded and specialist staff members were trained to see
that they performed at maximum effectiveness. The emphasis in the period was
strongly on the concept of the library as a teaching and learning resource. And
during this time, the concept of information literacy was developed:

one goal of education should be that students should know how to obtain information, how to use it in solving both familiar and unfamiliar problems … and how to judge both the consistency and the usefulness of information. Special importance should be given to individual study and research. … Pupils need to work individually with basic references and materials ... [they need] access to a wide variety of materials and will profit from different modes of working … The library is a coordination of teaching and learning services for a particular community. It is a centre of supply for the classroom program … It is a battery of learning media organised for access ... The school librarian should have a knowledge of objectives and processes in education ... as well as a knowledge of materials ... But the greatest impact must come not from the librarian's technology, but from his/her ideology, his/her thinking as a professional (Hughes 1969).

In spite of the progress which had been achieved in building school libraries, in equipping and supplying them and in training specialist teacher librarians, in the period that followed the attention to school libraries was reduced. The emphasis on the general funding of schools by the Commonwealth dominated attention through the Karmel Report (1973). This established Commonwealth funding for school education on the principle of 'need'. It changed the conception of Commonwealth government policy and its funding role in school education, initiating a system of funding that was still in operation two decades later. A major backward step during the past twenty years has been the dismantling of much of the mechanism set up during the 1970s and 1980s to provide support for schools. The initiatives of bodies such as the Schools Commission and the Curriculum Corporation were lost to schools until the Commonwealth government introduced new national bodies such as the National Curriculum Board to provide leadership throughout Australia and to develop the national curriculum, with the aim of achieving 'a world-best curriculum' (NCB 2009).

Unfortunately in that recent period of twenty years much of the benefit was lost which schools achieved under the Commonwealth Schools Libraries program. With schools, and particularly public schools, under increasing pressure to improve their effectiveness for all students the prevailing response was to reduce expenditure on areas outside the classroom and to achieve lower class sizes as the way to improve student learning. That was a mistaken approach. Class sizes were too large in the 1960s with ratios as high as 36:1 and changes were necessary. In the period that followed significant advances were made in reducing the ratio. Unfortunately, the process continued beyond the stage at which major benefits resulted. In the 1990s the changes were from 28:1 to 24:1. In a school of 560 students that change meant requiring 24 teachers rather than 20. That extra requirement was usually at the cost of auxiliary staff in the school, including teacher librarians. Little learning value comes from such a small change in student numbers in a class. But a major loss was experienced for schools in such a substantial reduction in auxiliary staff numbers.

The research into the effects of those changes in libraries sponsored by the Australian Council for Educational Research (ACER), with Michele Lonsdale, demonstrates the drastic impact.

> Using the standards developed by ASLA and the Australian Library and Information Association (ALIA) as a benchmark, Welch and Braybrook (2002) found that twenty per cent of schools in Victoria are staffed at a level equal to or above the recommended level and eighty per cent are below this standard, and that seventy per cent of schools in the survey operate below the recommended number of hours needed to staff school libraries. Reynolds and Carroll (2001) found that since 1983 the number of primary school libraries being staffed by qualified teacher librarians has dropped dramatically from fifty-five to thirteen per cent' (Lonsdale 2003).

That gloomy picture of one state represents negative changes which affected all, as the priorities within schools were narrowed. This was a significant loss to schools and students, and particularly so when every effort needs to be made to make more effective the education of the large group of students who are currently missing out.

> The context in which school librarians and teacher librarians operate today has changed significantly over the past couple of decades, with consequent implications for student learning. In particular, there has been an apparent decline in the numbers of qualified teacher librarians employed in school libraries in public schools in Australia; an explosion in information production and the development of information communication technologies (ICTs); changes in educational philosophy and practice, including a greater focus on learning outcomes, inquiry-based learning, evidence-based practice and school accountability; and changes in

the nature and role of the teacher librarian as a result of these developments (Lonsdale 2003).

In the period ahead, with a government whose major priorities include education, the next few years will be vital. In that period there is the opportunity to support the learning program in schools in a variety of ways. One very profitable way is through a systematic strengthening of school libraries, not just in materials and equipment but in staffing.

Where are we heading now?

The next few years will see Australian educators faced with the significant challenge of educating all students to a satisfactory level. However, we now know that it can be done. It is being done in countries with no more resources to devote to education than in Australia.

One major gain can be made through strengthening school libraries and the connections between the school and the community facilities. Sources both in Australia and elsewhere support a major effort to this end. There is now a massive amount of research which demonstrates the power of school libraries, appropriately supported by staffing and facilities, to enhance learning opportunities. Even more important the gain for students is greatest when their access to learning opportunities at home is limited – and these are the priority students. What is most significant is that the research indicates that good support for libraries in schools can help all students including those who come from lower socio-economic groups and this is the area of greatest priority.

The book by American researchers Sondra and Larry Cuban (2007) identifies a clash of cultures existing between schools and libraries. Their research showed that gaps frequently exist between the expectations in the two areas. In the period of the Australian libraries program a positive connection between the two was a major goal with the emphasis on the librarian as being not just a custodian of resources but part of the educational process in the school. Any gap between teacher and librarian is a major factor in a loss of learning opportunities for students, and in particular for students who lack good access in their homes to learning resources. Technological developments such as those described by Lee and Winzenried (2009) can significantly aid in such access and the results shown in their international research shows that this is successful in achieving more effective learning.

Lonsdale summarises her valuable survey and analysis of research into the worth of school libraries:

school libraries can have a positive impact on student achievement
– whether such achievement is measured in terms of reading
scores, literacy or learning more generally– in the following key
ways:

- a strong library program that is adequately staffed, resourced
  and funded can lead to higher student achievement regardless
  of the socio-economic or educational levels of the adults in the
  community;

- a strong computer network connecting the library's resources
  to the classroom and laboratories has an impact on student
  achievement;

- the quality of the collection has an impact on student learning;

- test scores are higher when there is higher usage of the school
  library;

- collaborative relationships between classroom teachers and
  school librarians have a significant impact on learning,
  particularly in relation to the planning of instructional units,
  resource collection development, and the provision of
  professional development for teachers;

- a print-rich environment leads to more reading, and free
  voluntary reading is the best predictor of comprehension,
  vocabulary growth, spelling and grammatical ability and
  writing style (Lonsdale 2003).

Lonsdale goes on to identify significant research, largely in the United States, to
indicate that a strong library program, with a full-time library professional, support
staff and a strong computer network that connects the library's resources to the
classroom, leads to higher student achievement regardless of the socio-economic or
educational levels of the adults in the community. She notes that the studies show
that libraries make a positive difference, particularly when a collaborative approach
between teachers and library professionals is adopted, in the areas of reading scores
and students' selection of reading material. It is the independence of positive
effects from a socio-economic level that makes the library of particular importance
in the search to develop ways to assist those for whom school is not always
effective.

The next ten years will be crucial to the future of education and to the life chances of a whole generation of Australian students. The intentions of the Commonwealth government offer real hope, particularly the will to make Australian schools 'world-class'. Achieving this, however, will demand a major effort from teachers, from administrators and from parents to take advantage of opportunities which come so rarely.

References

Betcher, C. & Lee, M. (2009). *The interactive whiteboard revolution.* Melbourne: ACER.

CSSLC (1969). *Standards for secondary schools libraries.* Canberra: The Commonwealth Secondary Schools Libraries Committee, AGPS.

Cuban, S. & Cuban, L. (2007). *Partners in literacy: Schools and libraries building communities through technology.* New York: Teachers College Press.

DEEWR (2009). Australia's National Report on the Development of Education.

Gillard, J. (2009). Speech to the National Education Forum, March 2009.

Hughes, P.W. (1969). The role of the library in the Australian secondary school. In Trask, M. (Ed.) *Planning of Australian school libraries.* ASLA.

Karmel, P. (1973). Karmel Report: *Schools in Australia.* Canberra: AGPS.

Lee, M. & Winzenried, A. (2009). *The use of instructional technology in schools: lessons to be learned.* Melbourne: ACER.

Lonsdale, M. (2003). Impact of school libraries on student achievement: a review of the research. *Report to ACER.* Hawthorn, Vic.: ACER Press.

Masters, G. (2007). *Restoring our edge in education.* Business Council of Australia.

McGrath, L. (1971). In *The role of libraries in secondary education.* Australian National Curriculum Board 2009. National Curriculum Board Website.

OECD (2005). *First results from PISA 2003.*

UNESCO Seminar, 1971.School Libraries. AGPS, Canberra 1971.(not referred to??)

UNESCO. (2004). *Report of the director-general.* Paris: UNESCO.

Scenario 4 Making dreams reality – the sustainable public library

Katie Hannan

There's a flash of red on my right as a bus overtakes me. I'm riding my bike through town. This has got to the best way to get around, I love it. I signal left and turn down the pathway that takes me to the bike parking shed in front of the library.

Somewhere in my bag is my wallet, there it is, down the bottom of my bag as usual. The bike parking shed is fantastic; all I do is scan my library card and the door opens. A solar panel on the roof powers the scanner and the lights for night-time. It's one of the many things that I love about this library. I'd rather ride an extra five kilometres each way just to come here, and I know my friends and family feel the same. Every time I ride into the library and park my bike in the shed I get green credits on my membership record. I can use these for any of the fee-paying services that the library offers. In fact last month I used my green credits to pay off my overdue fees. Ever since the library introduced the green credit scheme I've had to start coming to the library before work, otherwise I can't find anywhere to park my bike. The school kids love it.

If only you could have seen what this library was like ten years ago. The changes are almost unbelievable. While the exterior of the building is mostly the same, the changes made by the library staff and the local council to the way the library operates are wonderful. The services and facilities used to be fairly standard at all the public libraries in our area, so of course I used to go to the closest one, but that has changed now.

Last week I had an elderly friend of the family and her grandchildren visiting me from Western Australia. The friend used to use this library when she lived here thirteen-years ago. I decided it was worth using the car to bring her and the kids here and show them what it was like now. The friend couldn't believe her eyes. Perhaps I should describe what the library used to be like, and then you will understand why.

Imagine a dark red-brick building, constructed in the early to mid nineteen-seventies, surrounded by deciduous trees, lawns that occasionally were manicured and garden beds of flowering annuals. Winding pathways paved in the same red brick as the building led from the car park to the library and off to the rotunda, where community functions were held in the spring and summer. There was no bike shed, just a rack used sometimes by school children. The rack was rather too close to the library entrance and sometimes bikes were left in the walkway. As you entered the library, there were large shelves to your left, where people were expected to leave their shopping and school bags. The library didn't have a security system, and people weren't allowed to bring in large bags. The purpose of this was to stop people from stealing library material; the problem of course was that people stole things from other's bags.

If this isn't enough for you to conjure up a picture of a standard suburban public library of the late twentieth century, then I will tell you about the lack of natural light and the large sombre paintings on the walls. Year round, the lights were switched on all day because the windows let in very little natural light. On the walls hung dark paintings of historical community figures whose eyes seemed to follow you around the room! This gives rise to a rather gloomy picture, but the staff did the best they could with what they had. The public libraries that were the closest to my home and workplace were much the same, and, to be honest, have not changed much over the past decade.

So, what was it that made me return to this library? Let me think back. That's right, I remember now. A colleague of mine had bought a new house and moved from one side of the city to another and threw an amazing dinner party as a house warming. Yes, yes that's it. While there, I saw a 'Friends of the Library' spring book sale flyer on the fridge; the sale was the following weekend. I remember the day of the book sale almost as if it were yesterday. I'd treated myself to an early night on the Friday, after a hectic week at work and home. I was up early, refreshed. It was a cool morning and the sky was blue. I sat and ate breakfast on the back veranda; soaking up some sunshine and watching the chooks poke around in the back garden looking for bugs. With nothing urgent to do; well, nothing my husband couldn't take care of anyway, I managed to talk myself out of the routine Saturday morning sport trips and grocery shopping, so that I could enjoy a precious sunny morning to myself. The book sale flyer that I'd seen on the fridge the weekend before sprung into my mind and I decided that as it was such a beautiful day, I'd cycle out to the sale to see what treasures I might find. Before I set off, I quickly checked the street directory to see where I needed to go, it had been a while since I'd visited this library.

What I recall the most is the feeling of utter confusion that I experienced when I arrived at the place where I expected the library to be. After a moment of disorientation, I realised that the library was exactly where I thought it ought to have been, it just looked different. It wasn't just the library building that had changed; it was the landscaping and the car and bike parking area. I took a good look around me and realised that something revolutionary had happened at this public library and I really wanted to find out what it was and who was behind it.

The library was open already and after I'd discovered that there was a bike parking shed that could be used by members of the library, I decided that I'd better head on in and join up and find out more about the makeover that this library had received. I found the information desk and mentioned to the staff member working there that I hadn't been to this library for a long time, perhaps as long as eleven years, that I wanted to sign up and also find out some more information about the renovations that had taken place. The library assistant was more than happy to answer my questions, give me brochures about the library services, and take me on a tour of the facilities.

The original library had been a single storey building, with small windows and little natural light. This was no longer the case. To alleviate the problem, the entire roof of the library had been replaced. The new roof, instead of being flat like before, was constructed on a slant, to take advantage of the movement of the sun across the sky (Sands 2008). Any material that could be recycled or reused was made available for other community projects or taken to the council recycling depot.

A light-coloured roofing material was selected to minimise the solar heat absorbed by the building (Henderson 2009). The wall of the building that receives the most light was completely replaced by glass. Thermal shades were fitted. These can be raised or lowered, depending on the time of the year and whether or not the building needs to be heated or cooled. The area of glass that receives the strongest sunlight was fitted with double glazing. Zero-waste policies were implemented across the entire local council, including the library. These policies cover energy consumption, water and paper usage.

Computers can often be the major energy consumers in libraries. This usage decreases dramatically if they are turned off overnight, when they are not being used. The council has developed and installed a software program that allows all of the public-use computers to be controlled from a central unit, so they can be shut down automatically when the library closes. All computers are set to power down into sleep mode after a twenty-minute period of inactivity. Lights are controlled by motion sensors in combination with the amount of natural light in the building. The modifications to the roof and walls have so increased the amount of natural light entering the building that there are now only certain areas of the library where the lights are used. Solar panels have been mounted on the roof. When the solar panels generate more energy than is required by the building, for example on public holidays when the library is closed, excess power is supplied back to the grid. The revenue raised from this is invested back into the library budget.

The zero-waste policy states that all paper items that are purchased must be sourced from suppliers who stock 100 per cent recycled paper. All paper and cardboard that has been used on both sides is collected and recycled. In recent years, the publishing industry has revolutionised itself. The library only purchases books that have been printed with plant-based ink on recycled paper. There are many titles that can be supplied and printed using print-on-demand technology. This eliminates the need for the book to be transported from the publisher to the library, reducing the carbon footprint for each title that is purchased.

All of the bathroom and kitchen areas have been retro-fitted with water conserving tap fixtures as part of the zero-waste strategy. Water that is used in bathroom sinks and in the cafe is collected and processed via a grey water recycling system. To complement the water-saving initiatives, several large rainwater tanks have been installed to collect the run-off from the roof of the building. The water that is collected is used for a variety of purposes, for toilet flushing and for watering plants in the surrounding environment. The tanks have inbuilt volume sensors, when the tanks are at 80 per cent capacity, and the chances of rain are high (based on humidity and temperature) the water is diverted to be used for toilet flushing. An additional water storage and collection tank is located next to the entrance of the bike parking shed. This tank has been placed under cover out of the weather and mounted on the corrugated iron is a community notice board. The water tank sustains both the environment and the community.

As I mentioned before, a bike-parking shed has been installed. The shed can be used by library card holders. Every time a member rides to the library and parks in the shed, they receive green credits on their library membership record. These credits can be used for any fee-paying service offered by the library. There is also a solar panel on the roof of the bike-parking shed. This panel is used to power security lights and an anti-theft video camera. The external security lighting comes on automatically when the sun begins to set and the lights in the shed are activated by motion sensor, but only after the exterior light has switched on. The interior lights come on when the shed door is opened and stay on for fifteen minutes. If anyone is still in the bike shed after this time, the lights will be activated by a motion sensor. The shed is made from a wire mesh and transparent heavy duty plastic sheeting. This allows people to see how many bikes are in the shed and if there is anyone already in the shed.

The library cafe only sells ethical products such as fair-trade coffee, tea and hot chocolate. All other goods are either home made, or organic. The cafe has adopted a slow-food principle; where the entire menu is seasonal and nothing is sold that includes a fresh ingredient that has been sourced from outside of the country (Slow Food Australia 2009). The cafe sells 'enviro-mugs' to patrons, designed to keep hot drinks warm. The cost of getting an enviro-mug refilled is cheaper than if you get a disposable cup. The cups that are used are made from recycled paper. Any organic material is placed into a composting collection bin, which is collected by the council waste-management staff and taken to the council composting site.

Any technology-related waste, such as batteries, computers, photocopiers and so on, is managed through a central processing unit called 'techwaste'. As equipment, such as computers, is upgraded, or replaced, it is transferred to the techwaste unit. The staff of this unit rebuild any of the items that can be rebuilt and supply local community groups with any hardware items that have been reconditioned. The techwaste unit takes on trainees who are apprentices in waste management and it coordinates a community volunteer program.

In addition to the retro-fitting of the building, the landscape was redeveloped and replanted with native plants. This has the added function of providing a green corridor for native birds and insects, a place of refuge from the developed urban surroundings (Rudd, Vala & Schaefer 2002). The rotunda is now used as an educational space and features a public education campaign on gardening with native plants and information on the animal and insect inhabitants of the green space. The rotunda is named in honour of the traditional Indigenous custodians of the land.

These initiatives were why, after eleven years of loyalty, I decided to abandon my local library and its staff and travel the extra five kilometres to the next council area, so I could go to this library. The experience I had while visiting this sustainable retro-fitted public library was so amazing that I had vowed to return with my family and friends, and I did. In fact, I found out a lot more about what had changed at this library and in the local council electorate in order to make this tremendous change happen, but, perhaps that's a story for another time.

References

Henderson, M. (2009). Professor Steven Chu: paint the world white to fight global warming. *Times Online*, (May 27 2009). Retrieved from http://www.timesonline.co.uk/tol/news/environment/article6366639.ece

Rudd, H., Vala, J. & Schaefer, V. (2002). Importance of backyard habitat in a comprehensive biodiversity conservation strategy: a connectivity analysis of urban green spaces. *Restoration Ecology*, 10(2), 368-375. Retrieved from http://dx.doi.org/10.1046/j.1526-100X.2002.02041.x. doi:10.1046/j.1526-100X.2002.02041.x

Sands, J. (2008). Sustainable library design. Retrieved 16 May 2009 from http://www.librisdesign.org/docs/SustainableLibDesign.pdf

Slow Food Australia (2009). Retrieved 22 August 2009 from http://slowfoodaustralia.com.au/

Further reading

Borders UK Ltd (n.d). Our Living Earth: A Next Generation Guide to People and Preservation. Retrieved 21 August, 2009, from http://www.borders.co.uk/book/our-living-earth-a-next-generation-guide-to-people-and-preservation/1042827/

Green Building Council of Australia (2009). Green star certification process. Retrieved 22 August, 2009, from http://www.gbca.org.au/uploads/192/960/Certification%20Process.pdf

Lawson, G. (2008). Managing Your Library Construction Project: A Step-by-Step Guide, by Richard C. McCarthy -- Chicago, IL: American Library Association, 2007. ix, 172 pp. ISBN 978-0-8389-093-17. The Serials Librarian, 55(1), 312 - 314. Retrieved from http://www.informaworld.com/10.1080/03615260801971145

The Spinney Press (2009). Issues in society: News and views on contemporary issues: New August-December 2009. Retrieved 18 August , 2009, from http://www.spinneypress.com.au/pdf/ISSUES%20AUG%2009%20CATALOG%20DOWNLOAD.pdf

Scenario 5 The Centre – 2050

Sue Healy

Shelby has arrived at the Learning Hub – often called 'school' by previous generations – she is meeting a number of her friends in the Centre – a place where social interaction and information sources come together. Her grandmother worked in such a place almost thirty years ago when it was called a library. She imagines how different it must look compared to the place her grandmother described to her as a young child. It is 10am in the morning and the Centre is a hive of activity. The classes Shelby will attend today do not start for another half hour giving her time to electronically submit her history report for a plagiarism check before the submission deadline at 1pm.

The Centre is a large open space surrounded by a number of smaller enclosed working spaces where she and her friends often work together on class projects. There is still a significant fiction collection which can be borrowed when she wants to read a novel in a physical form or listen to a story in audio format. The physical forms available here, however, are not the same as the once popular printed versions which her parents still have at home. For Shelby and most of her friends, listening to stories is second nature and she often comes to the Centre and downloads stories purchased by the Centre to her latest iFone. Sometime Shelby and her friends borrow one of the digital books. This small paperback-like format is flexible rather than rigid like the early versions available in her grandmother's time and can be rolled up just like the twentieth-century printed paperbacks. They can hold thousands of stories or videos, but generally Shelby only requests two or three stories to be downloaded at a time as there is a royalty payment to the author for each title borrowed. No point in downloading and paying royalty on stories she might never read.

When Shelby has finished reading the story she will return the flexibook to the Centre. The great thing about this technology is that all stories are available in this format from the moment they are published. Every title is available from the Centre from the date of electronic publication. The Centre gets charged only when the title is loaned. These charges are minimal but important. In the early part of the twenty-first century there was a concept of copyright but few people took notice and many authors and songwriters lost access to a livelihood once their work was shared online.

At that stage there were no forms of effective online royalty systems in place. By the early part of the twenty-first century a royalty agreement was signed by all major institutions and organisations worldwide. In return for making all publications digitally available to places such as the Centre from the moment of creation, a small royalty payment would be generated for every loan. This meant that authors were now receiving payments directly from the subscription/circulation systems such as the one used in the Centre. With circulation payments being minimal, organisations were happy to comply. The ease of access to a worldwide audience meant authors now received significant royalty returns which in turn supported the creation of future works.

Shelby looks around for her friends who have still not arrived. She sits down at one of the many small internet pod seating areas which consist of a large circular table with an embedded multilayer digital surface. This table-top technology was first released in the early twenty-first century, but was limited in its accessibility because of its cost and availability. These early versions used single layer technology compared to the multi-layer versions now currently in use in the Learning Hub. Her grandmother often talked about how she controlled movement around a screen with a mouse. What a weird concept! Shelby has always used her finger as the preferred tool for movement around a screen space. Using her fingers to activate screens is natural to Shelby who has used this method to interact with technology all her life.

More recently Shelby has tried out a new form of 3D technology which uses thought control. She attended a technology demonstration session run by the Centre a few weeks ago and was amazed by the fact that she could control the digital activity on the large wall-mounted screen just by thinking. It worked by picking up specific electrical patterns in the brain which in turned controlled a switch. The information technology specialist used the analogy of going on a data walk with your eyes, creating a visual trail as you went. Each screen that was scanned with the eye did not obscure the previous screen but merely brought the new screen to the forefront for detailed viewing. As Shelby's eyes walked across the surface of an object, each image enlarged as she gazed at it and minimised when her gaze left it. This technology was in its infancy earlier this century when camera lenses that could automatically focus on whatever object your eye looked at through the viewfinder were first developed. Shelby slides pages across the screen assembling a tapestry of images that depicts the information story she is creating. Shelby also uses Dragon speech recognition version 32 to write to another screen page – thoughts that are barely vocalised.

Recently, Shelby overheard some of her teachers talking about how this technology will revolutionise student learning experiences. While Shelby found it took a bit of time to get control of the technology using her thoughts – similar to a time in pre-school when she first learned to fly in Second Life – she was amazed at how quickly she adapted to moving around this virtual space in real time.

Some of Shelby's friends who could not be there participated via the Centre's Second Life site. Shelby often attends information sessions run by the Centre in Second Life – the anywhere, anytime space which also stores class work and the information resources needed for her courses. She likes the fact that her learning life takes place equally in the virtual and real worlds. Sometimes she almost forgets the difference between the two as real people are always online and in real time she is often working in a virtual space. After the thought-control session Shelby and her friends were able to make a booking to use the technology and practise their thought-control skills. They are all eagerly waiting on the release of this technology in a palm communicator format.

The Centre is buzzing with the hum of student activity. Shelby reflects on the fact that all of the new technologies that have been introduced into the Learning Hub during her time there have been placed first in the Centre. It is the one place in the Learning Hub where there are information technology specialists who are always on hand to run sessions with staff and students on new technologies and advanced research strategies. They are key people in this space where much of the formal/informal learning and social interaction takes place.

The internet is a big place and when Shelby finds it difficult to locate what she needs for class she sends her information request through to the online InfoHelp desk. This service is staffed by information technology specialists from 7am until 10pm. The support from this service is immediate and provides her with new directions in which to pursue her research – this is usually just what she needs to help her get going on a project. Today she needs information which is often located in the invisible web. She did not know about the invisible web until she was talking to one of the information specialists via the Centre's help desk. She made an appointment to meet with one of the information technology staff after lunch to talk about effective search strategies in the invisible web.

At last her friends arrive. The three girls and two boys gravitate to the Centre cafe which forms part of the information technology complex. Shelby is reminded of a time when her grandmother was a student and food and drink were not allowed in such places. Fortunately for Shelby and her friends those times have long since passed and the cafe is usually their first stopping point for the day. The place is crowded – more than usual – due to the Dialogue in the Margin session about to start.

Dialogue in the Margin is an interactive reader's session run by the Centre staff each fortnight. These sessions bring readers and writers together using a type of blogging software which enables readers to read works in development and comment in the margins at the same time as the author is online. These online sessions create great discussions between readers and writers. Shelby has participated in many such discussions during her time attending the Learning Hub. She loves the way readers can influence the direction which stories take based on the readers' comments back to the author. Sometimes these sessions are synchronous (in real time) like today, and at other times they are asynchronous, particularly for sessions which involve readers and writers from across the globe spanning different time zones.

Today she will be reading the first three chapters of a new novel by a first time author. She imagines how she would feel if it was one of her stories which was being posted for discussion. Twenty readers have taken up the invitation to join the session which will start shortly. When she first told her grandmother about her participation in these groups her grandmother compared it to her experience of a book club back in 2009. But unlike the book clubs of the early twenty-first century, where readers generally came together to talk about a published book, the Dialogue in the Margin sessions gives an almost equal voice to author and reader. Shelby also likes the way the online sessions are captured for later review and dialogue can continue between sessions.

At times the story posted for discussion is unpublished, allowing readers to question the writer, clarifying plotlines and character development. These discussions have helped Shelby develop her own writing style. And she feels that her contributions have been influential in developing the plot of one or two stories that were posted to Dialogue in the Margin specifically to gain feedback prior to publication. Shelby enjoys these dialogues the most. At other times the group will come together, sometimes but not always with the author, to discuss a published story and reflect on the story elements from the perspective of different readers in the group. It always amazes Shelby how differently people can view the same story. Perhaps that is part of the appeal which continues to draw her back to this activity each fortnight.

Like most days at the Learning Hub time goes quickly. Shelby is rarely bored when there. The Dialogue in the Margin session has left her wanting to read the rest of the story, so she must make sure she downloads it from the resource catalogue to her iFone before leaving today. She must eat lunch quickly because she has an appointment with the information technology specialists in ten minutes. To make the most of the appointment time, Shelby needs to read over her notes and clarify what she wants help with. As part of her International Baccalaureate studies she has to write a 4000-word essay on a topic of her choice. The essay requirements stipulate that she must find a number of academic-type articles along with serious feedback from specialists' forums which focus on her topic. She has spent a number of sessions on her own looking for resources but feels that she has little useful material for her essay. Her mentor encouraged her to read the material written by one of the information technology staff about the invisible web and make an appointment to look at her search strategies.

The session with the information technology specialists starts off with an exchange of questions and answers about her topic and what she has found to date. Shelby is glad that she spent some time sorting out her topic notes and her queries so that she could move quickly to the problems she is experiencing in trying to locate information. She had already given the topic to the Centre staff when she made her online booking. They talk about the concept of the invisible web and begin to look at specific search engines that will pick up the resources she needs for her research. Shelby did not know about CompletePlanet (www.completeplanet.com), a search engine which trawls over 100,000 databases and specialist search engines. Nor was she familiar with Boardreader (boardreader.com), a search engine which locates forums on just about any topic. Together they found two forums on Shelby's topic after a search of this less well known (and hence invisible) search engine. Shelby was amazed at how much there was to know about effective searching. She liked the idea of Clusty (clusty.com) which offered clustered results from a selection of metadata searches. Every result on the first page was on her topic and nearly all from academic institutions. The information technology specialist walked Shelby through the Centre's SEI strategy (search engine invisibility strategy). Shelby now had enough information to locate the quality resources she needed for her research. They planned a follow-up meeting in two weeks time to see how she was going and to work on refining her note-taking skills. In the meantime, Shelby wanted to search the Open Archive Initiative (www.openarchives.org), a search engine which contained more than two trillion digital artefacts from 3500 institutions. This search engine would be extremely helpful for her next history essay which required Shelby to find a number of primary source images.

Afternoon tutor sessions passed quickly. Shelby's submitted her first history essay online after completing her plagiarism check. She managed to download a copy of the new book she started reading earlier that day and squeezed in another coffee before heading home. She had so much to talk about with her friends online that she wondered how she was going to get everything she planned to do finished that evening.

Further reading

21st Century Learning Spaces. http://edorigami.wikispaces.com/21st+Century+Learning +Spaces Viewed: April 2009

CeBIT Media Wall http://dvice.com/archives/2008/03/cebit-media-wal.php Viewed: July 2009.

if:book A Project of The Institute for the future of the book. http://futureofthebook.org/ blog/ Viewed: May2009

Microsoft Surface Like Wearable Computer That May Cost No More Than a Mobile Phone. http://www.labnol.org/gadgets/microsoft-surface-like-wearable-computer/8044/ Viewed: July 2009.

Mind switch could help disabled regain control. New Scientist. Vol 150 Issue 2028. 4 May 1996. p.6 http://www.mindcontrolforums.com/news/mind-switch-disabled-control.htm Viewed: May 2009.

NYU 21st Century Library Project: Designing a Research Library of the Future for New York University. http://library.nyu.edu/about/KPLReport.pdf Viewed: April 2009

Sony Flexi-OLED Display On Flexible Film. http://www.mydigitallife.info/2007/05/25/sony-flexi-oled-display-on-flexible-film/ Viewed: June 2009.

Stein, Bob A Book is a Place. The Age A2 Culture and Life (section) Saturday July 25 2009. P.14-15. Also available: http://www.theage.com.au/news/entertainment/books/a-book-is-a-place/2009/07/23/1247942011314.html

Scenario 6 The right library now!

David Warner

I went to our senior school library during the holidays in September 2009 to chat with young people there about libraries. I found some, like Al in Year 12, preparing for exams and finalising various assignments and others just passing the time. I also found Gil, one of our maintenance people, on the web during a break. Later the same day I went to the local public library and found a range of people there, including a number of our young people, doing exactly the same. There also was one student with a tutor going through one-on-one work preparing for a VCE assessment. So why were these people there?

These libraries were where the young people could do what they needed to do! They wanted to be there because it was convenient, the environment was conducive to the task at hand, that is, exam preparation and assignment completion, and they could communicate as they liked either using mobile technology or accessing friends and colleagues through Facebook or other social networking tools. Their social networks were relevant to the work they were doing because they were working with others. In fact two of the young people in the public library were communicating on Facebook with the person in the school library plus others. On occasions when library staff are unavailable, students will use the library without them.

Two younger siblings of those preparing for their final exams were in the fiction section, stretched out on the couches browsing books. Several others were on PCs 'googling' information they wanted. This was the school holiday period, but they were there, working and recreating! Only a skeleton staff was available, but that was alright, in the main, they needed little assistance.

Our library is an information resource centre. It has a good print collection, although increasingly print resources are directed to fiction and recreational reading. Non-fiction resources are more often purchased on need, particularly in areas not served well by the digital library and the internet. Increasingly our digital library holds traditional print material, including fiction. It has subject resources, films, plays, current affairs, news and requested media material available within the library. These resources are also accessible from anywhere else in the school and from home through the intranet, the Knowledge Network.

There is, therefore, a virtual aspect to our library. Library databases as well as internal resources can be accessed from common areas, classrooms and laboratories and from home or indeed, anywhere else in the world. This library is open, therefore, 356 days of the year 24/7. We do have staff and students who access the library through the Knowledge Network from all around the globe. I have just completed, for example, an ERIC search on future libraries.

During term time, however, this library and its junior counterpart have increased functions. The principal function is the provision of highly skilled professionals to work with young people in helping them develop their skills. The role of the teacher librarian is a key one in a school environment. I believe that librarians generally should have the skill-sets associated with teacher librarians. The teaching-learning role of the librarian is paramount, whether it be in a school or a public library. Increasingly, as we move to 'just-in-time' training, the role of the librarian in helping workers learn how to learn in this way is very important. The school has a learning focus on 'developing the disposition and skill to be a self-directed lifelong learner'. The library, particularly its professional staff, is an important resource in developing these skills.

Library staff members work formally with younger students, individually and in groups, to develop specific research skills, including how to reference online resources, how to better define research parameters, to develop research questions and so on. They also engage young people in dialogue about the material they are working on, acting almost like tutors. This happens too in the junior library, which serves the needs of prep to year 4, five to ten years of age. In the junior years, teachers, library staff and young people work in a seamless relationship.

Having a clear learning focus on developing the disposition and skill to be self-directed learners has given a strong strategic position for the libraries and library staff. The focus is based very much on past research that has shown that increasingly in the future people in the workplace will have to be learners. They will need to be able to re-skill and re-train just-in-time and many times over. The research also has shown that most people in the workforce are accustomed to being directed in their learning: the traditional classroom is what people know. This means that people are less accustomed to and skilled in self-directed learning.

Perhaps it is much more the disposition to be a self-directed learner that is the most important and certainly the hardest to develop. A simple illustration: I chatted to two tradespeople who now operate their own quite successful contract businesses. I asked them how long since they had visited a library and the answer was when we were at school! I asked them to describe their library experiences and, in brief, they said a dictatorially ruled environment where they couldn't talk or eat and had to sit quietly reading books that they had trouble understanding.

Disposition to learn and to use libraries, for example, for most young people is about finding enjoyable places in which to work, which are relevant to their needs and responsive to their learning. They need to feel that people who use libraries are just like them and that it is alright to be in a library. Tutoring goes on in the library and various aspects of learning support. Students with learning difficulties can feel that the library is a safe place in which to spend time and to engage in a range of activities, including learning. It also is about their recognising that they can learn in multiple ways and that throughout their lives they will find libraries useful and important to their lives. To develop this lifelong disposition to learn, young people need to enjoy using their library at school and to find that they can use it and access the information and resources they need.

Qualified library staff, therefore, is the key to effective libraries. Staff members need to be able to relate to young people. The sometimes traditional view that if you couldn't relate with people you became a librarian or teacher librarian could not be further from the truth. Library staff members need to be not only approachable but also proactive in relating with young people. Young people need to see the library as a warm, welcoming and interactive place. From this the capacity to work successfully with young people to help them develop their actual learning skills is possible. More than this, young people can feel good about learning and seeing the library as a good place in which to learn. Here then they can develop the capacity to question, to know what they need to know, how to access it and when accessed how to use it and make sense of it. Qualified teacher librarians, librarians and library assistants are as important as teachers in the school environment and have a particular importance in relation to young people developing the disposition and skill to be self-directed learners. There is some good research that supports these views (http://www.iasl-online.org/advocacy/make-a-difference.html; http://www.det.wa.edu.au/education/cmis/eval/library/value/val2.htm)

The junior library is within the junior years' neighbourhood and totally open so that young people can access it at any time during the day. For the very young, the print material is most important as they learn to read. While there are classes in library use, the library is an open-learning area with young people coming and going from their classes as they need to access resources held there, including library staff who are additional teaching-learning resources. This library is probably accessed more for the print materials than for the digital resources that are available throughout learning spaces; although this is not true in non-class time (after school, for example) when many students come in to use the PCs.

The senior library is open for years 5-12. It is a very busy place with individuals, small groups and sometimes class groups accessing it. I get excited taking visitors through the school when I come to the library because here I can best explain our notion of developing the disposition and skill to be a self-directed learner. It is generally full of people, most are there of their own volition. The library is a focus for many senior students because it is a welcoming and comfortable place for them to do their work. They also can use the PCs for internet access and gaming.

In fact, the library is the central point for young people after school if they have to wait for parents to collect them after work. Here young people are able to engage in recreation and feel comfortable operating in small groups. They can make reasonable noise and bring their afternoon tea from the senior cafe. This library experience helps create for young people a greater sense of relevance in libraries. They will be accustomed to using them happily. They also can do their homework and part of the responsibilities of library staff is to provide help, when it is needed.

The climate in the library is welcoming to all young people. It doesn't discriminate on talent: it is not just a place for the more academically oriented. People don't have to 'shush' because the librarians favour the 'quiet academic'. They favour all users and support and help all users. In fact, it is the young person who is pursuing a non-academic pathway that often need the most support. The library staff can make them realise that the library will be able to help them and is a good place in which to spend time. Its resources, print and non-print, must also be relevant and useable. The careful selection of material with the client in mind is essential. We were able to move this way quite quickly by introducing hospitality training as a major integrated program at the school from year 8. The library had to support it and its students.

The libraries also house software resources and key equipment that students need for continuous learning. The latter may include cameras, sound equipment and video cameras for media, multimedia, photography, music and so on. A library is the ideal place to host such equipment because it is accessible, unlike an office, classroom or laboratory. These things, such as software and other reference material can be hoarded by teachers, not shared or just not available because of the actual physical unavailability of the teacher. In a library they are available, provided of course the library is open. Our senior library is open from 7.45am to

5.30pm and for about 48 weeks of the year. It is not open at weekends except on special request. The junior library is open from about 8.15 am to 4.30pm.

This is an age where much software is free on the internet, but there is highly specialised software that individuals cannot buy and would never have access to if it was not for libraries. In an age where increasingly people are becoming independent contractors, maybe holding several jobs or providing services to a range of clients, public libraries, like school libraries, will hold software and other resources that is indispensible to people for their work and/or study.

Sadly, in the future, we may still distinguish between school and public libraries. I have to say that I have never come across a school where libraries are so busy that they could not cope with external clients. Yet, we often rationalise that external clients would disadvantage students or place them in danger. This is an age of great protectionism as far as young people are concerned. The fear that opening the school library to the public would bring paedophiles in is a bit of nonsense. Schools are able to manage child protection. The reality is we have hundreds of parents, contractors and visitors weekly. Those who harm children come from just such groups!

There is a dreadful waste of resource in differentiating between school resources and public resources. The library of the future should indeed have multiple client groups and there should not be any support for a school library resource that is only available during school time (35 hours week, 40 weeks a year)! Imagine the richness in combining school and community library resources. At the very least their e-resources need to be shared.

I have described our current libraries and how they are used. I have directed attention to their integral role in assisting young people to develop the disposition and skill to be self-directed lifelong learners. The libraries I have described are very different to the libraries I found when I first came to the school. They were traditional and did lack the culture that welcomed all and supported all to be learners. They are different to what they were three years ago and, indeed, to what they were like last year. For example, in the past the junior library had a door that could be locked thus potentially closing the chance for open interaction between classes and the library. So often the meeting between students and librarian had to be organised. Again as an example, the senior library this year is open to the chance encounter with small groups of young people as young as ten just turning up during the day to seek assistance in research for a project.

These libraries have change embedded in their culture and ... these libraries have a future! Why? They have a future because they have made themselves relevant today. Elliott Eisner, the curriculum guru from Stanford University, says:

> Preparation for tomorrow is best served by meaningful education today ... we will realise that genuine reform of our schools requires a shift in paradigms from those with which we have become comfortable to others that more adequately address the potential that humans have for shaping not only the world, but themselves (Eisner 2004, p.4).

I apply this to libraries because they are significant learning organisations and certainly perceived as pivotal to schooling.

The '2020' notion of government should not be allowed to dominate our thinking about education, particularly schools and their libraries. Young people are here now and need to develop with the future. We cannot accept the notion that they'll be right now while we prepare for the young people of the future. We adopt a philosophy that says 'If it is right for young people now then we need to make it happen'. Such libraries will be relevant because they are constantly changing to respond to their clients and the world they live in. They are focused on ensuring that young people have access to the resources for learning that they need and have the chance to develop the essential dispositions and skills for learning that they need now and to ensure their future.

I am not sure what the library of the future will look like. I do know that it will have a feel for its clients very much similar to what we have now. I do know that it will be responsive to the twenty-first century and its young people. This responsiveness will mean that it will be in a state of continuous transformation. It will be a place where people will want to go and where people will feel comfortable either recreating or working. They will be just like the libraries I have described today!

Feedback

I thought in completing this scenario, I would seek some feedback from staff and students. Below are student comments that endorse an ongoing central role for the libraries in their learning and social lives. They also express that libraries need to embrace change as part of their culture.

Hi David, I read the piece you wrote and have some feedback: – I agree that libraries need to be accessible and up to date – at all times of the school day, I am often in and out of the library from 7:30 in the morning and often don't leave until

6:00 at night. It is a very valuable source for students. I use the library for a range of reasons which you covered in the chapter. Without access to libraries (not just the school) I wouldn't know where to study, relax and read a book. Sometimes it's nice to get away from the common rooms and enter a new world when you dive into a book or study for upcoming tests. I know without libraries, and especially the school's, I wouldn't have done as well as I have so far in my schooling career. It is important for the school to offer an open, warm, friendly environment for study – and the library is it. You also mentioned that libraries have to evolve, it is important that the library grow both with the world and its students. As new technology comes along the library should be there to allow students to access it with the best support they can give. The world will be forever changing so it is reasonable that libraries follow.

Library staff – They are just as much help as the actual resources themselves. They can help you with writing bibliographies to helping you film your next media project. They offer so much information to students and are there when ever needed.

Combining public and school libraries – I thought that although it would be a good idea it would be a hard task to do. I thought the idea of combining online resources would be a good idea allowing students access to more information, further enhancing learning possibilities.

At the moment I feel libraries are a great source for not only students but the world, but as I said earlier, as the world continues to change so should libraries.

That's about it, there was nothing I disagreed with but I just thought that combining the public and school libraries would be hard, unless it was completely electronic which in that case would be an excellent resource. If though it was possible it would be another step forward, further helping students.

Hope the feedback helps. Regards Nicole

Hi David, It's really hard to say just where libraries are and the potential they have to develop. Ultimately I think it is important to have a range of resources available, keeping the option for books, multimedia, internet, magazines etc. open. Despite moving into a technology driven era, it is still crucial for our learning that we don't restrict our knowledge pathways by relying on this one form of resources.

At Eltham I believe that our library system is welcoming to all students because of the way it embraces student input and provides access to study and recreational spaces at any point throughout the day. Personally I feel that an open door policy is crucial to ensuring that students are using and valuing their library. It is hard to determine how schools and public libraries could be linked, but the idea of a shared intranet system or hard drive could be a starting point.

I hope that feedback helps. Thanks, Brit

The library of the future will only exist if the library of today is relevant and transforming itself continuously. In schools it will only be relevant and transforming if it listens to its clients such as Al, Nicole and Brit. If the library listens, then in twenty years time it will still be vibrant and relevant. The Als, Nicoles and Brits of the future will be saying very similar things. Our school has as its critical goal: redefining schooling in collaboration with the client (in our case the principal client is the student) and if we ensure that are our library keeps this as a critical goal then it should do very nicely in the future.

Reference

Eisner, E. (2004). Preparing for today and tomorrow. *Educational Leadership*, December 2003/January 2004.

Further reading

Aphek, E. (2001). Children of the information age: a reversal of roles, *Turkish Online Journal of Distance Education – TOJDE*, 3(4), October 2002.

Beare, H, (2001). *Creating the future school*. London: Routledge-Farmer.

Department of Education, Western Australia. (2010). Research: the value of school libraries in learning. Available at: http://www.det.wa.edu.au/education/cmis/eval/library/value/val2.htm

Drucker, P. (2000). Managing knowledge means managing oneself. *Leader to Leader*, 8.

International Association of School Libraries. (2008). School libraries make a difference to student achievement. Available at: http://www.iasl-online.org/advocacy/make-a-difference.html

Jackson, P. (1968). *Life in classrooms*. New York: Holt, Rinehart and Winston.

Warner, D.R. (2006). *Schooling for the knowledge era*. Melbourne: ACER Press.

Scenario 7 Dissonant voices – reclaiming the human against techno-fascism

Giuseppe Giovenco (forum leader)

Excerpt from student email that prompted the discussion

I am glad that you enjoyed reading my paper. I deal with students and staff in a library environment every day and I find some of the theory misses the point at times. I can see the benefit of ICT in libraries, don't get me wrong, but I think that there is too much emphasis on it at times, hence my arguments.

As I mentioned, I took a calculated risk as I was in a position to do so. I have never been a conformist, nor am I afraid to speak my mind. Sometimes we need to be put in a position where we see the world from a different perspective.

Response from forum leader

I have come across two or three students in the last couple of years that I feel are starting to represent the gathering wave of recalcitrants who are not happy with current or recent thinking ... especially since the panic of the internet hit in 1994 and the meteoric rise of techno-managerialism in institutions especially in higher ed. and, pointedly, in libraries.

I am so sick and tired of conveniently skewed and rationalised arguments and being ticd with techno-driven and idolising processes being rammed into place and being presented as the rhetoric of the 'new service' mantra.

As you correctly and appropriately pointed out, the 'service aspect' of libraries needs to dominate and drive the debate and development of library paradigms with the underlying and imperative factor of human connectedness (not techno connectedness). This is the underplayed feature of the Library 2.0 construct that has arisen ... one which no one really seems to have picked up on despite its having been argued for many years even before development of the web itself.

I am hoping that the backlash that is growing from all quarters will be lasting as the new generations rise.

However, being the sociologist and social anthropologist that I am (among other things) the misconstruing of service as tools, i.e., techno as opposed to service as relationship and need for communication, bonding, relevance and meaning will be soon kicked truly in the butt and find its way relegated to a history lesson on how 'NOT TO DO THINGS'.

People being people … regardless of generation are and will always be seeking relatedness, relevance, interaction, meaning and community … and this means … being and dealing with people!

The destructive trend, especially in libraries and related services is the stripping down, dehumanising, abandoning recognition of place, context and core identity. It is more an admission and condition of library managers and providers, in their self-conscious recognition of the parlous state they have allowed the service and profession to be devalued and misrepresented and degraded.

The moral and existential panic that the internet and Google (that demon!!!!) brought to the profession left them and their existence in tatters … pitifully clutching at straws for anything that may provide them with some (even if grovelling or pathetic) sort of process to revalidate themselves in a desperate scramble for survival … thus we have these ad hoc and senseless flagellations and delusions about the need for the profession (so we can save the world from itself … etc.) such as info literacy, info equity, educational partnering, community remodelling and info leadership …

The issue being presented today is not one of relevance or capacity of libraries to service or survive but is one of leadership and considered, service-based and people-focused management. The 'leaders' currently in power are those that have risen through the ranks, very often people phobic and staff distrusting / resentful and divorced from the ethic and grounding of relatedness and relationship. It is this mindset which easily and willingly takes on board the construct of 'industrial or techno' solutioning, i.e., 'modernist' and sees that issues and problems can be resolved by mechanistic, assembly line processes.

Just like the Medical model (… the drug and cut mentality), the Techno/Industrial model is not, nor ever was the solution, has never provided for holistic resolution and consideration, has created and ignored as many problems as it attempts to resolve and still leaves a huge swathe of dissatisfaction, dissolution and sense of meaninglessness, irrelevance and disavowing of user, their needs and recognition as self. The user and service staff are mere cogs or facets deemed necessary within certain frameworks to meet (meat … i.e., provide the corporeal substance) the needs of the system and organisation. In essence, libraries and library policy are being run by social misfits and vandals … who so fear the idea of the user or 'personal relationship' that they will justify any and all means as rational and valid approaches to service ethic and options. The product is 'information' in whatever guise they wish to conceptualise it and regurgitate it, regardless of whether it is what or how the user wants it or in which form it will be presented or made available.

How these can come about and have any basis when there is no fundamental philosophic grounding for the trade of librarianship (possibly arguably a discipline … but definitely nowhere near a profession) it is difficult to understand. Furthermore, these elements as noted above have always been in part as existent within the framework of librarianship contextual and relative to the time and environment in which and how they were expressed.

One could argue that learning to use the 'card catalogue' or understand printed indexes or analysing the quality of a resource, e.g., encyclopaedia, were equally acts of information literacy … however, at least these were conceptualised and applied in a context relative to the need and level of the user as defined and validated by the user themselves.

Now it is a demand and imposition for everyone, whether they want or see a need for it or not … and boy are you looked down upon or viewed with disdain if you dare to even think that it is not necessary or do not perceive it as vital a process as breathing … anyone in the 'trade' who dares to speak out against the mantras and rhetoric and techno-imperialism is very soon ostracised and finds themselves sitting in the 'no-future' corner … left to fester and deemed as problematic till they can no longer be borne by the organisation and conveniently and coercively shuffled away … if they don't do the honourable thing and leave on their own … at a very high cost often to the mental, emotional, career and financial health of the sacrificial victim … along with the impacts on service ethics, validity and quality that the users suffer due to such managerial mindsets.

I think the main reason why libraries and their ilk have been so hard pressed and in such internal and external strife is that there is, and has been, a disjuncture between the essential processes and reasons of library – why and how they were established – with the 'democratic' and 'social good' rhetoric and myth that has grown around them.

These rhetoric stances have been, from their inception, fairly much just that, rhetoric … libraries and ilk have never been representative of democratic or real 'social equity' processes … they have always been established and designed to serve and represent the dominant socio-political power paradigm or specific user client base (even at their most altruistic).

If we take modern libraries and see their development from arts, trade or subscription libraries, which were set up for particular clientele and with particular philosophic and outcome intents, then we see that the capacity for libraries to be truly democratic is severely undermined and flawed in this very basis.

Modern libraries have always only really catered for a small section of the population and revolved around middle-class constructs of appropriateness, need and users.

The non-users fell into two main generalised camps:

- the lower or disenfranchised classes who have always seen libraries as irrelevant, meaningless, pointless and a drain on their funds or inappropriate for their kind (a view and construct very much reinforced by library culture and environments) and who saw information and its relevance from a very differing perspective.
- the upper classes who saw public libraries as demeaning and irrelevant and at best 'a social good for those poor wretched souls' and who had strong control over their information gathering and needs based upon other underlings gathering it for them or from social/class/privilege networks.

Libraries have always struggled to attract, service and be relevant to all levels … and in many ways never really wanted to … it was only when public funding came into the equation and was coupled by the progressive development in various ways of alternate information gathering and educational levels along with more competitive and available alternate options … e.g., growing affluence and literacy levels making book shops or information style services (including some alternate public funded forms, e.g., community, neighbourhood or information centres) that such issues began to develop and be seen as a threat.

Anyone who has been in the trade prior to the demon internet, especially in public libraries will know that the angst over attracting and retaining users and being relevant was a growing and ever-present concern … especially in the area of adolescent (euphemised as 'young adult') services. I think it somewhat ironic now how it is the same young adult aspects that are actually driving the call for service and relevance, even to the strongly potential impact of disenfranchising the other users … especially the older ones.

It is no wonder that libraries were so quickly and effectively relegated to the level of irrelevance and invalidity with the arrival of the internet as generally accessible … and rightly so …

Anyway, now that I have dumped a whole lot of diatribe on you … I will get back to your original message.

As I commented in your paper, I wholeheartedly agreed with your work … but seeing that the subject is actually the educational representative of the 'techno' mechanistic model I was discussing above I was obliged to assess your work in that vein.

Be assured, however, there were various others who took the road you did and made the same expressions either in part or fully in their work ... so you are not alone in your concerns.

I am presently advising on a book being written and due for release by mid next year that takes on-board these issues, especially from a management perspective so there revolution is definitely developing a fervent groundswell ... perhaps then we may be able to develop the 'profession' into something more humane and aware of its real basis for existence and validation.

Let me applaud you in surviving in your nonconformist persona ... having been and continuing to be so myself (you may have noticed some elements of this). I fully appreciate what you are doing and saying. Retain this and keep going ... just be sure you build your resilience capacities as well ... as you know, being a nonconformist comes with its challenges and can take a toll as well.

Have a listen to the latest presentation of the Philosopher's Zone: How political idealism threatens civilisation.

> In the eighteenth century, advanced thinkers took up the idea that society was imperfect and that what you do with imperfections is get rid of them. The result was the growth of large radical projects aimed at transforming things –the French Revolution being a dramatic case. The basic issue was how to transcend conflict and achieve harmony. But is the search for harmony compatible with a free society? This week, Kenneth Minogue, Emeritus Professor of Political Science at the London School of Economics argues against harmony and puts the case for a contentious political life (Introduction, available at: (http://www.abc.net.au/rn/philosopherszone/stories/2009/2758369.htm)

The discussion, especially in the early parts regarding modernism, enlightenment etc. will be useful in informing the constructs of management discussions and representations. This is the sort of stuff that I allude to when I mention that LIS lacks a critical philosophical/political/sociol-anthropologic-historical grounding and understanding. Another thought that I have been playing with is the contexts and impacts of LIS conceptualisation and representation of information and information theory.

I see that the commoditisation of 'information' relative to service, together with and underpinned by techno-tyranny is missing the point of the role and value that interpersonal interaction creates the constructs of relationship and meaning in information seeking, transfer and perception. The role of LIS people is that of intermediary and facilitator between the information and the receptor. The more we devolve to techno-systems the more the meaning, value and relevance of the information are devalued, decontextualised and impacts on sense of relevance and relationship. We tend to forget that information is encased and contextualised by its social and interpersonal relationship meaning and facilitation.

Take this interpersonal aspect away and all you are left with is commodity leaving it open to whichever player best value adds that commodity to draw in the user/client. Therefore, libraries taking away that real and honest social relationship only leave them prone to disassociation and devaluing. It is no wonder that financial and other support processes are then progressively and inevitably drawn away from them to more apparently meaningful and valued service.

Removing or subverting the human and the interpersonal out of LIS is the seeds of its own destruction.

The less we relate and are seen and serve the less the service and facility is valued.

The less it is valued and perceived, the less it is likely to be seen as relevant and therefore not supported.

The fallacious concept of seeing a successful service as a threat that must be devolved, democratised or re-presented only goes to show how management concepts are out of step with user needs and perception of service/facilitation quality.

If a service is heavily used and is based on strong human-related interactions e.g., F2F Ref Service or circulations services, the common management response is NOT to say … 'hey what are we doing right here that people want and like our service' … but to say … 'this is an impost on staffing levels, management systems, productivity (however or whatever they may be perceiving that) and is inefficient.

They then seek to rationalise this into processes and constructs of effectiveness, rhetoric involving democratisation and ethical/equity issues. They then seek to change the process to redirect the impact from a managerialist/systems perspective of effectiveness and in doing so destroy the conditions providing for the success initially. Putting in alternate systems and service model aspects on this model is in essence a message to the users that they are not valued and that their needs are disregarded and worthless. This underlying message then gets transferred by the user to meaning 'that it's not a real service and what value are they to me anymore'. Management has then successfully broken the 'social contract' (Hobbsian philosophy, I think? ... also Rousseau) relationship and contexts of 'trust', duty, honour and care.

If you deconstruct or destroy that relationship then you create inevitable negative outcomes and more complicated problems which the profession and service models are now experiencing but not understanding.

It would be an interesting research project to investigate the constructs and underpinnings of why the internet phenomenon was so huge relative to perceptions of value and effectiveness of LIS.

I know there has been research done on this as a panic response to library structure contexts but I feel that there needs to be more done on the contexts of what is/was information and its meaningfulness to all stakeholders ... not just the idea information of the hallowed 'knowledge' that LIS touted but what all levels of stakeholder and how they perceived, engaged in and accessed information within a relevance framework. It would be interesting to get to the deeper nitty gritty as to what/why the inventors and conceptualisers of the internet and pre-internet perceived of and found lacking in the information environments that drove them down that path.

It would be interesting to get their impressions/perceptions of what LIS especially libraries were/are and how this may have impacted, even unconsciously on their actions and pursuits?

Response 1 to forum leader

My first reaction to this post was agreement with most of it as a statement generally but I wasn't sure it was relevant to my own public library experience. However, on reflection, I realised that it reflects trends and attitudes in a widespread way, and that the applications and reverence of technology in the public library is deep-rooted and insidious and the autocratic and powerful nature of senior library management is dangerous.

The shift in libraries to increased use of technology does seem to forget about the older user – not just older in age but older as in established. Libraries seem to not want to be left behind in order to be relevant in this online world but to me there is still a great need for the traditional role of libraries as recreational and cultural institutions, not just purely as providers of information. Despite the increase in electronic formats, I think the traditional products will still be required and should be around for a while yet, and I don't think library services and information as a product can all be lumped together as a uniform homogenous type of thing.

There are information needs, such as that assisted by ready reference, or information about a given subject, that is, information as a response or answer to a question; but I am concerned about the information as recreation needs where users want to pursue reading about something, or reading for its own sake as a pleasurable, recreational or escapist activity – reading fiction, favourite authors or genres, etc., or reading up on their hobbies or interests. Book readers are not just older readers. To me, these are the ones who may suffer at the expense of the online library and technology for technology's sake, including electronic products, internet and Web 2.0 advances which are constantly encroaching on our world and forced into our library environments. In the public library environment, I'd like to think books still, and will for some time, play a vital role. However, management decisions, in order to be seen as progressive, or for ego trips of kudos or power play, or for whatever reasons, can damage the tenuous thread that the traditional recreational and cultural aspects of libraries are hanging on with. Library managers and policy-makers can easily damage this delicate situation by poorly thought out decisions and consequences about users and intent of services, as costs of books and staffing soar. The temptation to increase online services and use of technology with the seduction of cutting costs and cutting staff, and to be seen as keeping up, must be huge. Online services and technology should support the recreational and cultural role of the public library, not replace it.

I'm in awe of the power the library manager can wield. I've heard ours proclaim many times, 'This is my library, I can do what I like!' I've seen service deterioration and staff morale plummet as a result of a whim. It is not uncommon for him to order a course of action then the next week overturn his decision, and chastise and bully staff for following the very instructions he had given. It appears he has absolute power as long as he provides suitable statistics to Council, and to do so usually requires cost cutting measures of cutting back staffing and resources, and demanding that staff work 'smarter', doing more with less … often with technology solutions to assist this process. Ultimately the cost is degradation of services as resources are stripped back, and staff become stressed and demoralised. He pays lip-service to the user and services, but the reality is a far cry from quality service with the user and staff being nothing more than faceless statistics.

Applications of technology are not always the answer and can cause more problems than what they were designed to 'solve'. An area of my own concern is the library's information retrieval system, specifically the catalogue. The catalogue has fallen into disrepute due to the wrong focusing of technology and resources. Other finding tools are attempted, using technology and online resources, in an attempt at bypassing or making up for the catalogue's shortcoming, often in an ad hoc way by unskilled staff, which can be ineffective attempts at virtually reinventing the wheel.

Whether the library has books on paper, electronic resources, or other mediums, the catalogue is one of the library's greatest resources. It is the key to the library but its quality, usefulness and maintenance has been one of the most neglected areas in library developments with the adoption of technology. There seems to be an assumption that with automation which has seen online catalogues, keyword and full text search facilities, copy cataloguing and downloading catalogue records from national databases, and even the potential demise of 'the book', that cataloguing and catalogue maintenance generally is of decreasing use and value. Resources are taken away from this area resulting in catalogues that are difficult to use, records that are unfindable and unsuitable. Large and powerful computerised systems are deployed in libraries with this or that wonderful feature – and the features become the driving force! They have forgotten about the catalogue as primary importance. The interface of the catalogue and cataloguing module of our current ILMS is such that the catalogue records have to be so corrupted in order to fit the system. Surely the ILMS should be written to take advantage of the catalogue? The database which is the catalogue is such a wealth of valuable information, that when the interface of the ILMS is removed the database should remain as the valuable, rich resource that it is, not so corrupted and bastardised that it's useless in the future. Rules, standards and tools can change, but the fundamental role of the catalogue as a finding tool and retrieval system to the collection should be maintained, developed and enhanced – but through neglect and focusing on the wrong issues, they have in effect, thrown the baby away with the bathwater.

Surely more resources should be focused on the development of useful OPACs and interfaces, which could maximise and utilise the incredible wealth of information developed in the library catalogue – including not just descriptions of resources (paper, electronic, or otherwise) but the wealth of data provided by the use of controlled vocabularies specifically designed to assist retrieval, and the training of skilled staff to create and develop tools that support the role and purpose of the library, rather than trying to reinvent them in different ways by the hotch-potch use of technologies that has created an attitude of, 'How can we use this?' rather than, 'How can we enhance and utilise what we already have?'

It is such a vulnerable time for libraries. They are caught between the cultural and historical values, and the current climate of technological innovation where maintaining these values is often beyond feasible realities of politics and economics.

(Jennifer Curtis, December 2009)

Response 2 to forum leader

On service

I work in the higher education sector and I often hear staff, both academic and general, expressing their ideas that the average student, and there is never a differentiation between undergraduate and post graduate students, is techno-savvy. In my experience, the average student is techno savvy – they are highly likely to be able to rip music from the web, are social networking experts and believe that good research involves clicking on at least three results from their Google search. What these students, and often staff, are lacking, is the ability to marry the technology with the academic. You can provide all the technology in the world, but if there is no way to learn how to use it, what good is it to you?

'Service' should not be seen as the provision of IT tools, nor even of the resources available within these tools, such as search engines, databases and word processing tools. Service is assisting the user to become familiar with these tools (since they are ingrained into our society, and I don't see us reverting to stone tablets any time soon) and helping them on a journey. For some it will be a simple upgrade journey, such as moving from Office 2003 to Office 2007. For many others, the journey will be quite epic – moving from a closed stack library collection to having to formulate a search strategy, look up an electronic catalogue, locate an item using a sorting system that is entirely foreign to them, using a photocopier or scanner, self-checking the item out from the collection and correctly citing references using a bibliographic software. The epic journeys are where the service provision of the library staff can have the greatest impact, as poor service in any of these areas can lead to the user not returning, or worse still in an educational setting, feeling that they cannot cope and giving up on their studies.

On Library 2.0

Library 2.0 is an interesting concept, and one that has not taken off in many areas. Whilst Web 2.0 is all about the user being involved, Library 2.0 is predominantly the library staff being involved, so is it really fair to call it a 2.0 phenomenon? It is still feeding information to the user – there is minimal interaction – Oh, what a different world it might be if we could allow our users to tag the catalogue, link to

YouTube videos of their local dramatic society production of Macbeth, or direct others to a Facebook page for fans of Thomas Keneally.

On technology

A number of years ago, in response to the online learning management revolution, my colleagues and I developed an online information literacy skills tutorial. It served a wonderful purpose, not because it was techno, but because we were able to justify our base level of knowledge. If students came to classes without having completed the tutorial, they were told that there was a base level of knowledge assumed, and if they did not understand components of the face-to-face tutorials, they needed to build this level through the online tutorial. It was an absolute god-send, as we could concentrate on the library skills – showing the students how to use the catalogue, taking them on a tour of the building and pointing out all the important things like toilets and photocopiers!!

The reality of this tool was that it was teaching a set of skills, and the technology behind it was simply a delivery mechanism. Exactly the same result could have been obtained using pen and paper, but this would then have required substantial input from staff to mark the quizzes and provide feedback to students for any skills areas that required some extra work. By making it available online, we negated the need for the human interaction, and an additional benefit to the students was that marking was instantaneous and the quizzes could be attempted as many times as they needed to.

On community and interaction

I have been with my current employer for over seven years, in several different positions. I started in a very user-focused position, dealing with thousands of undergraduate students each year. I valued the interactions I had with both students and staff, and took great delight and satisfaction from assisting them and starting many on a journey of lifelong education. Some have come straight from high school, others are international students for whom an open-shelf environment is quite foreign. I like to measure the level of 'community' and 'interaction' by the number of students who return to the service desk, asking for particular staff by name, delivering chocolates when they complete their PhD or just call because they know you can help. I am about to farewell two long-term customers when they complete their PhDs in the next few months, and each have invited me to the celebratory drinks – testament to the value they place in the relationship they have built with the library over time.

Despite the high numbers of students attending discovery tours of the library, many do not see it as a necessity, preferring the activities in the bar or scavenger hunt. I do wish I had a decent sum of money for each second-year student I heard saying they wished they had done the tour in their first year!! If only we could bottle essence of second-year student!

On attempts at degradation of service

With staffing levels and funding recently being drastically cut, and in a bid to rationalise services, middle management suggested cutting the information advisors' desk hours. There was an overwhelming vote from the service staff themselves that this was unacceptable and they would all take on extra shifts to maintain the service. This was only possible because the current manager is very user and service-focused, and also believes in a democratic staffing system. Service provision is driven by those at the highest level, but often with the least day-to-day interaction with clientele. Whilst I am the first to admit that difficult decisions often need to be made, consultation with those 'at the coal face' can have great benefit.

On technology (specifically internet and online)

There is a role for technology in libraries, but it needs to be seen as a partner arrangement rather than a replacement. Electronic catalogues and searchable databases have revolutionised the world of the academic scholar. However, technology needs to been seen in a holistic way. It is not just about the memory capacity or speed of internet access. The computing environment is a tool that needs to be mastered just like any other skill, but it is part of a greater picture. When we learn to drive a car, we don't just learn to accelerate – we combine all of our skills in steering, braking, indicating, changing gears and turning on the headlights to achieve our goal of travelling from point A to point B. Similarly, we need to see our typing and searching skills as part of the greater picture.

On information as product

A former colleague, Dr Megan Poore, presented a paper in late 2009 on the roles on digital literacy in relation to human flourishing. In it she links the current trends in social networking, blogs, wikis and the like to the need for a decent level of digital literacy using Pierre Levy's 1994 work on collective intelligence as a basis. There is food for thought that 'wealth is linked to literacy' and as educators we have a responsibility to assist our clientele to 'navigate the knowledge space'. Can we just find a better name for it than 'information literacy'?

Information literacy is the worst nomenclature ever invented! Only librarians know what it is, and even then some have difficulty explaining it.

On class

I disagree that libraries are classist. Perhaps I am living in a sheltered world in the academic environment, where only the brightest stars shine? However, I do agree that we struggle to be relevant to all levels. There are those who are the elite in their own field of study and feel that they know more than anyone else in their own area, and with careful marketing and public relations these barriers can be broken down. Similarly, the newer crowd of undergraduates can be ill-prepared for the journey ahead of them and do not see the relevance of the academic library to them. I have found, however, that an F grade on the first essay brings them scurrying in!

References

Lévy, P. (1997). [1994]. *Collective intelligence: mankind's emerging world in cyberspace.* Cambridge Massachusetts: Perseus Books.

Poore, M. (2009). Digital literacy. Human flourishing and education in a knowledge society. Available at: http://meganautpoore.files.wordpress.com/2008/01/digitalliteracyhumanflourishingproseversion1.pdf.

(Jacqui Kempton, January 2010)

Response 3 to forum leader

Without wishing to be branded 'recalcitrant' (after all, this library student looks forward to a future of cordial employment), I give a sympathetic hearing to the 'diatribe' in question. At the same time, I'm not sure it's fruitful to imply that rhetoric is something used only by them, and that we advocate exclusively for the profession's 'real basis for existence'. True enough, I can only wonder aloud with my training wheels on, but I'd sooner suggest that if we want to re-imagine what we do, and thereby renew everyday practice with a language that rings true (as opposed to one we affect, so as to shore up professional status, or to placate the Google-demon), then it's less a matter of trying to falsify the favoured lingo of the day than it is of creating a more convincing rhetoric, using a vocabulary that aims to synthesise differences, accommodate both change and tradition, and alienate as few 'librarianships' as possible.

'Will any man,' asked Dewey, 'deny to the high calling of such a librarianship [as he had in mind] the title of profession?' (Dewey 1876, p.6). Again, here I sympathise with the author of our diatribe, though I'd prefer to rework the way the point is made. As I read it, what's sought in part is a less self-serving appreciation of librarianship. This isn't to downplay, as I see it, the 'trade', the 'discipline' or the 'profession', but rather to encourage its cohort to put credentials to one side, shift focus somewhat, and increase the depth of the field, so to speak.

As a student, for instance, arriving fresh on the scene, one thing that struck me was the extent of the rumination on relevance, role and self-image by some practitioners, which indeed seemed to be symptomatic of an 'existential panic'. Now, I don't know, but perhaps panic of this sort is productive in a sense. Certainly the ubiquity of remarks about relevance made me re-examine my own assumptions about the career I'd chosen. At any rate, the inference I'm minded to make now (conscious, though, that I could be constructing straw men, looking on as I do from a 'lineside' position) is that some seem either unprepared or ill-prepared to defend 'the human and the interpersonal' in what they do, and instead – so as to counter the perceived threat of change, I suppose, or to stay in step with the 'hive mind' of the social web – reinterpret their roles as revolving principally around 'information', and measure their relevance against the yardstick of technology.

A different direction taken by those ruminating on their status (one which maybe manifests something of the 'desperate scramble for survival' that's been described) might well be epitomised by a set of statements that gained some press online last year; namely, the Darien Statements on the Library and Librarians, written by three such librarians inspired by a summit on the future of libraries in Darien, Connecticut, in March 2009. Here's an extract:

The purpose of the library

The purpose of the library is to preserve the integrity of civilisation.

The Library has a moral obligation to adhere to its purpose despite social, economic, environmental or political influences.

The purpose of the Library will never change.

The Library is infinite in its capacity to contain, connect and disseminate knowledge; librarians are human and ephemeral, therefore we must work together to ensure the Library's permanence.

Individual libraries serve the mission of their parent institution or governing body, but the purpose of the Library overrides that mission when the two come into conflict.

Why we do things will not change, but how we do them will.

> A clear understanding of the Library's purpose, its role, and the
> role of librarians is essential to the preservation of the Library
> (Blyberg, Greenhill & Trainor 2009, p.1.)

To be fair, the authors make a note of pointing out the intentional grandeur of their statements, though I'm not sure that even this explains how such notions could come into being. However, what interests me here isn't so much the statements themselves (which I'll leave the reader to ponder) but rather the philosophical and professional vacuum that these librarians seem to be trying to fill, partly with this awkwardly singular construction called 'the Library', which is presumably the Public One.

Perhaps such statements speak to the 'disjuncture' that's been described, between the practice of librarianship and its associated myths. Or maybe an absence of leadership at management levels has left a good many feeling disoriented. Another factor may be what is (or is not) being taught in library schools, such that there's room in the minds of graduates for fictions as to their functions. To take my own course of studies that I'm halfway through, yet am I to be prescribed, let alone pointed to, a single reading that could be said to address the history of librarianship or the philosophies brought to bear upon it.

Understand that I'm content to see librarianship subsumed by a contemporary framework. What I wonder, though, is how such an old 'profession' could endorse a curriculum that makes only passing references to the past that informs it, and no attempt at all to engage with anything like philosophy or critical theory. Maybe lines of inquiry like these are thought only to have a place in undergraduate degrees, and that there simply isn't time in postgraduate programs. Nonetheless, for my part it feels as though something important has been vacated here, leaving students to erect their own foundations, or to simply tag along uncritically with the status quo. To that end, I tend to agree with what's been written about the susceptibility of some to simple models of thought.

In the course of writing this, I came across a passage that seemed to tie up the threads of both my own disordered and admittedly nascent thoughts, as well as the sprawling nature of this discussion. The passage reads:

> [W]e are only in danger of being replaced by technology if what
> we do is the same as what technology does. 'Information
> professionals', I have tried to argue, approach information from a
> technological standpoint and in so doing create their own
> irrelevance (Litwin 2005, p.22).

As for whatever closing comments I can add, I'd like to think that as an almost-librarian, future employers reading this can rest assured that (as I channel Marshall McLuhan) if they don't like these ideas, I've got others.

References

Blyberg, J. Greenhill, K. & Trainor, C. (2009). The Darien statements on the library and librarians. Retrieved January 18 2010 from http://www.blyberg.net/downloads/DarienStatements.doc

Dewey, M. (1876). The Profession. *The American Library Journal*, 1(1), 5-6.

Litwin, R. (2005). Why our relevance lies in not being 'information professionals'. *Library Juice*, 8(7). Retrieved January 18 2010, from http://libr.org/juice/issues/vol8/LJ_8.7.html#3

(Denis McDonald, January 2010)

Response 4 to forum leader

What an interesting email you've sent. Your email forced me to think about what I do as a librarian, and what for me is an important aspect of the role.

With respect to using ICT in libraries, I agree that the service aspect of role is important, vital. Whilst I don't see ICT as a peril, if we use it at the expense of the interpersonal interaction, we degrade the service. I would say that it's more a matter of how can we use ICT to provide a relevant, meaningful, service to our clients.

For me, as a librarian (not a library manager), information literacy is one philosophy that underpins my dealings with TAFE students and staff (clients). I am also bound by the philosophical underpinnings of my employer (TAFE) such as ethical practice (equity of service to all) amongst others. Service plays a vital role in the delivery of information to the clients. The way I interact with them will have a bearing on whether or not I can help them meet their information need/s. ICT in its many forms and with its many tools, besides being a service that is offered to clients, is also a mode of delivery of information that allows the library service to reach many clients, at the same time, 24/7 (especially those that are studying flexibly, rather than face-to-face).

As an intermediary between the information and the receptor (client), my interpersonal communication with the client has meaning in so far as the way I interact/relate with the client to elicit the information need and can either enhance, or detract from their experience of the process. In other words, how helpful I am with the client (based on their perceptions) getting useful information, will often determine the client's satisfaction level. It also applies to all library services such as reference, loans (circulation) and ICT and will involve my communication skills, as well as my information literacy skills. As an intermediary, I take the role of a mentor, in a collaborative effort to enable the client to enhance their skills in the process of locating, assessing and evaluating information with mutual satisfaction in the successful outcome of that process.

The development of these services, including ICT, is not done for its own sake, but usually as a means to an end. That end relates to the client (I don't really like the word user), usually to facilitate access to services and information, or to become proficient in a subject or the use of a computer program or electronic database. For me, there is still that personal element, and a social context between the library staff and the clients. ICT is just another tool that can be used by me and the client to access library information and services.

For example, I use the library blog to collaborate with clients about new services or enhancements to existing ones, interruption to services, vacation hours, tips etc. Along with others, I use the library wiki to place various podcasts, videos, slide shows, and electronic versions of handouts, or guides, for clients to become familiar with the library.

Having said that, it's all very well to input into the blog or wiki, but it's not much point if no one is reading it or even if they don't know we have one, let alone the web address. It can become disassociated, as you say, and the process becomes impersonal, perhaps meaningless, even pointless. So for me this then becomes an issue of how to make ICT beneficial and also allow for human communication/feedback/collaboration, either directly from the ICT tool itself, or indirectly using other tools. In addition, it is for me a matter of being selective in which components/tools of ICT I would use, and for what purpose I would use them in the delivery and promotion of library services.

In summary, ICT has had a profound effect on all of us, and I'm glad that LIS has embraced it. Yes, it has changed our roles, which we have already had to adapt, and will continually have to adapt, to attract clients, remain relevant, and provide a service. Yet, it is constantly evolving with new tools being developed. I would expect LIS to also be involved with these, but they are just tools and we have to be selective in what tools we use and to what purpose we put them.

(Dennis Vukovic, January 2010)

Further reading

Andersen, J. & Skouvig, L. (2006). Knowledge organization: a socio-historical analysis and critique. *The Library Quarterly*. 76(3) 300-322

Beaudrie, R & Grunfeld, R. (1991). Male reference librarians and the gender factor. *The Reference Librarian*, 15(33) 211-213.

Birdi, B., Wilson, K. & Cocker, J. (2008). The public library, exclusion and empathy: a literature review. *Library Review*, 57(8) 576-592.

Black, A. & Muddiman, D. (Eds.) (1997). *Understanding community librarianship: the public library in post-modern Britain*. Aldershot, UK: Avebury.

Black, A., Muddiman, D. & Plant, H. (Eds.) (2007). *The early information society: information management in Britain before the computer*. Aldershot, UK: Ashgate

Budd, J. (2008). *Self-examination: the present and future of librarianship*. Westport, CT: Libraries Unlimited.

Bundy, A. (2004a). Beyond information: the academic library as educational change agent. *7th International Bielefeld Conference* Germany 3-5 February 2004, located at http://conference.ub.uni-bielefeld.de/2004/proceedings/bundy_rev.pdf

Bundy, A. (2004b). Places of connection: new public and academic library buildings in Australia and New Zealand. *Library Buildings Conference* Bournemouth UK 5-6 February 2004, located at http://www.bournemouth.gov.uk/library/pdf/leisure/libraries/places%20of%20connection.pdf

Buschman, J. (2007a). Democratic theory in library information science: Toward an emendation. *Journal of the American Society for Information Science and Technology* 58(10), 1483-1496.

Buschman, J. (2007b). Transgression or stasis? Challenging Foucault in LIS theory. *The Library Quarterly*, 77(1), 21-44.

Cavanagh, M.F. (2009) Making the invisible visible: public library reference service as epistemic practice, located at https://tspace.library.utoronto.ca/bitstream/1807/17737/1/Cavanagh_Mary_F_200906_PhD_thesis.pdf

Clarke, J., Gewirtz, S. & McLaughlin, E. (Eds.) (2000). New managerialism, new welfare? London: Sage Publishing.

Compaine. B.M. (Ed.) (2001). The digital divide: facing a crisis or creating a myth? Cambridge, MA: The MIT Press. Available at http://books.google.com.au/books?id=MbareJicwKAC&printsec=frontcover#v=onepage&q=&f=false

Coyle, K. (2005). Management of RFID in libraries. *Journal of Academic Librarianship*, 31(5), 486-489, located at http://www.kcoyle.net/jal-31-5.html

Doogue, G. (2001). Robert Putnam on community. *Life Matters*: ABC Radio National, located at http://www.abc.net.au/rn/talks/lm/stories/s422145.htm

Dutch, M. & Muddiman, D. (2000). Information and communication technologies, the public library and social exclusion. *The Network*. Working Paper 15, located at http://www.seapn.org.uk/content_files/files/vol3wp15.pdf

Farmer, L.S.J. (Ed.) (2007). The human side of reference and information services in academic libraries: adding value in the digital world. Oxford: Chandos.

Fleischmann, K.R. (2007). Digital libraries with embedded values: combining insights from LIS and science and technology studies. *The Library Quarterly*, 77(4) October, 409-27.

Garfield, D. (2007). A reading strategy for a UK university: reviewing the literature on reading, literacy and libraries, with particular regard to the HE sector. *Journal of Information* Literacy, 2(2), located at http://ojs.lboro.ac.uk/ojs/index.php/JIL/article/view/RA-V2-I2-2008-2/166

Goodson, P. (2008). Male librarians: gender issues and stereotypes. *Library Student Journal*, October, located at http://www.librarystudentjournal.org/index.php/lsj/article/view/100/187

Grafstein, A. (2007). Information literacy and technology: an examination of some issues. *Libraries and the Academy*, 7(1) 51-64, available at http://74.125.155.132/scholar?q=cache:QzeBOdRNRNwJ:scholar.google.com/&hl=en&as_sdt=2000

Green, L.V. & Clarke, R.A. (1995). Professional excellence and customer care: an academic library perspective. *Library Management*, 16(6) 16-23.

Haider, J. & Bawden, D. (2006). Pairing information with poverty: traces of development discourse in LIS. *New Library World*. 107, 9/10, 371 – 385, located at http://www.soi.city.ac.uk/~dbawden/jutta%20paper.pdf

Haider, J. & Bawden, D. (2007). Conceptions of 'information poverty' in LIS: a discourse analysis. *Journal of Documentation*. 63(4), 534-557, located at http://www.soi.city.ac.uk/~dbawden/jutta%20jdoc.pdf

Harris, M. (2006). Technology, innovation and post-bureaucracy: the case of the British Library. *Journal of Organizational Management*, 19(1), 80-92.

Harris, M. (2008). Digital technology and governance in transition: The case of the British Library. *Human Relations*. 61(5), 741-758, located at http://www.essex.ac.uk/ebs/research/working_papers/WP_07-07.pdf

Hawkins, M., Morris, A. & Sumsion, J. (2001). Socio-economic features of UK public library users. *Library Management*. 22(6/7), 258-265.

Hickey, A. (2006). Cataloguing men: Charting the male librarian's experience through the perceptions and positions of men in libraries. *The Journal of Academic Librarianship*, 32(3), 286-295.

Kuhlthau, C. (2008). From information to meaning: Confronting challenges of the twenty-first century. *Libri*, 58(2), 66–73, located at http://www.librijournal.org/pdf/2008-2pp66-73.pdf

Labaree, R.V. & Scimeca, R. (2008). The philosophical problem of truth in librarianship. *The Library Quarterly*, 78(1), 43-70 located at http://www.journals.uchicago.edu/doi/pdf/10.1086/523909?cookieSet=1

Landheer, B. (2007). *Social functions of libraries*. Amberg Press, located at http://books.google.com.au/books?id=Y6G6q1OMfBIC&printsec=frontcover&source=gbs_navlinks_s#v=onepage&q=&f=false

Library Leadership Network Peer Panel (2007). Libraries - Welfare for the middle class? January, located at http://pln.palinet.org/wiki/index.php/Libraries_-_Welfare_for_the_middle_class%3F

Lofgren, H. (1998). Libraries, new managerialism and economic rationalism: Remarks on the upheaval in Victoria. *Australian Library Journal*, 47(4), November, 327-33.

Loomis, A. (1994). Labor groups, Service to. In W.A. Wiegand,& D.G. Davis (Eds.) *Encyclopedia of library history* (pp.329-331). New York & London: Garland Publishing.

Luke, A. & Kapitzke, C. (1999). Literacies and libraries – archives and cybraries. *Pedagogy, Culture & Society*, 7,(3)467-491, located at http://eprints.qut.edu.au/5904/1/5904.pdf

Luke, T.W. (1999). Eco-managerialism: Environmental studies as a power/knowledge formation. *Living with Nature*, June,103-21.

Lyman, P. (1998). The poetics of the future: Information highways, digital libraries and virtual communities, located at http://people.ischool.berkeley.edu/~plyman/articles/Lazerow.pdf

Malone, C.K. (2000). Toward a multicultural American public library history. *Libraries & Culture*, 35(1), Winter, located at http://www.gslis.utexas.edu/~landc/fulltext/LandC_35_1_Malone.pdf

Marsh , M.S. (2008). Serving the patron: Tradition, ideology and change in public libraries. A master's paper for the MS in LS degree. May, located at http://ils.unc.edu/MSpapers/3393.pdf

McMenemy, D. (2007). Managerialism: a threat to professional librarianship? *Library Review*, 56(6), 445-449.

McMenemy, D. (2008) 'Or you got it or you ain't': the nature of leadership in libraries. *Library Review*, 57(4), 265-68.

Muddiman, D. (2000). Images of exclusion: User and community perceptions of the public library. The Network. Working Paper 9, located at http://www.seapn.org.uk/content_files/files/vol3wp9.pdf

Neem, J. (2009). Reviving the Academic Library. *Inside Higher Ed*. November 19, located at http://www.insidehighered.com/views/2009/11/19/neem

The Network: Tackling Social Exclusion in Libraries, museums, archives and galleries 2009, located at http://www.seapn.org.uk/

O'Brien, J. (1996). Breadth and depth of librarianship: Through the looking glass. *Australian Law Librarian*, 4(4), 303, located at http://heinonline.org/HOL/Landing Page?collection=journals&handle=hein.journals/auslwlib4&div=83&id=&page=

Pateman, J. (1999). Public libraries, social exclusion and social class. *Information for Social Change*, 10, Winter, 1999-2000, located at http://libr.org/isc/articles/10-public.html

Pateman, J. (2000). Public libraries and social class. The Network. Working Paper 3, located at http://www.seapn.org.uk/content_files/files/vol3wp3.pdf

Pawley, C. (1998). Hegemony's Handmaid? The library and information studies curriculum from a class perspective. *The Library Quarterly*. 68(2), April, 123-144.

Pawley, C. (2003). Information literacy: A contradictory coupling. *Library Quarterly*. 73(4), 422-452.

Popowich, A.S. (2007). The politics of public library history. *Dalhousie Journal of Information and Management*, 3(1), Winter, located at http://djim.management.dal.ca/issucs/issue3_1/popowich/index.htm

Quinn, B.A. (2007). Cooperation and competition at the reference desk, located at http://esr.lib.ttu.edu/bitstream/handle/2346/487/fulltext.pdf?sequence=1

Radford, M. (1998). Approach or avoidance? The role of nonverbal communication in the academic library user's decision to initiate a reference encounter. *Library Trends*, March 22, located at http://www.thefreelibrary.com/Approach+or+avoidance%3F +The+role+of+nonverbal+communication+in+the+...-a021239741

Radford, M.L. & Radford, G.P. (1997). Power, knowledge, and fear: Feminism, Foucault, and the stereotype of the female librarian. *The Library Quarterly*. 67(3), 250–66.

Reed, R. (2007). From librarian to information scientist: Technology and occupational change in a traditional woman's occupation, located at http://archive.wigsat.org/gasat/47.txt

Saunders, A. (2007). Ethics of economic rationalism. Philosopher' Zone: ABC Radio National, located at http://www.abc.net.au/rn/philopherszone/stories/2007/1923237.htm

Saunders, A. (2009). How political idealism threatens civilization. Philosopher' Zone: ABC Radio National, located at http://www.abc.net.au/rn/philopherszone/stories/2009/2758369.htm

Song, Y.S. (2009). Designing library services based on user needs: new opportunities to re-position the library. World Library and Information Congress: 75th IFLA General Conference and Council 23-27 August 2009, Milan, Italy, located at http://www.ifla.org/files/hq/papers/ifla75/202-song-en.pdf

Steinerová, J. (2001). Human issues of library and information work. *Information Research (IR)*. 6(2), located at http://informationr.net/ir/6-2/paper95.html

Talja, S. & Hartel, J. (2007). Revisiting the user-centred turn in information science research: an intellectual history perspective. *Information Research (IR)*. 12(4), located at http://informationr.net/ir/12-4/colis/colis04.html

Too, Y.L. (2010). *The idea of the library in the ancient world*. Oxford University Press, located at http://books.google.com.au/books?id=8OU4nTlcS0gC&printsec =frontcover&source=gbs_v2_summary_r&cad=0#v=onepage&q=&f=false

Townsend, K.C.. & Mcwhirter, B.T. (2005). Connectedness: A review of the literature with implications for counseling, assessment, and research. *Journal of Counseling and Development*. 83(2), Spring, 191-201.

Trosow, S.E. (2001). Standpoint epistemology as an alternative methodology for library and information science. *Library Quarterly*, 71(3), July, 360-382.

Trowler, P. (1998). What managerialists forget: higher education credit frameworks and managerialist ideology. *International Studies in Sociology of Education*, 8(1), March, 91-110.

University of Nebraska Lincoln Libraries (1988). Library philosophy and practice (LPP). Lincoln NE, located at http://unllib.unl.edu/LPP/

Vårheim, A. (2008). Theoretical approaches on public libraries as places creating social capital. World Library and Information Congress: 74th IFLA General Conference and Council 10-14 August 2008, Québec, Canada, located at http://ifla.queenslibrary.org/ IV/ifla74/papers/091-Varheim-en.pdf

Ward, R.C. (2007). The outsourcing of public library management. *Administration & Society*. 38(6), 627-648.

Weller, T.D. & Bawden, D. (2005). The social and technological origins of the information society in England 1830-1900, *Journal of Documentation*, 61(6), 777-802, located at http://www.soi.city.ac.uk/~dbawden/toni%20paper.pdf

Wilder, S. (2005). Information literacy makes the wrong assumptions. *Chronicle of Higher Education*. 51(18), B13, located at http://www.owlnet.rice.edu/~comp300/documents/ InformationLiteracy.pdf

Williams, G. (2007). June. Unclear on the context: refocusing on information literacy's evaluative component in the age of Google. *Library philosophy and practice*. Special Issue, located at http://www.webpages.uidaho.edu/~mbolin/williams.htm

Williams, P. (2006). Against information literacy. *Library + Information Update*, 5(7-8), 20, located at http://eprints.ucl.ac.uk/3844/1/againstinformationliteracy1.pdf

Wilson, K.M. (2006). Convergence and professional identity in the academic library. *Journal of Librarianship and Information Science*. 38(2), 79-91.

CHAPTER 4
Identifying the issues

The preparation of the foregoing scenarios was deliberately arranged so that contributors did not see each others' work until all the pieces were gathered together. This was quite intentional, so that each could present their own ideas and thoughts without being in any way influenced by the others (a slight modification, maybe, of the Delphi research technique). Authors wrote from their own situations, experiences and concerns. Remarkably, a considerable number of common issues can be seen in the scenarios, despite their coming from a wide range of sectors and situations.

One of the more obvious aspects of the exercise is the remarkable similarity between the papers of Johnson (USA) and Healy (Australia). Although written half a world apart, these texts show clearly how common some issues are among library professionals, at least in the developed world. Not only are the two presentations similarly built around the experiences of a single individual, but the buildings, processes, interactions and daily activities all bear a strong resemblance. To some extent this might have been expected as both authors function in comparatively similar sectors of the information field. However, both would be among the first to note also the significant differences between the American and Australian situations. Technology is a common theme with futuristic computing development occupying a very significant place in the pursuit of information and communication and, as a consequence, learning.

Beyond the more obvious there are some remarkable consistencies in all of these expert scenarios. Common to all the pieces is a complete understanding that 'library' has a viable future. A physical port of call for all those who wish to locate necessary information is an assumed given. The exact look and feel of that location does vary however. This centrality and continuity is vital as the authors look to the future. They are all equally positive that in future years there will be an important point at which assistance with the access and the interpretation of information will be provided. Rather critically, this point of contact with information will have a human face to it, even if computer-assisted, such that human beings can interact with other human beings as they make sense of the data that they need in order to live their daily lives.

Although its appearance may be different, it remains a point of focus for information seeking.

Technology appears in all of the scenarios to some extent or another. It seems that information delivery is now, for better or for worse, inextricably intertwined with technology. Whether it be as a facilitator for improved handling of e-materials as Law suggests, or the interface between humans and much of their information as Healy and Johnson would hold, it is an ever-present concern. Giovenco does well though to assign it to its rightful place as an information tool. The point he makes is further underscored by Warner and Hannan in terms of its relative importance to humanity and to the environment. There needs to be a considered balance rather than the presently dominant mindset that more machines and greater bandwidth must mean more learning and more information assimilated by knowledge seekers.

Technology may well be developed to include an emotional connection to humans taking into account their moods, emotional needs, and even emotional intelligence.

Despite these sorts of visions, there still remains a key role for human intermediaries. Though Johnson's Miles has his emotionally-hyped avatar, it is the people who provide a firm background on which he builds his knowledge. Though he is developing his 'sims' and their free will, it is his interaction with Dr Li, Dr Shahada and Jennie that remain highly important to his daily life. More than this, given his choice, he retains even an antique grandpa with stale jokes as an important member of his learning network. Similarly, Law points to skilled staff as offering the best chance for future e-collections and Warner believes in quality staff as essential to the learning future of young people. The skills may change in terms of technology, but the essential characteristic of considered and personal human interaction remains fundamental to information provision in the future.

Some years ago now, predictive studies considering future (then 2006) library staff, suggested that between 1996 and 2006 library staff would see a major reduction in clerical work as against a big increase in client services (Winzenried 2002, unpublished thesis, see figures 3 and 4).

These changes are now a fairly standard feature of library practice for most (Dowler 1997, Li 2009), and in a good many cases the reality has exceeded the predictions. If our scenarios are reliable, this personal intermediary role is set to continue further as the future unfolds. Certainly technology will also play an increasing part (though with the actual work carried out by experts rather than library staff), but the human contact will remain critical, especially for clients at either end of the age continuum.

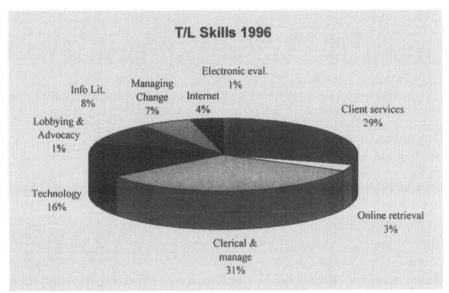

Figure 3   Teacher librarian skills in 1996 (Winzenried,2004.)

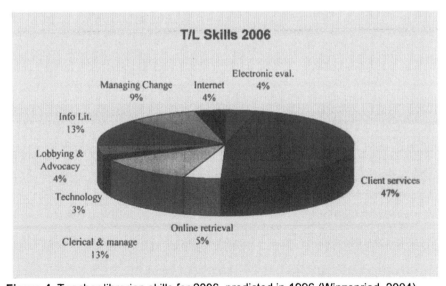

Figure 4   Teacher librarian skills for 2006, predicted in 1996 (Winzenried, 2004)

Change and information management have gone hand-in-hand for some years now. All round the developed world library staff have had to deal with considerable change from the time library automation began in the 1960s, and arguably before that. Incorporation of technologies meant that in many locations the library professional became one of the leading technology experts in their organisation. In terms of school libraries, particularly, it was frequently the teacher librarian who had to deal with computers first, developed early networks and subsequently pioneered internet use. Within a very short space of time the information expert became something of an all-round technology trouble-shooter. The high cost of employing emerging computer professionals made self-taught library staff invaluable for many of the smaller establishments – a situation that can still be found occasionally today. Each of the scenarios in chapter 3 assume considerable change – change in workflow, change in means of information access, change in technology and, particularly, change in clients. Innovative new directions are suggested for all of these aspects and for all sectors of the information provision industry.

One rather considerable change assumption made by all of our writers is that of digitisation. Increasingly information will become digital. Law would even suggest that this is quite vital to library survival and relevance. However, the actual work of digitising will not necessarily fall on the shoulders of library staff. Johnson suggests the work could well be done in developing countries – certainly somewhere where labour costs make it viable. Law is suggesting greater attention to aggregating existing and future e-materials into what he calls e-collections on the basis of using the opportunities we have now more effectively so there will be less to do later on. Healy assumes information online as a given for the world her Shelby inhabits, in much the same way that Warner considers it a non-negotiable certainty.

While Hannan would at first seem to argue against the digitisation process, given her green stand, it becomes important to offer as much information as is possible in a less environmentally destructive format. Her contention that there will be printed materials in the 'library' is not contradicted by any of the others. Everyone sees some print materials existing for many years to come. What is agreed, though, is that with information increasing at its current rate, and particularly with much of it being generated in non-print format, this digital information will necessarily become the major focus for the future.

Hughes raises a very significant issue in terms of education for all. One corollary of this that he cites as critical is that library access is for all. Giovenco reminds us that until relatively recently in our information history, library and access to information generally was rather socially biased. Frequently representing the predominantly socio-political systems in which they existed, it was only with the application of significant government money to library and the arts generally that considerations of democracy managed to enter the information scene. It is with this in mind, perhaps, that Hughes is so concerned that the current government initiative of education revolution does actually become truly revolutionary and start to address the education and information needs of all learners.

In summary, all of our contributors give library a central and crucial place in the lifelong learning paradigm. Representing as they do so many years of experience in a wide range of contexts, this is a significant finding. Libraries, contrary to belief in some quarters, are not irrelevant in the current age. Quite the opposite is true. Educationally important to Hughes, they are equally necessary as a way forward for higher education as shown by Law, as well as a pivotal aspect of general social interactions as outlined by Hannan. Warner notes the importance of library as it is central to the development of 'disposition and skill to be self-directed lifelong learners'. And Johnson's Miles and Healy's Shelby find a 'bricks and mortar' library a considerable focus for activity during their learning day. It is not only a part of their formal school process, but something that these young learners of the future carry with them everywhere with the help of various technologies that give them connection.

Centrality

One of the outstanding points of agreement with all of the contributors, regardless of their sector or location, is the centrality of library within the information landscape. In the past decade or two, much has been said and much has been written about libraries without walls (note, for example, the series of CERLIM conferences on this theme, Dowler 1997, Chartier 1993, Cram 2002), schools without libraries (e.g., Henne 1960, Zinn 2006), and the replacement of library by internet (e.g., Bradley 2007, Miller & Pellen 2006). So far, there has been only minimal movement in those directions. Some moves in the business sector in the early 1990s to save costs by removing their information mediators/library specialists and replace these with internet to every office desk (Miller & Pellen 2006) have seen a radical policy reversal in the first decade of the new millennium as productivity figures fell and staff struggled with the mass of information that presented itself (Barbera 1996, Rowse 1999, Edmunds & Morris 2000).

In more recent years, the arrival of learning commons at a number of universities is just one indicator that information users are searching for a location where they can interact with their information and, importantly, with each other as they do so. Where library managements have capitalised on this need, and combined the traditional role of library with a new and flexible social space where information can be accessed as well as social needs met, there is generally a successful and flourishing library as a result. Examples of these include the one-stop-shop concept used to design and operate the Saltire Centre at the Glasgow Caledonian University or the Heymarket Public Library in Sydney, Australia.

Hughes cites research in the USA by Lonsdale that supports the centrality of library in the formal learning cycle and Law notes the ongoing centrality in the higher education sector. The Lonsdale research though showed that while school libraries were critical to learning, they often lacked staff trained in the field of education. All too often the interface for learners was a technician rather than a teacher. Hughes cites Lonsdale, who in turn cites a study by Reynolds and Carroll in 2001, as finding that the percentage of Victorian schools having libraries staffed by qualified teacher librarians had dropped from 55 per cent in 1983 to 13 per cent in 2000. This step backward from a very different position in the 1970s came about as bureaucrats and managers ceased to fund on the basis of need and more on the basis of political expediency. It is this expediency that is one of the concerns, not only of Hughes, but also of many others, that the current education revolution may turn out to be less of a revolution and more a politically motivated window dressing. There does need to be genuine revolution and with school libraries at the heart of school learning, the revolution needs to have an important focus there.

Johnson and Healy let their imaginations run somewhat (just as I hoped they would) to the point where Johnson's character of Miles is assisted by his information avatar throughout the day and beyond (even to the extent that his library avatar wakes him in the morning!). That these artificial creations might have independent thought, and even some emotional aspects, is perhaps daunting for some, but perhaps it also highlights a need for the flesh-and-blood information professionals to remember they are dealing with real people who wish to be dealt with as real people. Relationships, as will be discussed shortly, are among the more critical aspects of future library.

Technology is a major aspect of the future seen by Law also, though his emphasis is different. The dilemma facing Miles and Shelby is coping with vast quantities of information so as to make sense of it in applicable ways. Law sees the same issue as regards the increasing quantities of information being produced in higher education. With most higher education establishments deeply committed to research and writing, the amount of material generated by them is colossal. Technical solutions to the gathering, storage and retrieval of these materials are the only current possibilities. Production has far outstripped non-technical management solutions. The human management problem though is much the same here as that suggested by Johnson, Healy and Warner. There needs to be flexible management and management policies that can accommodate the unusual, the highly technical and even the exponential growth.

Ensuring a future in the modern environment – called the post-literate age by Johnson – must relate to dealing with the information being produced in the most effective ways. Traditional management strategies and policies are unlikely to offer help with this; in fact, they would be more likely to prevent the rapid growth that is needed. Hughes alludes to this when he speaks of continuing revolution. He suggests that there must be a 'profound change' that for schools will see a substantial increase in resources and support for teachers. In higher education Law sees the same need, particularly in areas he summarises as 'user training, quality assurance of external resources and the building of e-collections aggregated with those of other libraries'.

This last point, one that is rather assumed by Healy and Johnson in particular, assumes a high level of interaction and collaboration (see below) between libraries. It includes the concept of a world IP databank introduced by Johnson, the e-collections that Law sees are so important, and the combining of physical libraries suggested by Warner. Such collaboration cuts directly across traditional 'storehouse' library views, suggesting the importance of sharing and collaboration with libraries as 'gateways' (a view strongly supported by Dowler and also Raitt for example).

In the final analysis though, each writer sees libraries having a real and positive future in an increasingly technical world. Despite all of the social networking activity that might suggest to some the possibility of a more anarchic and individual outcome, the physical library is seen as a viable reality. Hughes sees it at the heart of any moves to 'revolutionise' education – an essential provision for all learning development. Johnson, despite the technical nature of the information environment, sees the place as well as the relationships as focused on a physical library. Miles, in fact, is rather criticised by his girlfriend for the amount of time he spends there. For him, and for all the users of facilities that are people-centred, the library is a valued place at the centre of his information needs. It is a place where he has access to technology, which is vital, but it is the personal relationships with quality people that makes the library important to his life and learning.

Technology

Along with centrality, another consistent and critical consideration is that of technology. While not necessarily overt, it is implicit in almost every case. Johnson and Healy assume considerable development in terms of their holograms and thought control. Law builds his e-collections on the foundation of complex and reliable networks, Warner's 'young learners' depend on high-speed interactions and Hannan's green library needs working technologies so as to produce an achievable zero-waste policy.

Quite clearly, technology is going to play an ever-increasing part in the connecting of users with the information they need. In the modern age it also plays an increasing role in the connections between users, and thus in the connection of groups of users to the information. In every direction technology plays its part.

In the 1990s, even the smallest of libraries in the developed world (and in many cases well beyond that) were installing internet access to their libraries. CDROM technology had only just become readily accessible before the internet made its debut. Information sources moved beyond the four walls of the conventional library overnight. Staff within those libraries suddenly had to learn not only new technical skills but a whole set of information skills as well. It says so much for the flexibility of library staff that, on top of the relatively recent automation of catalogues, internet and computer networking was quickly incorporated into the library landscape. The rate of change to hit libraries during the last thirty years of the old millennium was unlike that in any other era. That rate of change has just kept going into the new. Raitt projected some of these changes into the future in this way:

> For libraries to stay in the game, they will not only need to become learning centres and make their collections and stock available electronically over the world wide web and other online services to people who want to get their information and knowledge from their office or home, but they will also have to contend with documents in this new media. This all means an enhancement and augmentation of library and information services, making them more community-based (and this can be the community formed by

all people in an organisation as well as those in a given city or
region) and bestowing added-value upon them (Raitt 1997, p.7).

At the time he wrote, the age of digitisation had begun and the general euphoria
surrounding the sharing of the world's information resources was in full swing. It
would not be long before that generosity of spirit was to receive a severe setback as
established publishers realised the full impact such moves would have on their
incomes. However, the technological innovations swept on.

The introduction of common broadband followed quickly behind. In the first
five years of the new millennium, computer use in libraries was, for many, the
major use of the library. Everyone was heading for the millions of amazing
websites that offered the information that was previously the sole domain of the
library, but now with added bells and whistles. Then in 2006, with the advent of
social networking, it all changed again, almost overnight. Three-fifths of all traffic
on the internet was made up of peer-to-peer connection as social networking
became the commonest use of the medium (Harkin 2009, p.97). The social
networking dreamers and theorists of the 1960s saw their vision fully realised.

Thus in the past twenty years so much has changed in terms of access to
information, its organisation and the expectations of users. This last item may well
be the most important. Students in schools today are growing up in a very different
world, and consequently with some rather challenging expectations.

On 7 September 2009, the Seven Television Network (Australia) ran an item
on two girls (aged 10 and 13 from memory) who became stuck in a drain. They
were rescued quite quickly because one of the girls carried a mobile phone that
allowed her to update her Facebook entry. Outlining her predicament on Facebook
resulted in a rather speedy rescue for both of the young persons. The interesting
'news' for information managers to note from this is that neither girl rang the
police or emergency services directly. Rather than dial 000, they chose another
option. Facebook was the way to contact people, they thought, and in doing so they
did solve their problem.

I recently walked in to a year-five information technology class. The teacher
was laboriously rehearsing the different tools that were available in MS Word and
what they did. 'This is the print icon and what it does is ...' The class was, to my
mind, a little on the noisy side. I don't mind some noise if it is working noise, but
this was a little more. Turning to two girls seated close to the door I asked if they
had heard the teacher. Ignoring my question, they asked if I would like to see the
movies that they had produced and edited for their blog sites. They both had been
blogging for more than a year, and to judge by their movies had developed some

quite amazing skills in animation and movie editing. Drawn animations, video from their phone cameras and over-dubbing of audio were all present and impressive. And still the teacher continued to expound on the print icon. It was no wonder that the class was not paying attention.

This is the environment then envisioned by the scenarios. Information users of the future will require, perhaps demand, ever more sophisticated solutions to their information needs. Johnson's Miles is working with sims that have a conscience and uses personally programmed bots to assist him search through the vast amount of information that is available. Healy's Shelby communicates freely with friends and assistants around the globe. Information delivery for both is instant. Clearly there is the assumption of high speeds and huge bandwidth, together with ultra-reliable networks. Warner's learners rely on internet delivery for their information needs, with multimedia assumed as standard. Again, reliable and high-speed networks are expected.

When it comes to technology there would appear to be two contrasting issues at stake – the client and the technical system. Both need to be carefully assessed and both need to be developed. There is not a great deal of point having a high-tech system, for example, if users are unable to understand it and use it. The best technical systems can sometimes be the worst as far as the users are concerned.

One particular situation I have seen again and again in the school context is where principals and/or business managers have opted to have computer networks installed and maintained by highly skilled technicians without any reference to teachers. The result in almost every case is a very complex system that has little or no relevance to teaching or curriculum. What pleases the technician is not necessarily what the teachers need. They are denied the operations they need and the learners fail because necessary resources are either not included or are hidden behind impossibly complex systems.

By contrast, and perhaps even more prevalent, especially in the smaller schools, are the systems that are installed piecemeal with little long-range planning by 'skilled' teachers. While superficially a very sound idea (the teachers do know what is needed), these systems frequently fail, are riddled with collisions and otherwise cause grief for many years. False economy very often leads to disenchantment of both learner and staff. Continual system failures ('computers down today') do not build healthy attitudes to learning or technology.

The most successful systems are those where competent and trained technicians work as a team with highly skilled teaching staff members who have a modest understanding of technology. Importantly, these 'techno-teachers' are quite often found in the library – the teacher librarians. These often overlooked and much maligned folk have quite regularly been working with significantly complex technologies for many years more than many classroom teachers. They understand the rudiments of networks and systems because their library software requires considerably knowledge and they also have a sense of broader curriculum. Many successful systems in schools and public libraries can be clearly traced to a successful cooperation between technicians and trained librarians/teacher librarians. Together this team will know what is wanted and collaborate to develop the system that will be most reflective of the client's needs.

Clients, even younger ones, can quickly detect the flaws in computer networks and become disenchanted with faulty ones. Similarly, they are early appreciators of those that are successful and of the power that strong systems can provide. Warner notes a comment by a student who, though voicing concern at technical efficiency, also sees the potential of effective systems:

> I just thought that combining the public and school libraries would
> be hard, unless it was completely electronic which in that case
> would be an excellent resource (Warner, chapter 3).

System reliability is a major requirement for efficient, well-managed information provision.

Lurking behind each of the scenarios are a further two major assumptions as regards technology; adequate bandwidth and high-speed processing. For Miles and Shelby, as well as for e-collections, lifelong learning, quality resources and green libraries, there is the assumption that connections will not only work reliably but also quickly. Speed is critical to the handling of large amounts of data. Those who can remember back to the early days of database use might recall the wait times involved while the prehistoric (almost) machines churned their way through the tapes of data. For collaboration to work on the scale of Warner's combined libraries or Johnson's holographic connections between America and Amman, speed both of machine and of network becomes critical. Healy notes, regarding her Shelby, 'More recently Shelby has tried out a new form of 3D technology which uses thought control'. What are the implications for networks if this becomes a reality?

Today's clients are not well known for their ability to sit and wait for things to happen. They require connectivity here and now and at speed. Failure to deliver on this may well lead to their being disenfranchised – perhaps lost forever as regards developing key information-seeking skills.

There are pitfalls of course. Frequently provision of network beyond a single location becomes the subject of political debate. One such example is the national high-speed broadband network proposed in Australia. Despite the existence of several models overseas, Australia's politicians are promoting the new network on the basis of its enormous potential bandwidth. This is an attractive proposition to most voters. However, they have moved into contract stage and yet still have not seriously considered or offered for public debate the key issues of what will be using this bandwidth, the cost of connecting to it and, particularly, the cost of maintaining such a system for householders, schools, universities and libraries (among other potential users). The solution superficially is great, but the application leaves so much to be decided and is most likely to lead to massive cost blowouts or no improvement at all for users who are unable to pay the much larger costs.

In summary, then, there are some very serious issues to be faced by information professionals if we are to make the giant leap forward into the world of Miles or Shelby. Many issues need to be considered and considerable strategic planning needs to take place. This is not to say that building the biggest system possible should become the sole objective of the future information manager or professional. It is to suggest though that, despite its rather 'black hole' nature, a solid technology base needs to be planned for and provided. Money will need to be spent – quite a lot of it. The issue is, where is it best spent?

Of course this does raise the issues of access and equity. These are important and I will deal with them shortly, but in the meantime it is important that library future does include a serious and well considered plan for the future that is as 'future proof' as it can be. Such a plan needs to be built firmly, not on what magic technology can do or even the latest super softwares, but on what can be actually supported (initial cost and ongoing maintenance) as well as what the clients most need. In our book *The use of instructional technology in schools: lessons to be learned*, Mal Lee and I discuss the quite considerable range of technologies that have been directed at schools over the past 100 years. Quite regularly there were (and continue to be) outbreaks of 'impetuous technophilia', well-intentioned educators who saw some value in each and vigorously pushed them at their schools and students. Frequently governments were persuaded to spend considerable public money on aspects of technology. All too often in both of these cases, little thought or study has been given to whether the technology involved really creates a difference in learning. Technophiles are too often attracted by the latest and greatest gadget and governments by what wins votes. Neither of these is a sound basis for improved learning.

As with schools, so with libraries generally. The latest gadgets are not necessarily those that the client needs. The client's needs must be at the forefront of managers' thinking and planning. Such planning must be carefully carried out, well researched and thoughtfully implemented. Mistakes are costly both in terms of credibility and cost.

Consider ...

The research on technology in education stresses the importance of the teacher in making technology more accessible. The teacher becomes especially important when home background is not supportive or when students are finding school unhelpful. A longitudinal study over fifteen years, involving 20,000 students, clarifies the role of teachers (Abbott-Chapman & Hughes 1995). The study confirms that the socio-economic status (SES) of students is strongly related to their school performance and that the strength of this relationship increases over the period of schooling. However, 16 per cent of that cohort succeeded despite adverse backgrounds and circumstances. For these students the influence of particular teachers proved to be very significant. This group of teachers effectively acted as 'circuit-breakers', breaking the cycle of social disadvantage/educational failure/increased disadvantage. These teachers were quite varied, showing considerable individuality, but did show two common factors: their conviction that all students could succeed and also their capacity to use a wide range of teaching approaches. These teachers could not be classified under any of the common classifications: progressive, constructivist, traditional, progressive or learner-centred. Rather, they had a great range of teaching approaches, covering all these different categories but with the capacity to adapt their approaches to different circumstances and individuals.

The overall conclusion from this project was that the special qualities and characteristics of effective teachers are related less to teaching styles and such dimensions as the progressive-traditionalist spectrum than to the nature of the teacher-student relationship. Mutual respect and rapport with the students were seen as pre-requisites of effective teaching (Holloway & Abbott-Chapman 1992, source: Phillip Hughes 20/9/09 email.)

Does this hold for library leaders as it does for teachers? Why?

Bandwidth is not cheap, but in an increasingly connected world it is of vital importance. Fast computers do cost more, but their speed can be weighed against client satisfaction. Computer numbers need to be carefully calculated – too many and you have wasted precious budget, too few and your clients will go elsewhere. Have your computers networked to needed softwares and databases and you will have satisfied clients. Connect them to a series of pay-as-you-go databases and you may well be asking for trouble.

Amid all the technical assumptions and dreaming, Giovenco sounds a timely warning. It is a serious error to place all of the emphasis on the technology. Simply making more connections or faster ones is not going to assure information is available to users, clients or 'customers' in a way they can use. He uses the term 'techno-imperialism'. I would prefer to call it 'impetuous technophilia'. What ever you choose to call it, there has been in the recent past enormous concern, angst and often dismay at the way technology has appeared to hijack library – and education generally perhaps. Like it or loath it, technology is here to stay and is set to play an ever-increasing role in our lives, and especially in areas where repetitive tasks are involved such as searching for information.

The issue is that for some the technology has become the major focus. The individual is lost in the equation. That can happen so easily in the field of information provision. Despite working in a highly automated world, Miles still finds satisfaction with his emotionally charged avatar, Marian. There is something of a personal connection there. He continues to mix with real people even when faced with the possibility of using alternate means of sourcing information. However, one further aspect is suggested by all his activity – a certain measure of complexity, some might say chaos, in the whole information landscape. There is no simple solution to the effective connecting of client with the information they require, when they require it. Change is all about us and has been for some time, while the picture is becoming more complex daily and, as Fullan points out, just a little chaotic (Fullan 2001b, p.ix).

Change, complexity and chaos

> For any given organisation, the important questions are
> 'When will the change happen?' and 'What will change?'
> The only two answers we can rule out are never, and nothing
> (Shirky 2008, p.23).

Fullan says much the same thing when he notes 'The more complex society gets, the more sophisticated leadership must become. Complexity means change, but specifically it means rapidly occurring, unpredictable, nonlinear change' (Fullan 2001a, p. v). There seems to be little doubt that we are in a time of major change. We only need look at the 'Make Poverty History', the Global Warming Debate and other worldwide movements to see that large proportions of the world's population not only assume change but feel they can make a change.

As I write these words, there is an international conference taking place in Copenhagen, Denmark, at which global leaders are attempting to take a leadership position as regards the global warming threat. The expense and difficulty of holding such a meeting is enormous, and yet the perceived climate changes are sufficient to justify it all. Coupled with the official conference are thousands of spectators and protestors who have also made the trip to Denmark. Their presence argues two things; they recognise change is taking place and they also believe that such change can be controlled or managed. Not only is their attitude to change an accepting and perhaps optimistic one, but their activities, along with that of the official meeting are be available fairly instantly across the globe in a wide variety of forms from internet news, to blogs, to twitter, YouTube, Myspace, Flickr, and so on. The 'protestors' are clearly convinced that their presence will produce results, that they can make a difference.

Change has become an accepted phenomenon in many areas. The information provision field is no different. The moment human information moved from spoken to written word (or was it the case even before that?) information management began to get complex. From the moment in the 1980s when automated library systems began to be more usual, the nature of library and the role of its people began to change. In the modern world it is bordering on the chaotic. Wikipedia shows one example of an attempt to channel that chaos. That change continues.

Hughes cites a study by Lonsdale reported in 2003:

> The context in which school librarians and teacher librarians operate today has changed significantly over the past couple of decades, with consequent implications for student learning. In particular, there has been an apparent decline in the numbers of qualified teacher librarians employed in school libraries in public schools in Australia (Lonsdale 2003, cited by Hughes above).

Hughes, Warner, Healy and Johnson see the challenges to the education context clearly. The future they suggest has recognisable aspects but there are also some significant differences. Without doubt they see a more complex situation with some very important challenges that need to be negotiated in the very near future. The arrival of social networking as a common aspect of life has greatly complicated the learning transaction. There is a new dynamic that Miles and Shelby are a part of; one that reaches outside their respective physical situations to take in wider, global perspective. 'Managing' this sort of change is the challenge that confronts information management right now as the moves have begun right now. Johnson notes, 'libraries will be relevant because they are constantly changing to respond to their clients and the world they live in'. Warner puts it in a very similar way, 'Such libraries will be relevant because they are constantly changing to respond to their clients and the world they live in.'

Changing technology has brought changes in work flow as well as role differences. Not only were staff wrestling with internet, they were quickly dealing with highly motivated and technologically capable learners. Into the mix was added the new levels of information creation that the technology produced. Every internet connected individual became a publisher and new ways of tracking, accessing and ordering these materials needed to be developed. It is not that long ago that library staff had either to pay considerable money for the services of a web designer or learn coding for themselves. Within a remarkably short period of time this changed with the arrival of web authoring software and then, an equally short time later, blogs and wikis tended to make specific softwares unnecessary.

The paradox of complexity is that it makes things exceedingly difficult, while the answer lies within its natural dynamics – dynamics which can be directed and stimulated in the right direction, but can never be controlled (Fullan 2001a, p.3).

Fullan sounds a note of warning regarding the whole deal on change. He argues that change cannot be 'managed'. 'It can be understood, and perhaps led, but it cannot be fully controlled' (Fullan 2004, p.42). It is the nonlinear and rapid nature of change in the modern world, he contends, that makes for greatest 'messiness' (p.39). One of its key characteristics is its unpredictability (Fullan 2001a, p.13). Johnson describes a rather different information environment to that we know today. There is a 'natural progression' feel to his view and so we can identify how this might become reality. We can see how the changes might come about that lead from our present to his future. What neither he nor Healy offer though is clear direction as to how these changes might be 'managed'. They seem to be very much supporting the Fullan view that change will happen so rather than trying to do the impossible, that is manage it, the best option is simply to take advantage of what it offers. By 'making the best of the situation' managers can meet client needs in new ways and stay relevant to their users. It is this relevance that is so important in the view of Warner as far as ensuring a future for library.

Difficulties arise when library staff and management try to control change or even deny it. Fullan cites emotion as one aspect of behaviour noted by managers when considering why their people resist and sometimes sabotage change (Fullan 2004, p.76). In the classic tale, 'Who moved my cheese?' one of the characteristics of the situation was the growing tension accompanying change. Hem and Haw became frustrated and angry with each other as their situation deteriorated. Under stress they blamed each other for their difficulty rather than consider what might be done to rectify the situation (Johnson 1999, p.40). Relationships are at the core of these reactions to change.

Democratisation of library

Each of the scenarios assumes that, in the future at least, library will be accessible for all. This is not to say that everyone will have equal access though Hughes and Warner tend to argue the case for it as a corollary of equal access to quality learning. The democratisation of information access has been some time coming, and may be some way off as yet for the majority of the world's inhabitants. Not everyone has the same access to digital information in particular. Physical library construction is not yet equal. For the time being at least, democratisation of library is more likely an ideal than a realisable outcome.

Historically, access to information was to the literate (fairly naturally). In the early days of books, only the very wealthy could afford to own them. The 'advent' of a social conscience did not extend to the very poor for quite some time. Charles Dickens, and those of his age, saw education as the way out of poverty, but with most of the poor also largely illiterate and unemployed they missed out on the new move to provide workingman's libraries, usually in the form of Mechanic's Institutes. These establishments, the predecessor of modern libraries were fine as far as they went but the intention was not to provide everyone with access to information. Those who had money were not considered to be in need of the access. Those who had nothing went without. Democracy, at least as far as access to information was concerned, did not yet mean available to ALL.

Library management and indeed the staff themselves were organised and trained in such a way as to best serve this portion of the community. They did not direct their attentions or their processes towards the illiterate or underprivileged who could not afford to support their 'business' in any way, neither did they offer any real values to the wealthy who could afford their own books and their own research when that was needed. Born in the Industrial Age, these managers modelled the moralities of their time. Industry required hard-working folk who knew their place and stayed in it. They were, like the children, expected to be seen and not heard. The age of Quiet in the library had arrived.

The arrival of public money in the mid twentieth century and increasing government interest in learning for all has begun the necessary process of democratising libraries. Democracy became more generally seen as 'for all' and the digital age late in the century created new environments while the Knowledge Era demanded new work styles and more flexible, thinking and discussing workers.

All too often though, information managements have not changed accordingly; material is still purchased with certain styles or readerships in mind, material is still prepared by a limited social group or ignored if it does become available from other sources.

Libraries have never been representative of democratic or real 'social equality' processes. Even at their most altruistic, they have always been established and designed to serve and represent the dominant socio-political power paradigm (Giovenco 14/11/09).

Evidence that this past is still with us can be seen in the attitudes often taken in developed countries as regards less-developed countries. On one memorable occasion I shared an international conference with, among others, a Ghanaian university library director. A US academic library director was speaking at some length of the responsibility his library was taking for developing countries. Among the highlights mentioned were the numbers of containers full of books weeded from his library that had been sent from the US to African universities and schools. The comment in my ear was not entirely printable but in essence indicated that most of these had been consigned to landfill. Africa needed current works not the cast-offs from other countries. Our American cousin was clearly convinced that anything he no longer needed would be received with gratitude and pleasure – less developed countries would, he suggested, welcome his weeding output.

I believe that this sort of reasoning is becoming rarer every year. I hope so, but I know for a fact it is not dead yet. For a century or more though, library has evolved through the different stages from philanthropic to self-help, and even self-directed (Warner). It is set to become democratised more effectively. Will that happen completely? Giovenco has his doubts and Hughes a few reservations. Both are hopeful there will come a time when this is the case and high quality education will become a reality for all students. Miles and Shelby live and work in highly technical environments. Will the world ever reach the stage of development where all communities can indeed share the same opportunities?

Consider ...

The interaction between Amman and the US that Johnson imagines does seem to be some way off yet but are management plans and the training of future information professionals preparing for this possibility?

Is your library ready to interact through your existing interactive whiteboard, for example, with people in other cultures and other lands?

To what extent is the democratisation of information a reality now? Do library collection policies, for example, reflect equality?

How would the current management have to change and in what areas, for this to be possible?

What developments are underway right now in your library that are bridging the social and economic divides in your community?

How many of your clients are in the top 5 per cent wealth bracket for your country? How many in the bottom 5 per cent? Do you know? How is your information provision planning dealing with this?

Is the whole digital divide issue merely a myth?

Giovenco alludes to the way 'modern libraries have always only really catered for a small section of the population and revolved around middle-class constructs of appropriateness, need and users' (Giovenco 14/11/09). To some extent he is being rather provocative, and yet how many times has the term 'digital divide' been used and has anything been done about it? There may well be far more truth in Giovenco's statement than the modern information professional wishes to acknowledge. Hughes, Giovenco and to perhaps a lesser extent Johnson and Healy see a future for library only as it becomes more effectively democratised so as to provide best possible service to its clients. That this service is a collaboration between many libraries and many informational professionals worldwide is taken for granted. Democratisation is not a political arrangement based in particular ideology but rather a state of mind for managers and a level playing field for all users.

Hughes cites Masters (2007) as calling for 'all students' to 'receive a high quality education no matter which school they attend'. He links this democratisation of library very firmly to success in lifting the quality of education. The school library, or learning resource centre as it is accurately called, can play an important central role in the massive effort to make Australia one of the countries where 'Education for All', the key aim of UNESCO, becomes a reality.

Democratisation of library, as reflected by the scenarios in this book, is aimed at all users having access to high quality information no matter which library they walk into (or log into).

Access and equity

Within the scenarios there is also an underlying assumption that libraries are not only democratised, but that access is for all on an equal basis. This is more an implied or assumed consideration than a discussed one. Law's e-collections are only possible if all libraries have the same high levels of access to the resources and to collection building mechanisms. The future that Shelby and Miles populate is one of considerable technical complexity. The assumption is that all of their contemporaries share the same levels of access (otherwise how would the link between the US and Amman be possible). However, the digitisation that Miles relies so heavily on was completed in Ghana? Does this suggest some different degree of access – one that is not necessarily equal?

Interestingly, although our writers have been working in the profession for many years, certainly long enough for them to be aware of the long-running debate on the digital divide (Lighthall & Haycock 1997), no one mentions it. While at the present time there is significant evidence of regions that are information rich and others that are information poor, in the future scenarios above there is an assumption that any such issues have been resolved. They are clearly optimistic about what the future holds for library and one corollary of that is a belief that problems of now will find a resolution.

For the present, though, a digital divide is one problem that current information professionals do need to address. Back in 1997, Lighthall and Haycock collected presentations from an international school library conference that considered the inequity of information access. The conference title was 'Bridging the Gap' and the collected papers were titled 'Information rich but knowledge poor'. Presenters debated both the transition from information to knowledge and the inequity of access to information in the first instance (and thus to knowledge). At the time these themes were attracting a lot of attention.

Since then not a lot has happened to change the situation. Bandwidth has expanded for many, but not all. Machine speeds are improved, but their cost, while lower overall, is still problematic even for some areas within developed societies. Certainly the digitisation of information should have a wider availability potential, but this assumes that sufficient technology is in place to access that material. In the days when newspapers and pamphlets were only available in print format, access could be limited even to one person (as they might take the copy home). Digitisation opens the field rather more but not necessarily universally. Law tends to suggest the critical aspect here. If information is correctly aggregated by those who do have that ability (or location) then dissemination becomes so much easier.

Johnson speaks of a world IP databank – an aggregated collection of 'nearly 99.9 per cent of intellectual property in all formats' as the basis for information clients in his future. Establishment of this collection has been a result of collaboration and, it could be assumed, of some cost-sharing arrangement. The collection arrangement includes payment for intellectual property and thus would also suggest the assumption of some degree of shared legal responsibility. If the costs involved in collection and ongoing maintenance are shared under some form of global agreement (something like that being considered for dealing with global warming) then equity of access may be managed by a global cost-sharing mechanism.

It does rather beg the question though of possible cost recovery for such a major undertaking. Johnson and Healy do not deal with the possible ongoing costs involved in a high-tech knowledge sharing situation. Do only the rich pay? Is that the level of equity to be expected? What cost would there be if there were a single collection somewhere in cyberspace?

To a large extent, this may be taken out of the hands of information management. Present systems such as Wikipedia, argue for a cost (to the user) free possibility as regards what might be termed 'free to air' information. The internet contains unknown numbers of digital items that are available without charge. The issue becomes more difficult once the aspect of intellectual property and publishers rights enter the debate. Recovering costs for users (touched upon briefly by Johnson) infers that there is a charge somewhere along the line for users. Would this then only perpetuate the digital divide we have with us today?

Given the political realities of the current age, a fully universal cooperation may not prove achievable. If this is the case then one single and universal databank remains a little way off. For the future library/information manager though, it seems important that the arguments Law uses as regards higher education and the formal schooling situation noted by Warner do tend to both encourage a greater collaboration and interaction. This collaboration would then form a basis on which to work more globally. Warner offers a somewhat radical suggestion by suggesting the possibility of combining school and public libraries to afford suitable economies of scale. Seeing little difference in the actual function of the two, he offers the possibility of cutting down on duplicate facilities and services by developing school libraries into more public facilities. There is much food for thought in this suggestion though I can imagine that there would be a few managers of these establishments who reading this might be somewhat outraged by the suggestion.

All of the scenarios above are based on greater degrees of collaboration between information professionals than in previous times. One aspect of that collaboration will need to be a rationalisation of what equity of access is all about. It may mean far more than simply sharing your establishment's database with a library down the road.

Certainly we have never had such globally levelling technology as we do have today and it is set to become more so. The potential for a global databank is considerable. It is at least a theoretical feasibility.

A global databank may be a future possibility but access to that bank could remain problematic for some time yet in terms of actual communications technology – its limits and its cost. Rather like the issues that have been raised regarding climate change, if there were to be a shift towards a global information system, there would most likely be a lively discussion on the extent to which developed countries should assist undeveloped or developing nations. There are costs involved and while that remains the case there may well be many problems yet to be solved. The scenarios though tend to see these problems as being resolved in the future so that a greater degree of collaboration and sharing is possible. They remain very positive.

It could be argued that the digital divide might not be so much an issue of cost as much as one of relationship. Collaboration between information professionals would appear to be quite considerable (for example, Law and Warner, above, also Dowler 1997, pp.17-34). However, there are still managements that do not naturally share or collaborate. Quite frequently the rather antique issues of possession do make their presence felt. Perhaps this is a factor of capitalistic thinking, perhaps it is a relic of the past storehouse mentality (Dowler 1997, p.xiii). Either way it can make access and equity rather difficult.

Writing particularly of the formal schooling context Warner comments, 'I have to say that I have never come across a school where libraries are so busy that they could not cope with external clients ... The library of the future should indeed have multiple client groups and there should not be any support for a library resource in schools that is only available during school time (35 hours week, 40 weeks a year)!' For him, access and equity are both possible and even non-negotiable aspects of information provision for learners. He seems to suggest that it is far more often the attitude of current library managements that is getting in the way of access and equity.

Quality staff

To ensure a future for library, staff needs to be of high quality both in terms of personal skills and also ability to deal effectively with the information problems of clients.

Hughes and Warner make one thing very clear; for library to survive into the future and for the best possible learning outcomes (formal or informal) libraries need quality and qualified staff. Hughes in particular notes the past forty-year history of government commitment, or lack of it, to library in this context. In the 1960s and 1970s the Australian government committed itself to increase resources for high quality education. One critical aspect of this resolve was a refocusing on library. Quality resourcing was seen as an important part of ensuring quality learning. Since 1975 that commitment to library has eroded and recent studies by Lonsdale, Reynolds, Carroll and others have shown unfortunate trends in this regard.

Reynolds and Carroll (2001) found that since 1983 the number of primary school libraries being staffed by qualified teacher librarians has dropped dramatically from 55 to 13 percent (Lonsdale 2003, cited by Hughes above).

Hughes goes on to note significant study in the United States that supports the value of professional qualifications for library staff.

> a strong library program, with a full-time library professional, support staff and a strong computer network that connects the library's resources to the classroom, leads to higher student achievement regardless of the socio-economic or educational levels of the adults in the community.

This last item is rather important. If there is a digital divide, and the case is very strong if the concerns expressed by Giovenco are well-founded, and they appear to be, then it is this group of socio-economically challenged learners who are disenfranchised most in the current learning and information context. The very groups still outside the democratisation net are those most likely, Hughes is suggesting, who would benefit by having access to quality library staff. Achievement levels are something that the current Australian government wishes to address with their education revolution initiative. However, one of the critical contributing factors to the raising of those levels is not included in the current policy directions. It was in the 1960s. It is not now. The value was demonstrated back then and is supported by research now, but does not rate a mention as part of a move to raise educational achievement.

Within the context of the current concerns with literacy and numeracy, this neglect in policy is extremely worrying. If learners are not being given every opportunity and assistance to develop both a love for reading and a competency in it at this early stage, what future do they have in the adult world? Of all the stages when additional encouragement towards a competent literacy is needed, primary years must surely be the most formative. Why is government ignoring this situation? How can an education revolution not commit to some serious assistance for developing learners in their younger years? Can revolution be expected to be successful when inadequate weapons are provided? Warner sums this up nicely.

> Qualified teacher librarians, librarians, library assistants are as important as teachers in the school environment and have a particular importance in relation to young people developing the disposition and skill to be self-directed learners.

And again:

> Qualified library staff, therefore, is the key to effective libraries.

At the other end of the education spectrum, Law notes that the same quality library staff are needed in the higher education sector. Among the keystones for building a library future that he concludes as essential are quality assurance of external resources and aggregated e-collections. Both are essential and both require quality staff who will 'embrace the challenge'.

For all learners, and this includes all information-seeking persons, it is important to have a clear point of access to the most appropriate information. For a large proportion of the population this means access to individuals who command respect because they are clearly seen to either have that information or know how to get hold of it quickly. Lloyd, in her research on fire-fighting information, noted the frequent frustration of probationary fire-fighters when their senior colleagues 'went silent on them'. Needing the information that the more experienced fire-fighters had gained through many years of first-hand experience, the probationers recognised their authority and sought the necessary information, but were often denied it. Thus, quality information was available but access to it was not. Without the necessary information, the probationary fire-fighters remained 'outsiders to the community of practitioners' (Lloyd 2007, p.185).

Lloyd's study makes it very clear that qualified people are critical in all areas of information provision, formal and informal, library and workplace. As Lloyd found in her study 'you can't develop fire sense just by reading about it' (Lloyd 2007, p.188), so it is the recognition of experience and practical ability that a client will look for in their library/information professional. Quality information provision will usually be recognisable and will attract clients, but that attraction needs to be based firmly on clear links to the client, and not simply on a perception of what the client wants. Service needs to be directed very firmly towards the client and their very specific needs. Selection of new items for acquisition needs to be based on soundly constructed, client-focused selection criteria. Further there does have to be every effort made to build and maintain strong relationships between library staff, their clients and all the other likely stakeholders.

Healy makes this point for formal schooling and the school library of the future:

> The internet is a big place and when Shelby finds it difficult to locate what she needs for class she sends her information request through to the online InfoHelp desk. This service is staffed by information technology specialists ...

For Shelby one very critical aspect of her successful search for information was the ability to form some relationship, even a point of first contact, with a qualified person – someone she could rely on to help with her specific information need.

The need is twofold – first, qualified staff with a real ability to help, and second, quality staff who are client-focused.

Client focus

Warner has much to say on the topic of client-focused library. In his view, library will only 'have a future because they have made themselves relevant today'. This relevance is to the user, client or customer, call them what you will. The concern he has for library future is that it might continue the faults of the past. One of the people he talked to about library reflected negatively on their past experience. They recalled library as, 'a dictatorially ruled environment where we couldn't talk or eat and had to sit quietly reading books that we had trouble understanding'.

Hannan goes a little further in terms of client-focus when she considers the importance not only of catering to client's information needs, but of doing so in an environmentally responsible way. For her, response to the needs of the client reaches well beyond the immediate to the global. There is an element of this in Johnson's vision of Miles, who lives in a world that is part real and part virtual. Not only are his intellectual information needs met in various ways, but so too are some of his emotional needs. While technology is totally integrated with daily routines, his information provision includes an emotionally charged avatar who helps organise his day and keep him on track.

Johnson is also very clear on the physical aspects of information provision. His 'library' includes places for coffee breaks, 'naps', green plants and general socialisation as well as the more conventional aspects of information provision. He would most likely support Warner's comment about libraries needing to be 'enjoyable places in which to work, relevant to their needs and responsive to their learning'. The need to enjoy comes over very strongly with Warner and clearly finds an echo in Johnson as indeed in Healy. For Healy, the presence of a cafe at the Centre is a vital part of the whole information provision arrangement. It is a focus for socialisation, a place where Shelby can meet with her friends and socialise generally or take in more directed discussions.

> The three girls and two boys gravitate to the Centre cafe which forms part of the information technology complex. Shelby is reminded of a time when her grandmother was a student and food and drink were not allowed in such places. Fortunately for Shelby and her friends those times have long since passed and the cafe is usually their first stopping point for the day.

The concept of food in the library is a challenging one for some present library/information staff. So too might be the concepts of socialising and napping. There are already some clear trends in these directions. A visit to almost any library outside those in formal schooling (and even a number inside it) will show how many current library clients are using facilities for social networking, physical or cyberial. A quick visit recently to the State Library of Victoria reading room showed more than half the many computer terminals there were being used for email, chat, Twitter, Facebook, and so on. Fewer than half were being used to search the internet or the catalogue. Similarly, visits to most of the larger book retailers in most developed countries will find that precious sales space has been allocated to cafes and comfortable chairs. In a highly commercial and competitive market place, retailers are appreciating that clients will use these resources and sales will be positively affected, despite the risk that new and unpaid for books might have drinks spilled on them.

Johnson highlights the importance of client focus as he describes the way that Miles is able to change his digital information gateway to suit his specific needs and comfort.

> What makes the portal especially valuable to Miles and others in his school is its customisability. Using open source APIs (application programming interfaces) and programming scripts, Miles has rearranged the standard library layout, deleting some components like the annoying electronic posters and adding features like a real-time Arabic translation avatar, a collection of rare Tagalog documents, doorways to several research labs, and a hidden door to a representation of his bedroom at home where he can work on personal tasks.

In the future suggested by both Johnson and Healy, the customising of personal information environments is a vital step towards client satisfaction. Warner underlines the reason why this is so important when he claims, 'disposition to learn and to use libraries, for example, for most young people is about finding enjoyable places in which to work, which are relevant to their needs and responsive to their learning'. However, the personalisation of library websites and portals may not be welcomed by those library staff members who lack the flexibility to put client needs before their own long-term habits and preferences.

It is critical, Warner, Healy, Johnson and Hannan suggest, that current and future library/information personnel seriously consider their clients and make changes accordingly. Flexibility, the ability to change direction on the move rather than be locked into past structures, is increasingly important in the rapidly changing information landscape. To cite Warner again, libraries will be 'relevant because they are constantly changing to respond to their clients and the world they live in'. And again:

> The library of the future will only exist if the library of today is relevant and transforming itself continuously. In schools it will only be relevant and transforming if it listens to its clients... If the library listens, then in twenty years from now it will still be vibrant and relevant.

Giovenco puts the issues even more bluntly as he comments, 'removing or subverting the human and the interpersonal out of LIS is the seed of its own destruction'.

It is clearly important that libraries face change head on. These changes may, and probably will, challenge even some of the most iconic of beliefs – such as those on food and silence. It is vital though that information provision structures are created which can move out of past traditions quickly and into a more flexible mode of practice. Giovenco puts the case rather strongly, and perhaps a little confrontingly, when he suggests that current library policy is often being driven by:

> social misfits and vandals … who so fear the idea of the user or 'personal relationship' that they will justify any and all means as rational and valid approaches to service ethic and options.

Strong words, but in many cases fully justified. There are too many parodies and stereotypes of library out in the wide world of media that live and even thrive on the rather indefensible mores of past library practice and policy. If the rules were more socially justified, these characterisations would not have the popular attraction that they do.

Meeting the information needs of the clients might be a little less confronting for some. These are perhaps more easily dealt with inside the 'normal' library framework. However, as Healy and Johnson suggest, in the future technology of all types is set to play a much more prominent role. Here too there are some challenges highlighted. Law points out the absolute necessity of coordinating and collaborating so as to effectively deal with the unprecedented quantities of digital materials. Collaboration within libraries and between libraries is going to become increasingly critical, he argues. Warner sees a future in which public libraries and school libraries in many places merge physically and where school libraries are open to the general public over extended hours. Again, these are ideas that represent considerable change of focus for all those concerned. If meeting the needs of clients requires these changes, and our contributors are strongly suggesting that they do, then it is important that information professionals, now and in the future, consider them most seriously.

All of these suggested changes rest on one very important aspect; that of correctly assessing the client needs. In chapter 5, this issue will be further explored and some practical suggestions to help with this will be offered. Here, it is important to note that the Shelbys and Miles of the future are having their needs meet in all of these different ways. The key to their success in their quest for information is a flexible and reliable structural framework to their information world, one that is populated by a fair share of real people who are absolutely client-focused rather than precedent-driven. Abiding by rules formulated in the past is not likely to help any information provision system into a successful future. How the client needs are assessed and how the systems can become flexible enough to meet those needs will be considered later. Both are vital for library futures.

Importantly, Giovenco highlights one aspect that will help to make or break success in this area. Relationships are fundamental to the future of information provision. Libraries need to establish strong working relationships between their staff. They also need to develop significant relationships with their clients to the point where, as Hannan puts it, 'I'd rather ride an extra five kilometres each way, just to come here, and I know my friends and family feel the same way'.

Relationships

If our contributors are correct, the future of information depends heavily on the development of new levels of collaboration, communication and consideration in the face of the overwhelming growth in information itself and the increasingly complex technology often used to both produce it and to investigate it. Relationships in this complex and often almost chaotic landscape are critical. Rarely do people who don't 'get on' together endeavour to collaborate or communicate with each other. Rather they will purposely set out to find fault or 'white-ant' proceedings, thus affecting the establishment of a learning community. In cases like this, it is vital that improvements are made in relationships before change will be embraced. In her investigation of fire-fighter training, Lloyd noted:

> Learning to become a fire-fighter is a complex construction that
> threads together information from a constellation of sources within
> an information environment. The process of learning to become a
> fire-fighter does not simply occur through an engagement with
> external and codified sources of information (i.e., text). It also
> requires a relationship and experience with information that is
> socially afforded and physically located (Lloyd 2007, p.181).

To Lloyd, then, relationships require social affordance and physical location. These two aspects show clearly in the future world of Miles and Shelby. They also see considerable expression in Warner, as his young people socially network in an environment of support and acceptance, and in Hannan, where the physical library reflects clearly the values of the client and forms relationships on common belief structures as regards the world and its sustainability.

From our scenarios, relationships occur on several levels. Miles and Shelby show clearly how personal relationships with library staff and or 'experts' are vital to what might be termed 'library satisfaction'.

> The session with the information technology specialists starts off with an exchange of questions and answers about her topic and what she has found to date. Shelby is glad that she spent some time sorting out her topic notes and her queries so that she could move quickly to the problems she is experiencing in trying to locate information.

Warner seconds these views wholeheartedly.

> Library staff work formally with younger students, individually, in small groups and classes, to develop specific research skills, including how to reference online resources, how to better define research parameters, to develop research questions and so on.

These personal relationships extend to library staff, to peers of the clients, to their immediate support groups and well into the world around them. Miles is encouraged by the information 'establishment' to form a personal learning network (PLN). This group, made up of people he has chosen, is occasionally challenged so as to keep it flexible and highly relevant as well as becoming a vital part of his learning and information landscape. His fellow students are included, as are members of his family and of wider social groups.

> Miles considered his PLN. The school requires that all students have a 'formal' personal learning network of twelve members. (Like other students, Miles's informal PLN has more than 100 members at any one time accessed by a variety of networking tools.) For their formal PLN, some students create expert groups from specialised fields of high interest; others form a group with as diverse a representation as possible. Librarians are a part of nearly every student's PLN and they take this responsibility seriously.

In their own separate ways, each of the contributors is suggesting that library staff need to be a part of each learner's personal learning network. If this outcome could be achieved, then not only would learning be more successful but libraries would have an assured and central future for generations to come.

All too often though, as Giovenco warns, relationships are replaced with technology. Where 'techno' takes the place of relationships, libraries will fail. This is perhaps one of the concerns that Hughes sees as he reflects on the current

Australian government education revolution initiative. If service becomes translated into more technology or faster connections, so much will be lost, yet this is often a standard feature of government action. Lee and Winzenried note that as regards technology in schools, it is often the number of computers a school has that, politically, becomes equated to the amount of learning going on there (Lee & Winzenried 2009, pp.30, 95). In the world of information provision it can often be the case that more computer access and faster internet speeds becomes an improvement in 'service' and an end in itself. Somehow this is seen as proof of more effective information provision.

Giovenco's warning is well timed. With governments seeking to catch votes with free computers and the general euphoria surrounding technology, it must be remembered that information provision generally, including every aspect of library specifically, must remain relationship driven. 'Service as relationship and need for communication, bonding, relevance and meaning' need to be foremost in planning and policy.

> People being people, regardless of generation are and will always
> be seeking relatedness, relevance, interaction, meaning and
> community. This means being and dealing with people (Giovenco,
> chapter 3).

Library deals with the needs of real people. Relationships with those real people and between those seeking to assist them are vital. What are needed are 'genuine relationships based on authenticity and care' (Lewin & Regine 2000, p.27). Johnson notes, 'Research on adolescent sleep needs convinced the library advisory committee that napping is a legitimate use of library resources and that library policies should reflect this'. His library management of the future considers client needs, checks on their authenticity and then changes policy to meet the genuine needs effectively. Regardless of traditions, mores or normal policy, library management reflects strong commitment to the client-information relationship in every one of its many dimensions. Authentic interaction between real people will be at the very heart of library futures.

Nowhere are authentic relationships more necessary than in the area of collaboration. Law see collaboration as vital on two fronts. He notes (quoting Bradwell 2009), that:

> Through their institutional capital, universities can use technology
> to offer more flexible provision and open more equal routes to
> higher education and learning. We need the learning and research
> that higher education provides. But this will take strategic

leadership from within, new connections with a growing world of
informal learning and a commitment to openness and
collaboration.

Here are relationships with a vengeance! Suggesting that senior libraries should
resolve their differences and cooperate closely to establish shared collections rather
cuts across generations of 'storehouse' mentality (Frye 1997, p.4). While
information professionals have not necessarily been backward in the area of
interaction, any collaboration has generally been on the basis of interlibrary lending
rather than anything else. Increasingly though, the pressure is mounting on them to
provide leadership and direction towards the e-collections that Law considers vital
and to the world databank that Johnson envisages. Law argues that in this sort of
development library should be taking a leading role.

> It should be a central task of the library to manage this activity. It
> may or may not hold the material but it should certainly be seen as
> the central and expert arbiter of preservation standards and
> archiving policy.

There are some distinct advantages on offer that make these moves valuable as
libraries look to increase their range of offerings to clients. Law notes the aspect of
learner collaboration as one area where library could have a much higher profile.

> There is growing evidence of young researchers using social
> networking tools for collaborative research – OpenWetWare is a
> prime example of this – and again the library has a real possibility
> of helping promote those tools and services.

Improving relationships between libraries is seen by some as one of the great
challenges or opportunities of the new millennium.

> Convergence, in physical and virtual form, is deemed as one of the
> major issues facing libraries in the 21st century ... Convergence
> reinforces the library's role as a social hub and demonstrates
> another 21st century phenomenon: that of the library becoming the
> 'third place', a destination essential to individual well-being, after
> home and work. In the country, as the ALIA submission to the
> 2020 forum (2008) noted, 'Libraries are often the strongest and
> most sustainable source of support' (Robinson 2009, p.11).

Convergence such as is suggested by Robinson has its echo in the views of Warner
particularly. But in all the essential ways, it is implicit in the thinking of Johnson
and Healy. For all of them, the convergence of information locations makes much

sense. As the world moves in an ever-more digital direction and social networks become the 'norm' there ceases to be the need for duplicate facilities. Thus, the need for new relationships within the industry, as well as between industry and client, become much more compelling.

One further relationship is clear from the contributors – that of library and home. To take Miles again as a case in point, his information connections include strong home–library ones. Given the digital environment, he can access the information and communicate with its specialists and his personal learning network from home as easily as anywhere else. This situation already exists, with many 'workers' currently working from home, and the trend is set to continue (Drucker & Khattak 2000, p.108ff). In the same way, learning and information seeking is no longer fixed to any external point of contact. Library in the future will need to connect more effectively with clients' homes, offer more serves online and establish new policies and procedures to make this possible. Warner cites the Knowledge Network of his school as an example of school-library-home interactions.

> Increasingly our digital library holds traditional print material, including fiction. It has subject resources, films, plays, current affairs, news and requested media material available within the library. These resources are also accessible from anywhere else in the school and from home through the intranet, the Knowledge Network.

Given the growing reality of our living in 'cyburbia' (Harkin 2009), new relationships will need to be built and old ones revised if we are to retain our clients and the relevance of libraries in the future.

Digitisation

Modern technology does present some significant potential for change in how information is stored and retrieved. This in turn presents the information professional with some very significant issues to confront. Take digitisation for example. To what extent is information likely to be digitised in the near future? There are moves afoot at the present time to digitise all printed materials and place them into a global bank (note the concept of a world IP databank presented in Johnson above). What are the implications of his suggestion and what is the potential for a commercial organisation having control of such a bank?

Johnson's scenario raises some very challenging and very specific consequences of the continued trend towards a digital future.

> Only one thing seems to be missing in Miles's school library –
> books, magazines or any paper information source. The last print
> books – school yearbooks and some local history publications–
> were sent to Ghana to be digitised five years earlier. All those
> materials are now available online.

Books are one of the more contentious issues among information professionals in the first decade of the new millennium, and discussions can often become tense and emotional. To some extent, this is something of a reaction to the challenge to established order and expresses a deep reverence for past traditions. A book-less library is a concept that some management and staff simply do not want to contemplate. However, Johnson as well as Healy clearly see the time when this will be the 'norm'. Healy suggests that:

> ... for Shelby and most of her friends, listening to stories is second
> nature and she often comes to the Centre and downloads stories
> purchased by the Centre to her latest iFone. Sometime Shelby and
> her friends borrow one of the digital books.

Consider ...

Recently it was announced that Google Books would seriously commence digitising recently published works on a major scale. Below is an extract from a lengthy posting by Rick Prelinger, a key figure in film archiving. It may be a bit extreme but is rather thought provoking.

'If something close to the draft settlement (with Google) is approved, there will be very little reason for most libraries to retain most out-of-print books, and Google will be the sole source for millions of books on terms that they dictate.

In the case of books, an innovative, intelligent and powerful external entity encountered the three-hundred-year-old world of US libraries and, a mere five years later, is within sight of rendering this world nearly irrelevant. In essence, the message of Google Books is that collections of old physical materials possess no inherent entitlement to respect.'

Two Australian information professionals responded to the idea thus ...

1) 'Google isn't in the business of respecting 'old physical materials', and why should they be Mr Prelinger?

They are however funding the world's largest digital preservation programme which will provide each partner library with a preservation-quality digital copy of each text. Who is losing out here? Through the Google Books programme more eyeballs than before will be able to access these texts and preservation-quality digital surrogates for long-term preservation will be secured at each library.

Is Mr Prelinger concerned about preservation or about access? Either way I don't see that we lose out on either. The problem is that it is a private initiative that has sufficient funding to take the lead with the preservation of this textual heritage; however, what right do libraries/outspoken archivists/the public cultural elite have to complain about this when they haven't done it themselves. Sure it gives Google competitive advantage but that's what fuels innovation.

What should we be more concerned about – the format of knowledge or the knowledge itself?'

2) 'Mr Prelinger is concerned about libraries and archives ... and their continued existence. He can see that in ten years time or whatever, when 50 per cent of the Bodlean is digitised, Oxford University will say – why are we bothering to spend millions of pounds on funding the library when most of its collection is now available online via Google. We will cut its funding to a minimum and keep it as a museum ... keep the pretty books on the shelves and whack the rest into 'deep' storage – the admin staff can manage the database subscriptions (if that model still exists), IT can manage the preservation files ... and users will never darken its door – it will all be online.

It does indeed make vast collections hugely more accessible but it is at a cost ... and the libraries while trying to do the right thing and make their collections more accessible may, at the same time, be creating the tools for their own demise ... thus we need to radically rethink, especially academic/research libraries, their roles, to ensure that indeed there is a role in the future.

What does the possibility of a single commercial entity having control of the majority of published information suggest for libraries in the future? Is it simply a case of format?'

In arguing for e-collections, Law includes implicitly a far more digital future. Giovenco and Warner take a stand for the client and their needs as paramount and thus allow for whatever future the client, not the information professional, sees as of value. Given the current high level of digital involvement of the so-called 'digital natives' it would seem a foregone conclusion that they will look for a digital future that delivers now and to wherever they happen to currently be.

A consideration of the implications of a move to digitisation is beyond the remit of this current work. However, it is not all that long ago that protests similar in nature were made regarding the arrival of pocket calculators. Not long ago also there was a real fear that spell-checkers would make future generations unable to spell and thus unable to communicate. Given the stunning growth of social networking this latter concern seems to have been a little wide of the mark. In essence, these concerns and many others like them (how about, for example, a specialist medical opinion, given sometime around 1850, that people's heads would be blown off by trains going faster than 25 miles per hour!) are passing fears that usually prove to be emotional reactions to change rather than actualities. Society changes, in the present context, very rapidly, and one skill or format might seem doomed only to be replaced by a different one.

One of the present problems confronting digitisation of existing sources is that of copyright and ownership. Healy suggests that solutions will be found.

> By the early part of the twenty-first century a royalty agreement
> was signed by all major institutions and organisations worldwide.

There is an underlying assumption in her work, as well as in that of Johnson, Law and Warner, that some solutions will be found. They are positive about a digital future and look to see those positives rather than criticise. In fact, all of the scenarios and comments made by the contributors are more positive than anything else. As regards the debate of print versus digital, they accept on the basis of client focus that what will be will be and that the most likely future scenario is digital.

Various issues will push this trend, as well as the simple one of client need. Johnson sees the trend as not only one leading to increased flexibility, but one also necessitated on the basis of cost.

> Miles's school library does not own or lease any information
> sources. But it has built, using freeware APIs, a powerful portal
> and guide to the databank.

Just as Warner sees collaboration between libraries and even the merging of libraries as a result of growing costs, so Johnson sees the digitisation as one way of keeping costs down.

Law tends to see digitisation as a serious matter of survival. With more and more information every day being produced in digital format it does not make any sense to store it in any other format. Sheer quantity will force a digital future on information provision facilities. The issue of scale is quite likely what will push most forcibly towards digitisation in the future. With the unprecedented increase in digital publishing, the balance between digital and hardcopy will move quite rapidly away from print materials. The future would seem to be quite literally, a digital one. Johnson offers his summary thus:

> Jennie and Miles are capable readers. Due to an early childhood educational programs, both, in fact, could read before entering kindergarten. But like the majority of their peers, they nearly always choose other media for nearly all their information and entertainment needs. Even video and audio are increasingly less popular than gaming. Miles and his peers demand engagement – not just entertainment – and engagement requires interaction.

It is a most likely outcome but also a very challenging one.

Physical property – real

On the evidence of our contributors, there are some mixed messages as regards a physical, 'bricks and mortar' library in the future. While Johnson and Healy both see a technological future for information provision, Johnson tends to argue for a largely non-physical library (though not entirely) and Healy for a physical one. Hannan reflects the opinion of Healy in that she's for a 'real' rather than a virtual library, though of significant 'greenness'. Warner also, while presenting future libraries as digital rather than print-based, argues for a physical library building. Law does not directly address the issue, but his attention to e-collections and the need for establishing suitable protocols and collaborations tends to suggest that library remains physical, although its roles and work may look different. Giovenco leaves his options open in that library may look like almost anything in its appearance, but it will certainly reflect the needs of its users.

Each of the contributors sees some form of physical information interface populated with information specialists as the way forward. Perhaps most ethereal is the position of Johnson, with his emphasis on information from home, school, international and on the move. Library is where his Miles makes contact with the necessary intermediaries who offer him the support he needs as he needs it. Suggesting that physical library will be closely linked to user needs, he notes that:

> Neither of these schools have either physical or virtual libraries or librarians. (Miles's first podcast that earned him databank payments was a commentary arguing that sending children to traditional schools should be considered child abuse.)

This is a rather interesting comment, particularly the last part. Physical library depends very much on the need of the client and the type of locality, either physical or virtual, in which it is placed. Some learning programs need a physical library, some do not. It is wrong, Johnson seems to be saying, to assume that all learners need a physical information point. There is some echo to this in Hughes (though I feel he would see a physical library quite necessary to formal education contexts), in that library is essential for top quality education. Despite the rhetoric of the education revolution, we do not yet have top quality education. Library provision with quality resources and quality staff, will hugely assist in the move to raise current quality.

> ... libraries make a positive difference, particularly when a collaborative approach between teachers and library professionals is adopted.

Both a real library presence and strong collaborative relationships between all stakeholders are vital to Hughes' vision for quality education. Given the nature of some current education establishments, it might just be that he would even agree with Miles on the 'child abuse' nature of some traditional schooling. Change is needed and, whether as radical as Johnson might be suggesting or otherwise, library is at the heart of quality improvement.

Healy and Warner follow on this theme, though they seem to be arguing in favour of a physical library to which learners come for help. By inference, they would also suggest, as does Hannan, that adults too have a physical library resource that they can approach.

It is most likely that there will be physically existent, real-life libraries for many years to come. The shape that they will take is far less clear perhaps than their role in society and specifically in the formal learning paradigm that is such a concern to Hughes.

At this point it is worth noting the picture of current library painted by Hannan. Far from being a place where the client's needs are met in a highly motivational way, or where learners have their enthusiasm and interest in lifelong learning developed, she sees all too many of them in a much less positive light.

> Year round, the lights were switched on all day because the windows let in very little natural light. On the walls hung dark

> paintings of historical community figures whose eyes seemed to
> follow you around the room!

Perhaps the image is somewhat characterised but there is more than a small
element of truth in this description of the public library, and not only those in
regional areas.

One quite significant issue that appears either directly or indirectly in most of
the scenarios is that of opening hours. For some time now, information providers
have been considering the times that they open their doors to clients quite
seriously. Even in the formal setting of schooling, where hours might be expected
to be most limited, this trend is noticeable. Warner notes that his current school
provides considerably extended hours:

> Our senior library is open from 7.45am to 5.30pm and for about 48
> weeks of the year. It is not open at weekends except on special
> request. The junior library is open from about 8.15 am to 4.30pm.

Universities worldwide are beginning to open learning commons (or similar);
places where students can gather to work collaboratively socialise and study. Many
of these are open twenty-four hours a day and are being accessed every one of
those hours.

In some cases these learning commons are arranged within the confines of the
established library structure. In others, they are quite separate entities. Either way,
they tend to be suggesting that today's clients are willing to work more flexibly if
they have that opportunity. More needs to be done to study this development and
ascertain exact client needs in terms of space, resources and support staff that they
look for.

Access to library, study area, learning commons, or whatever the name might
be, has sometimes in the past been seen as problematic outside 'normal' hours.
Setting aside the questions as to what 'normal' hours might be, and who is actually
normal and who decided what normal might be, it does seem odd that conventions
might be seriously disadvantaging learners and that this might be in fact socially
condoned. Is there a case for discrimination if hours are set within tight parameters
that might be unsuitable to some users? Perhaps the old traditions and mores that
Giovenco refers to are in fact the real problem. Warner clearly infers that some of
the concerns might involve the safety of minors – a concern of some significance in
the current world. However, he points out that in practice this is unrealistic.

> The fear that opening the school library to the public would bring
> paedophiles in is a bit of nonsense. Schools are able to manage
> child protection.

The wasted resource of closed libraries is, on the strength of our experts at least, unlikely to be sustainable in the future. With increasing demand for connection to information, growing familiarity with extended technologies and progression of the instant gratification that marks the current generation, it seems unlikely that libraries can continue with their restrictive access for much longer.

Physical property – green

One aspect of the physical library that does get some mention by our contributors is that of sustainability. In the current context of concerns regarding global climate change this is perhaps not surprising. However, as Hannan suggests, the green library is a relatively new debate in many ways. To some extent, and very possibly closely linked to its very print-based past, library has tended to be a considerable user of consumable materials – particularly power, plastic and paper.

Hannan suggests that library futures will give greater attention to zero-waste policies and renewable energies. This will be part of a general trend, she suggests, and not simply a single unit construction.

> Zero-waste policies have been implemented across the entire local council, including the library. These policies cover energy consumption, water and paper usage.

These policies will extend to library suppliers as well as guiding decisions within the specific library itself.

> The zero-waste policy states that all paper items that are purchased must be sourced from suppliers who stock 100 per cent recycled paper.

Thus the library of the future as Hannan sees it will be a socially and environmentally responsible unit that represents global and community values as it dispenses its information to clients. This is not to suggest that such facilities are in any way deficient in terms of client access or comfort. Hannan is quick to point out that library will continue to welcome clients, encouraging them to be green (thus the bike 'credits') and providing high levels of service. Access to information follows the same pattern outlined by other contributors – a growing trend to digitisation, computer access, high-tech solutions to problems and personal attention.

Johnson sees a similar picture when he notes that Miles and his friends have a common understanding of the need and importance of environmental responsibility.

Heads nod. (85 per cent of all energy needed to power the school is generated by projects designed by the students themselves over the past 15 years.)

Environmental concepts will possibly make considerable difference to the physical look of libraries.

Roof lines and materials, provision for tank water, solar heating, energy devices and the like will mean a 'different' look to libraries generally. While there are examples that already exist of this sort of building, libraries have been slow to change. The future is looking as though it will be greener.

There is a strong element of social and global responsibility that comes through all of the scenarios offered by the contributors. Law is making the point for collaboration and sharing of resources so as to offer the best information in the most responsible way. Warner considers library as critical in shaping young people for a responsible and caring future. Giovenco sees the need for change so as to ensure a more holistic approach to the real people seeking information and thus he supports a more globally responsible and personal information system.

Combining libraries, sharing school libraries with the wider community, opening university libraries to the general public – all these are possible. The world of Miles and Shelby may be closer than any of us think. The world of Warner's young learners is already with us. What happens next?

Where next?

What are the implications for library management in the face of these challenges and a mostly chaotic information environment? Can it be managed at all? Are the days of managers now past? Can we be leaders of developments or simply the puppets of technical advances that are out of our control?

Among many others, Fullan suggests that there is a distinct possibility that having a coherent view of the theory of organisations will give some meaning and direction to our actions. He suggests that while it is certainly challenging to manage and lead in an environment akin to 'pell-mell innovation', failure to do so will end in extinction (Fullan 2001a, p.v). He set about to provide some basis on which leaders could lead in 'messy conditions'. The issues already mentioned in this chapter and drawn from the scenarios presented above are part of the current 'messy conditions'. Technology, in particular, is often seen as leading us on a merry dance over which we have no control. There frequently seems to be no way to stop the tram and get off. In schools and libraries where finance is limited, and often politically manipulated, this technology tightrope can make management of any sort extremely difficult. The whole information situation is complex and chaotic. Old established relationships are changing, particularly the teacher–student one.

A paper published by the Australian Council for Educational Leaders (ACEL) and written by practitioners MacNeill and Silcox (2009), suggest schools are facing some 'pedagogical wars'. Along a teacher-centred to student-centred paradigm, there has been much change in the last twenty or thirty years. From the 1960s, they suggest that formal learning in developed countries has gradually changed from the teacher-centeredness, characterised by Charles Dickens in *Hard times*, to a more student-centred model. The change has not been easy but it has been worthwhile (see, for example, Warner 2006; Caldwell 2004; Beare 2001, 2002; and others).

However, MacNeill and Silcox (2009) see the growing political calls for standardised testing as reversing that trend. In an age when student engagement is hardly optional, can we return to the situation of drilling for tests results? The implications of this manoeuvring for the information professional are considerable. Is the information to be provided as black-and-white answers to a set of preset requirements or are we preparing learners to spend the rest of their lives learning flexibly in an ever-changing environment?

There is fortunately still a space where those of us who become in some way 'responsible' for managing access to information and in particular for those attempting to lead learners through the information minefield – relationships!

Shirky, in his rather special book *Here comes everybody*, talks of the power of organising without organisations. In a world of Facebook and Twitter more and more individuals are using their social networking skills to achieve so many things that previously were the work of established organisations – libraries, for example. Taken to its natural conclusion, where does that leave the organised school library (or the school for that matter)? James Harkin looks at the growth of social networking as something of a migration. Speaking of the Facebook, Twitter, YouTube, and so on, developments, he suggests:

> In an entirely spontaneous flight, which occurred over the space of just a few years, masses of ordinary people around the world quietly migrated to a vast electronic terrain where they could rub along with other online peers. Hitched to a continuous online information loop for long periods of time, they moved to Cyburbia (Harkin 2009, p.99).

It is into this world that Johnson's 'Miles' and Healy's 'Shelby' have stepped – or rather they have grown up in the middle of it. But in both cases, it is a normal part of their lives – a seamless part of everyday activity and as natural as eating or breathing.

Summary

So, as far as our contributors are concerned there are some very specific and significant issues to be addressed by information leaders if they are to have a future. Client focus, relationships, vision, successfully coping with ever-changing technology, changing client expectations and a host of other vital issues are a daily consideration. How then does the information professional establish a framework for their future that can incorporate and act on these issues?

I wonder if our libraries have something to learn from these different scenarios. The issues that they raise are only a few of the factors that contribute to the context in which schools, school libraries and libraries generally operate. Despite all of the new and perhaps bewildering recent developments, so many current library managers consider their work to be focused around the old pastimes of cataloguing, sorting and borrowing. What are the real situations in our learning communities, and do we really take the time to explore them honestly?

Take one pet issue of mine (shared by a few others too); in a time when almost every new book shop is incorporating a coffee shop into the precious sales space (and thus setting up the potential for coffee all over a new and unpaid for book), school libraries still hold to 'No food and drink in the library!!!' WHY? Our students borrow books from the library (we encourage that) then they take them away to what? Quite possibly to the nearest cafe for a quiet read with a can of drink or a cup of coffee, the book in one hand and a hamburger in the other. What is the message that we are sending out? Don't do in our library what you do everywhere else? Is that going to make friends for our library?

You are welcome to disagree with me (and I am sure some of you will), but I challenge you to review most earnestly the rules that you base your daily operations on. Your clients are the key to your future. The more that they use your library and its resources – including the best one of all, YOU – the more assured you are of having a future library. In the big scheme of things which is better, a damaged book that has been read and enjoyed or an undamaged one sitting safely on the shelf unborrowed?

Given the wide range of issues raised in the scenarios what then is the response of the 'future library manager' to be? In an information world that is chaotic, complex, dominated by technology and a demanding clientele, what are the possibilities?

In an age when social networking tools make it so easy for our clients to organise their own information networks, we need to make library central to our clients. This will take vision and will need commitment. We must proactively prepare to offer the Miles and Shelbys of the future the services they need, in the way they need them and at the time they need them. It's a huge challenge but cannot be allowed to become an impossible one.

References

Abbott-Chapman, J. & Hughes, P. (1990). *Identifying the qualities and characteristics of the 'effective teacher'* (pp.1-95). Hobart: Youth Education Studies Centre, University of Tasmania.

Barbera, J. (1996). The intranet: a new concept for corporate information handling. In Raitt, D. & Jeapes, B., *20th International Online Information Meeting* proceedings, London: Learned Information Europe Ltd.

Beare, H. (2001). *Creating the future schools.* London: Routledge.

Beare, H. (2002). The future of school: seven radical differences. *Principal Matters*, November, pp.40-45.

Bradley, P. (2007). *How to use web 2.0 in your library.* London: Facet.

Caldwell, B. (2004). *Re-Imagining the self-managing school.* London: Specialist Schools Trust.

CERLIM (Centre for Research in Library and Information Management) Libraries without walls series of conferences commencing in 1995. Retrievable in May 2010 from http://www.cerlim.ac.uk/conf/

Chartier, R. (1993). Libraries without walls. *Representations* 42, Spring 1993, pp.38ff.

Cram, J. (2002). Whose knowledge? Whose management? Cognitive considerations for the provision of virtual library services to school communities. *School Libraries Worldwide*, 8(2).

Dowler, L. (1997). *Gateways to knowledge*, Cambridge, MT: MIT Press.

Drucker, J. & Khattak, A. (2000). Propensity to work from home. *Transportation Research Record*, 1706/2000, 108-117.

Edmunds, A. & Morris, A. (2000) The problem of information overload in business organisations: a review of the literature. *International Journal of Information Management*, 20(1), 17-28.

Frye, B. (1997). Universities in transition: implications for libraries. In L. Dowler (Ed.). *Gateways to knowledge* (pp.3-16). Cambridge, MT: MIT Press.

Fullan, M. (2001a). *Leading in a culture of change*. San Francisco, CA: Jossey-Bass.

Fullan, M. (2001b). *Change forces, the sequel*. London: Falmer Press.

Harkin, J. (2009). *Cyburbia*. London: Little, Brown.

Henne, F. (1960). Toward excellence in school-library programs. *The Library Quarterly*, 30(1), pp.75-90.

Lee, M. & Winzenried, A. (2009). *The use of instructional technology in schools: lessons to be learned*. Melbourne: ACER.

Lewin, R. & Regine, B. (2000). The soul at work. New York: Simon & Schuster.

Li, L. (2009). *Emerging technologies for academic libraries in the digital age*. London: Chandos.

Lighthall, L. and Haycock, K. (1997). *Information rich but knowledge poor? Emerging issues for schools and libraries worldwide*. Seattle, Washington: IASL.

Lloyd, A. (2005). Information literacy: different contexts, different concepts, different truths? *Journal of Librarianship and Information Science*, 37(2).Is this referred to ???

Lloyd, A. (2007). 'Learning to put out the red stuff: becoming information literate through discursive practice. *The Library Quarterly*, 77(2), 181-198.

Lonsdale, M. (2003). Impact of school libraries on student achievement: a review of the research. Report to ACER. Hawthorn, Vic.: ACER Press.

MacNeill, N. & Silcox, S. (2009). The 'pedagogical wars': a challenge for school leaders. *Perspectives on Educational Leadership*, 4/April 2009, Melbourne: ACEL.

Miller, W. & Pellen, R. (2006). *Libraries and Google*. Binghampton, NY: The Haworth Information Press.

Raitt, D. (1997). *Libraries for the new millennium: implications for managers*. London: Library Association Publishing.

Reynolds, S. and Carroll, M. (2001) Where have all the teacher librarians gone? *Access*, 15(2), pp.30-34.

Robinson, L. (2009), Convergence: rural libraries lead the way. *InCite*, 30(12), 1-12.

Rowse, M. (1999). Only connect: the role of linkage in information search and retrieval. *23rd International Online Information Meeting*. London: Learned Information Europe Ltd.

Shirky, C. (2008). *Here comes everybody: The power of organising without organisations*. London: Penguin.

Warner, D. (2006.) *Schooling for the knowledge era*. Melbourne: ACER.

Winzenried, A. (2002 or 2004). Unpublished thesis. Charles Sturt University.

Zinn, C. (2006). Bootstrapping a semantic wiki application for learning mathematics. International Conference on Semantics – *Semantics 2006*, Vienna, Austria: November 27-29. Retrieved November 2009 from http://www-ags.dfki.uni-sb.de/~zinn/Publications/semantics2006.pdf

CHAPTER 5
Conclusions

'The library is a coordination of teaching and learning services for a particular community' (Hughes 1969). While Hughes is confining himself to library in a formal school context, this quotation may very well suit the whole library context. Library as a connection point between information and the user is all about learning. People seek information in order to satisfy a particular need and advance their learning accordingly. As a point where learning takes place, library needs to be central to the community, high on any government agenda and an instance where the community can place their confidence in quality staff and processes.

The scenarios in this book tell very similar stories. Information provision is all about relationships. The quality of those relationships will have more to do with the meeting of individuals needs (and thus the long-term relevance of library) even than the quality of the information provided. Again to quote Hughes:

> But the greatest impact must come not from the librarian's technology, but from his/her ideology, his/her thinking as a professional (Hughes 1969).

That said, quality of information is also a priority, and so there needs to be, in the future and beginning now, higher levels of collaboration between libraries, funded by a more effective set of government priorities.

Services and spaces within the libraries need to be highly flexible so as to anticipate change, while client needs must be far more effectively assessed and met on a regular basis. In many cases, old notions of management, old practices and priorities, need to be reviewed both in the community and in the library. Again, it is the client needs that must drive these considerations and not specific management styles or previous practices.

While it is perhaps very unlikely that accurate predictions of library future can be made with specific physical detail (though in her attempt to do this, Hannan does present some rather topical ideas) it is clear that if library is to have any future at all, that future must start now – with a clear recognition of the client it is serving and a clear picture of their specific needs. In many cases these needs are not currently being recognised or met. Their needs may in fact be seriously challenging to current library management practice and policy. Personnel in libraries that aim to be future proof will need to become, if they are not already, highly skilled at recognising personal needs and in connecting the individual with the information they require in a way that is meaningful to the individual. This last point is a serious flashpoint, given the current rather general government trend to staff libraries with well-intentioned technicians rather than with those more highly skilled in personal learning.

Heller's thought of management as almost invisible remains valuable (Heller 1985, p.9). The key to library future is an almost invisible management but a highly visible staff. Many years ago I took over management of a group of school libraries at a large independent K-12 school. One of the first clear moves made was to remove a number of internal walls in the principle library (mainly serving secondary students). Numbers previously using the facility had been low. Under the new arrangements the students and teachers became more regular in their visits and more likely to call in just to chat. They could react with real people spread throughout the library rather than a single 'on desk' person totally preoccupied with lending items and maintaining quiet – spelled QUIET!!

However, the reaction of the staff themselves was less enthusiastic. Never before had they been asked to work 'in public' and it was more than several could deal with. Though prepared to take their time on the desk, for the most part they sought refuge from clients in a back room. When questioned on what the clients needed, there was little they could offer apart from item loan. Beyond that all was a mystery and, generally speaking, the staff were happy to keep their distance.

A number of years later, the loss of walls was a distant memory and staff were working comfortably in public, ready to offer help, chat and otherwise interact with clients. Each could give quite detailed accounts of the needs of many students by name. Library use was high, there were clearly positive attitudes from clients as well as staff, and a comfortable working relationship was clear for all to see. The library was relevant, relationship-based, and in every likelihood set to remain that way. I believe it still is. The key to the change was a rigorous review of client needs. Changes were made, not for arbitrary reasons, easier management or the whims of the accounts department, but because that is what the clients asked for.

Leading in a change ecology

One does not have to read far into the information literature before realising that change is the one big factor challenging the professional today. The scenarios themselves highlight this clearly, and show in some cases a very confronting information environment, even ecology, as future possibility. It isn't just a case of environment as it is more a case of ecology – an ecology in which every aspect of information consumption is linked in non-linear ways to every other aspect. The relationships are complex and moving.

Leaders in the new ecology are just another part of its dynamic. There are no options for not acting, not participating, the result of this is extinction.

Flexible management and spaces

It would appear unwise to suggest that there is any particular single solution to the question, 'What does the library of the future look like?' In the foregoing scenarios and discussion, relationships have continually been stressed. Library needs to be built around these and their nurture. Spaces need to be incredibly flexible to allow for individual choice – the democratisation of space if you like. Management structures similarly need to be totally flexible – the democratisation of management. Old management rules and practices must be reviewed in the light of what our clients need – not as we see it but as they do. Rules such as the 'No food' oldie must be reassessed, and quite possibly consigned to the dustbin of history. Many are legacies of the industrial era and do not have a place in the digital one. They will only serve to make your library irrelevant to the very people who need you most and who will ensure your future most effectively. Warner's note is significant in this context:

> Here young people are able to engage in recreation and feel
> comfortable operating in small groups. They can make reasonable
> noise and bring their afternoon tea from the senior cafe.

Clients need to feel valued and supported. They need spaces that they can 'control' to at least a certain extent. If able to manage their learning to a considerable degree they are more likely to learn and to respond to library materials and sources. Structures and furniture need to reflect this need for flexibility. The more internal 'set-up' in your library that is movable by the client the better. Even with the youngest children there is increased satisfaction if they can place a cushion where they want, pull a chair up to their friend or adjust the environment in any way that is suitable to them. They need permission to do so and provision to do so. This is not unreasonable. We all arrange our furniture at home to suit our needs and often move things to fit changing circumstances. Why should libraries be any different?

When planning new library facilities, be visionary and also consult with clients. Too often libraries are planned in the dark recesses of power without any of the consultation that is so empowering. One of the best examples of this arrangement would be the Saltire Centre at the Glasgow Caledonian University (www.caledonian.ac.uk/thesaltirecentre). Opened in 2006, this multi-purpose resource centre incorporates the library into virtually every need of the student. For example, the student fees are paid in the library. Counselling is available adjacent to the cafe and a host of flexible work and social places are available throughout the building. The library was conceptualised as student-focused, and students met regularly with the architects and had a major role in the design of the building There is some degree of separation between traditional library function areas and more general areas. For instance, the main student contact area, called 'the Base', is located on ground-floor level. Most of the reading and stack areas are on higher floors. However, on all levels there are areas where furniture can be moved to suit individual needs and technology is wireless throughout in order to assist this.

While the scale is large (16,000 students in 2007), the principles carry over to the smallest locations. The name of the game is consider the client before all else and give them some ability to shape their own learning. They will respond to this with a loyalty to your establishment that will see lifelong learning become more of a reality as well as give your library a greater chance of longevity.

Information literacy

Among serious considerations here is the aspect of information literacy. This is seen by many at the present time as one aspect where the teacher librarian has influence and importance, because they 'teach' information literacy. I would argue that by doing so we are not putting the client first. While there are generic skills for more efficiently accessing and identifying information, and a clear case that having these skills will increase a learner's confidence in sourcing the information they need, the assimilation of those skills, appropriating and internalising them, is an intensely personal arrangement. For the most part, such teaching is an extension of the Industrial Age model of learning – 'you need this skill-set to survive, here it is, do it and all will be well'. The process of teaching information literacy as a formal process remains an authoritarian one. Law suggests that while instruction is needed for users to get away from the google mindset, it will not be successful as an 'eat your spinach' arrangement.

From the evidence that is now being gathered (Fullan 2001a p.55ff) it seems that instead of planning classes, the staff of libraries need to be building relationships one by one – slower and perhaps more challenging, but in the end the only way to ensure the client will find what they need when they need it and also to ensure they come back next time. Johnson has Miles calling in for formal training in semantic web, but he is there in response to a need he has perceived in himself. Miles is involved because he feels that there might be some information that is of immediate interest to him. He has the skills to 'know' what he needs or wants to know, and he has a relationship with the library and its presenters that means he will approach them for that information.

Similarly, Healy's Shelby interacts with 'information technology specialists', but she does so having first determined what it is she wants to know. Basic information-finding skills are perhaps already present, but it is the 'on time, need to know' that is her basis for activity. As such, it is likely that she will be far more effectively provided with further tools and skills to make the next steps.

> **Consider ...**
>
> Two teacher librarians wish to assess the information skills of their class. Both gather the students around the interactive whiteboard in their library (touch sensitive variety).
>
> TL#1 asks students to list ways they might find out about whales. She writes the responses on the IWB for all to see.
>
> TL#2 asks the students to list ways they might find out about whales. Students come to the board one at a time, select a colour stylus, write their response and return to their places.
>
> Which group of students will remember the discussion best? Why?
>
> Perhaps, there is a strong metaphor here for the way we all develop our information handling skills.

It is quite usual that the on-time nature of most effective skill development will be more effective as a learning device. In the case of interactive whiteboard use, it is when the learner actually physically makes contact with the board that they are most engaged with their learning and thus most likely to retain that learning (Lee & Winzenried 2009, pp.193-8). Similarly, it is when the skills are most needed that the learner will best appropriate those skills and will most need to be offered them.

It is not ideal to present them en masse at certain levels of formal schooling or in quantity at any time.

Both timeliness and personal readiness are critical to developing the learners' information skills. Neither of these are necessarily considered in the case of structured information literacy teaching. Significantly, it is often the case that examples of such teaching come from locations where testing is part of the basis for proving such teaching is needed in the first place and effective in the process (Nimon 2001). This is despite the growing documentation that testing does not actually measure learning all that effectively (see, for example, Shepard 2000, O'Connor, Radcliff & Gedeon 2002). Necessary skills are often very difficult to measure.

> The demands of the today's world require students learn many skills. A knowledge-based, highly technological economy requires that student's master higher-order thinking skills and that they are able to see the relationships among seemingly diverse concepts. These abilities – recall, analysis, comparison, inference and evaluation – will be the skills of a literate twenty-first-century citizen. And they are the kinds of skills that aren't measured by our current high-stakes tests (Edutopia 2008).

Relationships – a reprise

One relationship not mentioned thus far is that between the various tasks and duties of the information manager/intermediary. A quick overview of the scenarios and of much that is discussed in this book might tend to suggest a heavy bias towards non-print materials. This is in no way deliberate. Rather what I hope you have taken from this work is that many professionals would rather put the emphasis on the user and their needs rather than on any particular duty.

While it is outside the scope of this work, when it comes to the current tasks faced by information professionals I would argue that they need to focus on these tasks much less than in the past. Some tasks indeed are becoming less necessary and certainly if non-print resources are to become the more normal situation, a number of the older occupations of library staff will vanish almost completely. However, this work does not recommend anything of this sort unless it is in the direct and provable response to user needs. What is perhaps implicit in the current work and very clear in the scenarios is that library staff will be expected to be more visibly more of the time, involving themselves directly with the clients.

In the past it has been the case that school libraries retained back rooms in which skilled and talented staff hunched over computers managing cataloguing, serials, special collections, and so on, while a single overworked and overwrought desk jockey tried to meet all the face-to-face needs of clients. And, despite the current economies of staff, there are still some examples of this in existence. The messages this sends to users, and the obvious inefficiencies as far as the user is concerned, need to be seen as far greater imperatives than having fully completed MARC (or other) format with all the different fields correctly and fully completed. Good and all as clean catalogue records might be (and they are good), if the client out the front does not have their needs met satisfactorily and personally with positive and friendly attention, they are far less likely to return. For better or worse we do live in an era of instant gratification. Despite having the most detailed and correctly catalogued collection possible, a library could well find itself redundant all too quickly. As Giovenco said in his forum discussion (chapter 3):

> People being people, regardless of generation are and will always
> be seeking relatedness, relevance, interaction, meaning and
> community. This means being with and dealing with people.

It is this relatedness and relevance that information professions planning for a future need to review most urgently. Those tasks, previously so important to library operations and managers, that are not related directly to people will need to have their importance reassessed. For the most part they still have some relevance, but the 'people' aspects of operations need to be promoted into a clear prominence.

Positive and effective relationships with clients are absolutely essential now. They are going to be far more important in the future. All staff need to be vitally preoccupied with this relationship, and in smaller libraries ideally they need to be working in a position where clients can approach them at all times and they need to maintain an approachable demeanour at all times. This is particularly true where younger users are involved and where staff numbers are small. Failure on this point could condemn your library to oblivion very quickly.

Two final scenarios

In closing, it might be germane to offer two final exhibits for your consideration. There is perhaps much that we can learn from them both. Both of these are current situations known to me (but before you ask, I am not in a position to share details of locations).

Exhibit 1 – the Outy

This first exhibit I consider to be something of a library in the school – what might be termed an 'Outy'. At this particular location, the teacher librarian moves about all week going from classroom to classroom with a library trolley arrangement on which are all the necessary books and materials needed for the day. Their time is spent teaching with the classroom teachers either on themed class work, or in the more 'usual' library areas of literature and information literacy. Their goal, and this arrangement came at the insistence of the principal, is to integrate both library and themselves into the everyday classroom teaching.

Computers in every classroom (three or four as a rule) provide facility for online searching and this is generally handled in small groups. Students are relatively focused as to their information needs, because they have the assistance of both their class teacher and the teacher librarian. At this location, the arrangement has another value, classes are large and so the occasional help of a second adult in the room does give the class teacher valuable assistance. It also gives the teacher librarian first-hand knowledge of the information requirements of the students. They are part of the various projects and 'experiences' at all stages.

A library space still exists at this school. Used for borrowing and reading it is operated by a library technician. Most of the activity there as far as students are concerned takes place during non-class time. It is a quiet place where much cataloguing can get done. Teachers and students need never visit the actual library space because they have the 'library' brought to their door. The teacher librarian is still 'in charge' of the library, but in practice this is more of a remote arrangement with much of the daily housekeeping maintained by the technician working independently for the most part.

The whole arrangement has been brought about at the insistence of the principal and in pursuit of some very clear goals in the school's mission statement.

Negotiation with library staff was minimal, though not at all unfriendly. Information provision has become a very practical, 'applied' arrangement built around classroom activities.

Exhibit 2 – the Inny

The second situation that comes to mind is rather like a school in the library – I tend to think of it as an 'Inny'. The library is located at the apex of all student and staff movement within the school. It is open in almost every direction without security systems and with multiple entries and exits. Largely by the conniving of the teacher librarian, it is the best furnished place in the building. Leather bucket arm chairs complement tables and comfortable, flexible seating for work, eating, sleeping, chatting or even reading.

In the hope of offering a student-friendly environment, furniture was sourced from mainstream furniture sales locations with some specific items including the library desk and the newspaper storage cabinet bought from a long-established office furniture supplier. By choosing this option, furniture was selected that did not necessarily have that traditional 'library look'. It was also considerably cheaper. Using a supplier who had connections to a manufacturer, custom-made items like the newspaper store could be sourced for considerably less than from conventional library suppliers. Importantly, clients related better to the 'office' feel than they did to the more 'library' feel of the library on a different campus.

The library is lunch room, conversation area, teacher meeting area, function centre, and so on. Students use the library as a point of informal contact with each other, with staff and with visitors. Study runs alongside coffee and cake (occasionally provided by the library) and cleanliness is maintained (very well) by students themselves. Students themselves requested cleaning materials be on hand so that tables could be wiped and any spills cleaned up. They have corporately taken on board that this is 'their' library and so keep it remarkably clean and tidy without having to be dragooned. Their 'ownership' of the location has been a principle goal of library staff.

One consequence of all this is that the library is seen by everyone as a place for serious study and academic help as well as for relaxation, snacking and reading. The raised profile of the library has engendered new respect from both students and staff, but especially as a place to ask questions, raise issues, discuss their future and generally get help and friendliness. Staff, from principal to bus drivers, meet regularly in the library either for formal purposes or simply to lunch with the students and other staff (a rather relaxed way of negotiating on budget and facilities). School bus drivers choose to sit and read while waiting for their passengers and grounds staff will join in at lunch times when their tasks permit.

The library has become a common bond for all of the school population and rather than resenting their presence, students appreciate other peoples' views. When an information need arises, a question has to be answered or some sympathy handed out – the library is seen as the place to go. This location supports all the usual social networking tools but gives a positive 'real world' context – all the comforts of home while living in 'Cyburbia'.

I would suggest that this particular library will not only survive long into the future, but will also make a difference in the lives of many people. Firmly established with the clients of this library is a feeling that the library is 'the place to be' – for friends, for comfort, for sharing and for information. Most of all, they are showing a new willingness to ask for help, to approach staff with their needs and to look to them for the skills they need in acquiring information. Library for them is building a positive feeling that will affect the way they look at libraries and information location once they have left the formal school environment. This should dramatically increase the chances for lifelong learning.

And finally ...

The bottom line is that library needs to cater for client needs, whatever they are. Leaders in library need to be visionary and plan to meet needs now and into the future. With the future so uncertain, great flexibility is required of people, policies and physical surroundings.

Information provision is very much a timely arrangement. For maximum benefit, it must be provided not only as the client needs it but also when the client needs it. Shelby (Healy) and Miles (Johnson) are not unique individuals. They represent all of our information-seeking clients. They look for the information they need, in the form they need it and at the time they need it. Technology may provide future clues as to where their information is found, and perhaps even the form that it is delivered in, but it is the relationships that are formed with the information professionals and their staff that will especially 'condition' them to have positive lifelong attitudes to information. As a specific locatable gateway to their information, library needs to be a key part of the process if it is to have a future.

To ensure survival we need to have a very clear moral purpose for our information practice and an organisational model that effectively reflects the specific needs of our clients. Both purpose and model need to be effectively communicated to all stakeholders (users, staff and supporters – all of them) who in turn, need to be involved in the decision-making process. There must be a strong spirit of teamwork throughout the organisation. There need to be strong relationships within the library, and these need to be consistently transferred to all clients and stakeholders.

Johnson's Miles cites his grandfather's summary of library past, present and future in this way:

> You know I talked to Grandpa just now ... He said about the same
> thing – that the tools and roles of the librarian have changed so
> dramatically, especially in the last 20 years or so. But then he

added something. He said that the tools librarians use change, the importance of certain tasks that librarians perform changes, and even the services libraries offer to support their schools and communities change. But some things, like the librarian's mission and values, remain constant. Librarians still support intellectual freedom and fight censorship. Librarians are still about open inquiry and access to information and ideas. Librarians are still about helping people find and use information that is reliable and help them use it to improve their lives. And librarians have always been about helping people help themselves by learning how to be lifelong learners and informed decision-makers. And Grandma Annie, who was listening in, added that librarians have always wanted people to find enjoyment, fun and excitement in learning and reading.

If we can achieve these then our future is assured. If we fail in any one of these, we might not have a future.

References

Edutopia. Available at http://www.edutopia.org/comprehensive-assessment-introduction on 29/01/10.

Harkin, J. (2009, *Cyburbia: the dangerous idea that's changing how we live and who we are*. London: Little, Brown.

Heller, R. (1985). *The new naked manager*. London: Hodder and Stoughton.

Hughes, P.W. 1969. 'The role of the library in the Australian secondary school' in Trask, M., ed. Planning of Australian school libraries. ASLA, 1969.

Lee, M. & Winzenried, A. (2009). *The use of instructional technology in schools: Lessons to be learned*. Melbourne: ACER.

Lonsdale, M., Impact of School Libraries on Student Achievement: a Review of the Research, Report to ACER, ACER Press, Hawthorn, Victoria.

Nimon, M. (2001). The role of academic libraries in the development of the information literate student: the interface between librarian, academic and other stakeholders. *Australian Academic & Research Libraries*, 32(1), May 2001 at http://alia.org.au/publishing/aarl/32.1/full.text/mnimon.html

O'Connor, L.G., Radcliff, C.J., & Gedeon, J.A. (2002). Applying systems of design and item response theory to the problem of measuring information literacy skills. Available at http://faculty.wiu.edu/JP-

Stierman/Information_Literacy/assessment/applying%20systems%20design.pdf, visited 29/01/10.

O'Keeffe, D. (2009), Much ado about nothing, in Education Review, Nov 2009.

Shepard, L. (2000). The role of assessment in a learning culture. Available at http://edr.sagepub.com/cgi/pdf_extract/29/7/4, visited on 29/01/10.

INDEX

Printed and bound by CPI Group (UK) Ltd, Croydon, CR0 4YY

13/05/2025

01869549-0001